SPORTING BIRDS
OF THE
BRITISH ISLES

SPORTING BIRDS OF THE BRITISH ISLES

Brian P. Martin

Paintings by
Rodger McPhail

David & Charles
Newton Abbot   London   North Pomfret (Vt)

To my wife Carol and sons
Spencer and Ross

The maps were drawn by Ethan Danielson from material supplied by the
British Trust for Ornithology. This included the detailed breeding distribution
maps from *The Atlas of Breeding Birds in Britain and Ireland* by
permission of the publishers T. & A. D. Poyser of Calton

British Library Cataloguing in Publication Data
Martin, Brian P.
   Sporting birds of the British Isles.
   1. Game and game-birds—Great Britain
   2. Shooting—Great Britain—
   Amateurs' manuals
   I. Title
   799.2'4'0941   SK185

   ISBN 0-7153-8447-3

Photoset by A.B.M. Typographics Ltd., Hull
and printed in Great Britain
by Butler & Tanner Ltd., London & Frome
for David & Charles (Publishers) Limited
Brunel House   Newton Abbot   Devon

Published in the United States of America
by David & Charles Inc
North Pomfret   Vermont 05053   USA

CONTENTS

INTRODUCTION

Bird shooting has a very short history, but during some five centuries the quarry list has been whittled down from potentially the whole of our avifauna to, in Britain, a mere few dozen species. Of these just thirty-three are of sufficient sporting interest to be included in this book, though most are also shot for the pot and the remainder under the heading 'pest control'. As there are several hundred species which either reside in or visit the British Isles regularly, this is a situation which could not have happened without the overall co-operation of our very large sporting community, for no other group of people has a greater desire to keep its own house in top order.

If in this book I am occasionally guilty of romanticism then I own up, for shooting wild birds is the most exciting of traditional pursuits, but I am confident that such an outlook is never allowed to cloud the accuracy of what is basically a natural history concentrating on certain aspects of behaviour of a select group of birds. My chief aim is not to help the shooter take big bags but rather to stimulate his interest in the birds which he seeks to shoot in restricted numbers. However, increased knowledge of the birds will make the shooter more effective. Above all, knowledge of feeding habits is essential, for the unending quest for food dominates every day in every bird's life.

I have concentrated little on courtship for most shooting takes place in winter and there must be an emphasis on winter biology. With such a wealth of literature available selective information has been inevitable but I hope that not too much bias has crept in. Where there is conflict of source material I have selected that which I believe is most likely to be correct. I am sure that many shooters will be surprised at what fascinating lives their quarries lead and I hope they will think more deeply about each bird's status equally from the sporting, pot and pest points of view.

This book is not for the 'social shooter'. He has no place in my field. Also it is not significantly concerned with rearing and release, for there are many expert works on that subject, but there is some mention of this where wild birds are affected. In any case, captive behaviour, generally with intense rearing in an alien environment, is often quite different from wild behaviour.

It has not been my intention, either, to point out every loophole in the law so that the shooter can go in search of as wide a list of quarry species as possible. This could be against the spirit of the law. Thus I have not detailed those species which are commonly the subjects of special licences to kill, though there are legal notes (see Appendix II) to help anyone with genuine control problems. Such birds are not the concern of the sporting shooter unless his expertise is enlisted in undertaking control.

Thirteen species were removed from the quarry list through the Wildlife and Countryside Act 1981 and since then there has been considerable bitterness, disillusionment, confusion and frustration in the shooting community as shooters see their sport eaten away. However, although many of us did not agree with all the new restrictions, such as protection of the curlew and redshank (which we hope to get back and fall in line with Northern Ireland), for some were based on emotion rather than scientifically based logic, there was a need to assess many wide issues. It was a bold start which should not be condemned out of hand and should not be looked upon as a nail in the coffin of bird shooting but rather as the beginning of a period of consolidation and development in the sport.

This book gives the latest position for every recognised quarry species hunted throughout *most* of the British Isles so that the individual shooter can make up his own mind which way he wants to go.

History

Today's quarry list was not designed by a committee. It is the legacy of tradition, fortune, necessity and compromise, but it is not always rational in relating a species' 'shootability' to its population. Complication began with the passing of the Game Act 1831 which did not foresee the adaptability of species but did register the importance of shooting at that time. Since then shooting has played an increasingly important role in preserving extensive areas of woodland, moorland and otherwise rapidly diminishing wetland for the benefit of many species of birds, animals and plants as well as quarry birds.

Guns were probably first fired at birds in fifteenth-century Europe. Early weapons were very inefficient and impact on populations was negligible, but development was rapid. At the beginning of the sixteenth century came the wheel-lock but when wildfowl were killed with guns in Norfolk in 1533 the crossbow was still the main field piece. The flintlock followed in 1635, and by the end of the seventeenth century was in general sporting use.

The great increase in guns in the eighteenth and nineteenth centuries coincided with a tremendous human population explosion and, coupled with extensive land drainage, brought great pressure to bear on our birds. Along came the breechloader to provide greater firepower; driven shooting took off, with access to wild places made easy by trains and cars, and many wild bird populations began to plummet. For the sporting community a particular black mark was the demise of birds of prey, anything with a hooked beak being seen as a threat to gamebirds. 'Pest' birds were virtually wiped out in some areas. Many thousands of skins were taken for the taxidermy trade in the new age of the collector. Attitudes have improved this century, but in a largely urban-based society which has spawned the 'anti' movement there has been tremendous compromise as the sporting community responds to the whim and manipulation of the day.

The need for subsistence shooting virtually disappeared with most of the professional wildfowlers earlier this century, and the general emphasis has changed to sport shooting. However, even today there are many shooters who would not kill unless there was a meal at the end of it, whether for themselves or someone else, and I have a firm belief that every sportsman should prepare and eat at least some of his bag. Oddly enough, shooting simply for sport is more likely to conserve bird populations because the sportsman wishes to safeguard his interests more than the pot hunter who is less likely to care about tomorrow. Both contributed to the decline and even disappearance of species but generally it has been sporting interests behind reintroductions and revivals.

Subsistence shooting was concerned primarily with the certainty of killing and there were no qualms over shooting sitting birds. On the contrary, they were easier to hit and therefore stalking was particularly important. Puntgunning was a form of stalking but today this misunderstood activity is purely sporting. Now there are few places where puntgunning is either practical or allowed, even though the small group of enthusiasts are among the most responsible, hardy, dedicated and skilful sportsmen in the world. Their combined effect on bird populations is negligible. Long may they continue.

Altogether, then, it has been shooting that has had the greatest impact among methods of taking birds. Snaring, trapping and bow shooting were relatively insignificant. However, development has not been the same the world over. Although puntguns are allowed here, many countries restrict guns to 12 bore or less and it is only recently that Britain came into line with other governments in imposing restrictions on semi-automatics. Motorised boats, too, are now forbidden in immediate pursuit of birds in many countries. The sale of dead wild geese was banned in Britain from 1968, but North America took this step in 1918 because market hunting had a dramatic impact on bird populations there. However, this is still permitted in many European countries, in most of which market hunting is uncommon.

Finally, we cannot overlook the important part played in history by agricultural development (which itself is related to a changing climate), in influencing expansion and contraction in bird populations. One has only to study the recent success of the very adaptable woodpigeon.

A Dynamic Population

In coming to the present we must remind ourselves that in dealing with birds we are concerned with dynamic, mobile populations and must be prepared to look for and respond to change. We must allow for bad years with crop failures and high mortality as well as good years with record harvests and subsequent high populations which cannot be sustained. We must also remember that many British birds are migratory, and take an interest in their overseas breeding success.

Some winters will be severe, mortality will be high and breeding populations might be affected. Nesting will be late in cold springs and early when warm. In any case we must allow for altitude and latitude in considering breeding times. Scotland, for example, has a very different climate from that in the South.

Population fluctuations are mostly related to juvenile rather than adult survival. Most adults die through predation, accident and occasional disease, and not starvation, whereas when the season of greatest food shortage comes and the population is too high then the young die first through lack of experience. Remaining birds stand a better chance of survival. Therefore, we cannot look at shooting in isolation. In sporting and pot shooting we should achieve no more than an easily replaceable cull. However, pest control might involve an overall depressive effect on a population through sustained high level shooting or 'relief' through local control. In addition we have to consider the varying 'responses' of each species to environmental change. For example, the Game Conservancy has suggested that the 'shootable surplus' varies from 50 per cent for the redlegged partridge to only 8 per cent for the pinkfooted goose.

None the less, there are constant factors in birdland. For example, the majority of young are born at the time of optimum food supply. To understand fully a species' natural history we must study its adaptation to certain foods. Energy intake determines everything — including anatomy and where the bird will be at certain times of day and year. For example, the wildfowl shooter should remember that a species' roost is less variable from day to day than its feeding ground and that is why flight shooting concentrates on the roost, undesirable as this often is.

Environment and Habitat

In looking at specific populations the bird shooter should not lose sight of the main battle — to protect and enhance the environment while maintaining and improving a wide variety of habitats. On a personal level he will naturally care for the countryside, taking home cartridge cases and minimising disturbance. He will be aware that his is not the only disturbance of wild creatures and wild places. With increasingly efficient communications, faster travel and growth of leisure pursuits he must take into account many other interests, including birdwatchers, ramblers, yachtsmen and anglers. In pursuit of quarry birds he may also disturb protected species. In the breeding season he should be particularly careful, for if he disturbs any wild bird included in Schedule I of the Wildlife and Countryside Act while it is building a nest or is in, on or near a nest containing eggs or young, or disturbs dependent young of such a bird, he will be guilty of an offence and liable to a special penalty.

We can all play a part in helping towards a gradual improvement of coast and countryside by remaining alert to development and pollution. Above all we should be aware of changes in agricultural practice, for farming controls over 80 per cent of the land.

The Individual Shooter

Most shooters, other than the very youngest, have probably often asked themselves why they kill birds, whether for sport, the pot or pest control, or any combination of these reasons. The sport hunter may frown on the pot hunter shooting a 'sitter', but *he* is not necessarily preoccupied with pursuit of the rarest, biggest or fastest. He is usually simply happy to enjoy the shooting environment, and often delights in stacking the odds in the birds' favour. For many shooters the 'pest' woodpigeon has become the major sporting bird. Mere 'blood lust' should never be a prime motivator.

The shooter is traditionally a good naturalist. Outside for long hours in all weathers, he witnesses many aspects of behaviour which the fair-weather man will probably never see. His understanding of patterns of birdlife will increase his enjoyment of the natural world and increase his bag. Many famous natural historians started out as bird shooters, from Reverend Gilbert White in quiet eighteenth-century Selborne to Sir Peter Scott in the twentieth century.

Whatever his motivation, the bird shooter engages in a pursuit shared by about three-quarters of a million people in the British Isles and he must therefore behave reasonably to ensure its continuance. First, it is his duty to know the law thoroughly but treat it as a *minimum* standard. As well as major points of legislation, including those outlined in Appendix II, he must be aware of regional and local by-laws and restrictions. Employers too should know what their keepers and other employees are allowed to do.

Correct identification is obviously important if the shooter is to avoid breaking the law. In this book the colour paintings are so fine that long, tedious descriptions of plumage are unnecessary. Instead I have chosen to describe each bird's features which are the best pointers to rapid identification. Weights are to the nearest ½oz. Some species, such as the 'grey' geese, are difficult for the beginner to separate, so practice in field identification with an experienced shooter is essential before a shot is fired. At first the novice should try to memorise particular bird features and after a while the 'personality' or 'jizz' of a species will become indelibly stamped on his mind. Time of day and weather conditions will play tricks of light but *if you are in any doubt about a bird's identity, do not shoot*. Their calls will often help.

Apart from what the shooter *must* do there are a number of things that he *should* do. First, he should always observe etiquette and shoot only where he has express permission to go, taking only those species which have been mentioned. He must not damage crops, frighten livestock or cause any nuisance. If making a hide he should leave the field or marsh exactly as he found it. Courtesy to strangers is vital.

Shot size should be large enough to kill efficiently, birds shot at must be well within killing range of any particular gun and any wounded birds must be dispatched as quickly and as humanely as possible. Local bag limits must be strictly observed of course but, in addition, within these limits the shooter should stop shooting when he has taken what he knows to be a reasonable quota on the day.

Pest control can be important on a shoot but there is no need for all-out warfare on any bird. Some people argue against any control of predators such as crows, saying that removal of some, which are likely to be the less efficient survivors, increases the chances of survival of the remainder and the long-term vigour of the species. Between these two extremes there is room for a happy medium and it is always useful to remember that there are individuals in birdland just as there are among humans. Watch out for illegal poisoning and trapping of birds too, for that will only get all sportsmen a bad name.

The shooter is in a unique position to assist ornithologists with bird research by participating in various studies such as the wing surveys organised by the British Association for Shooting and Conservation (BASC). This will help to determine age and sex ratios in bird populations and provide information not usually available through observation alone. Even simple bag returns contribute to our understanding in many ways. Rings recovered from shot birds should always be returned to the addresses embossed thereon and will always be gratefully acknowledged. To know where such birds have travelled adds a new dimension to one's interest in the sport.

The Club Shooter

Increasingly the best bird-shooting PR is propagated through clubs, especially through wildfowlers whose coastal marsh is generally in the public eye more than any other habitat. Birds are the most beautiful, obvious and exciting elements of our wildlife and will always arouse concern among the local community. Any fears must be allayed.

In addition to national legislation most clubs impose at least a few extra rules tailored to meet local conditions or even to compensate for what they believe to be shortcomings in legislation. Bag limits are quite common but in any case every shooter should have his own idea of a fair bag. This will be taken bearing in mind the species' local status.

Many clubs have wardening rotas, not only to keep an eye on their own members but also to watch out for the infamous 'marsh cowboys' — totally irresponsible poachers. In some cases warden fowlers also police nature reserves voluntarily. Perhaps most important, they guard against over-shooting. Some wildfowlers do abuse the privilege of being able to go to a marsh whenever they wish to, and then the wardens must caution them. It is surprising, perhaps, that more clubs do not restrict numbers of visits, for protected as well as quarry species can be disturbed and bad PR is bound to follow, as well as spoiled sport for those who can shoot only infrequently. Obviously what constitutes a reasonable number of visits is a matter for only local determination. Other restrictions might include no shooting of some birds usually on the quarry list, limits to the times of day and year when members may shoot and a limit to the number of cartridges per visit.

In recent years the trend in wildfowling has been for clubs to move away from the early interest in rearing and release schemes to concentrate on the management and improvement of habitat. This benefits all creatures as well as quarry species and is excellent PR.

The Shooter's National Responsibility

Many of our wildfowl species are migratory, spending the winter in the British Isles before returning north or east to breed. In some cases Britain hosts large percentages of the species' world populations. Obviously this must be borne in mind when bags are taken. In the past British wildfowlers have been very insular and it is generally only since the 1950s that most have been forced to join clubs. Today it is absolutely essential for the wildfowling community as a whole to take increasing interest in each species' world status.

Apart from self-restraint, British shooters are increasingly concerned with international legislation, agreements and conventions. The wide-ranging EEC Bird Directive (first draft 1977) was an important example that galvanised hunting organisations into action and instituted further international liaison to protect our interests. Overall, more countries are coming into line regarding basics such as seasons, which are generally being shortened, but there must always be room for interpretation to meet local conditions. Few countries now allow shooting beyond February for that would reduce the breeding stock, whereas many of the birds shot earlier in the season would die anyway. Night shooting has been banned in some countries but continues in Britain, subject to various local restrictions. It is said that this increases the number of crippled birds and that identification is harder, but the small number of hardy souls who go moonflighting tend to be very experienced wildfowlers who have clearly demonstrated their collective responsibility and have put forward many powerful arguments for continuance of this exciting sport.

Forever Changing

Many shooters are traditionally very conservative and dislike change but at last there is increasing realisation that with man's great influence on the environment nothing will ever stand still. The quarry list, for example, will always be subject to alteration. Generally it has been reduced, but there is nothing to stop us thinking more positively, and continually reassessing putting a species back on the list as its population increases. The brent goose is currently under discussion.

Climate, too, is always changing. At the moment we are in a cooling phase which began in the 1950s after an unusually warm fifty years. This has been distinctly beneficial to some of our duck and, who knows, if it continues it may well add further variety to future bags. It will also help the cold-loving ptarmigan. On the other hand it might have a depressive effect on some gamebirds.

Then there are introductions, reintroductions and escapes. The Bob White quail was introduced to Ireland in 1982 and approval has been given there to attempt the reintroduction of the black grouse. Several exotic pheasants and ducks, not to mention the rose-ringed parakeet, have established feral flocks. All need constant review

Apart from the birds themselves we must look to other creatures which share their habitats. One of the most important changes in recent years has been the rapid spread of the feral mink, a great predator of water bird eggs and chicks.

Finally, we must continually review our methods in so far as they impinge on the environment. Until now lead shot has traditionally been used but the toxicity of lead has been causing concern. In Britain the chief anxiety has been over anglers' lost and discarded lead which is picked up by swans as grit. In some American states soft iron shot is now mandatory in cartridges, though it is said to lack the range penetration of lead and thus might lead to increased wounding, though the difference is minimal.

Scope for Expansion

Despite everything I believe that there is scope for development of bird shooting in the British Isles. Game shooting is more simple for it responds directly to the amount of leisure cash in the economy and has a major reliance on rearing and release schemes, but there is great potential, too, for improvement of habitat to help wild game. Woodpigeon shooting will continue to attract more participants as leisure time increases just so long as agriculture provides the food the birds like. Most wildfowling clubs have waiting lists for membership but some have become under-subscribed during the recession despite their greatly under-rated value for money. The coast cannot take much more pressure and agreements by councils formed from local user interests will become more common. However, there are great opportunities to improve and expand inland duck shooting through provision of many more flight ponds and efficient management of exist-ing waters, many of which are simply too bare.

I hope that we never need to adopt the 'points' system as used in the USA in which rarer species have higher values, yet that could easily become necessary here if self-restraint is insufficient. However, perhaps we should look more at the American Duck Stamp scheme in which hunters' money is channelled into acquisition and management of refuges. A sore point in Britain is that the re-venue from game licences is swallowed up by bureaucracy and does not go back into shooting. Without sufficient strategically placed undisturbed roosts birds such as geese will be unable to exploit new feeding grounds.

The International Waterfowl Research Bureau is already trying to rationalise current shooting legislation. We might well have to join in area bag quota sys-tems related to local populations for migratory species. But this would have to be flexibly related to fluctuations in breeding success in order to avoid further species going on the permanently protected list.

To conclude on development, I would like to see Sunday shooting become universal for any species, including game. Let the shooter choose! These bans, such as in Scotland, constitute an anachronism of no significant value to the birds and are a positive hindrance to the 'working' shooter who is tethered to his workplace for at least five and often six days a week.

Where Are We Going?

In the 1980s, when such wide issues as world conservation strategies are being discussed, the average bird shooter feels as lost as anyone. But if he treats his own little patch with respect, as a microcosm of the grand scheme, then he will not go far wrong. The major battles remain — human population control and wildlife habitat preservation and development.

Shooters must never give in to illogical 'anti' pressure, though always be wil-ling to compromise and lay the gun down temporarily when a species is threatened. There is always the danger that increasingly restrictive legislation will bring undue pressure on remaining quarry species.

Guns have changed very little over the last century and are unlikely to change much in the near future. However, it matters not whether we hunt with a ray gun in the next century just so long as the execution is humane and we retain the natural choice to eat meat. Shooters will always remain in the van of environ-ment watchdogs for we care for and share the excitement of our wild birds as much as anyone.

BRIAN MARTIN, BROOK, SURREY

PHEASANT
(Phasianus colchicus)

Numerically and economically the pheasant is established as Britain's most important gamebird, some ten to fifteen million being released annually by under 3,500 full-time and many thousands of part-time gamekeepers. Its shooting is no longer the sole preserve of wealthy men but is also enjoyed by 'working' sportsmen. Together they manage great areas of countryside specifically for the 'comet' but in so doing also provide safe habitat for hosts of other creatures and plants.

HISTORY: There is no firm evidence of introduction by the Romans, but pheasants were probably kept in Romano-British households towards the end of the occupation when they were widely reared for the foreign table. Remains have been found in Roman excavations at Corbridge in Northumberland but it is unlikely that the species then went feral here.

The first British record is from 1059 and it is probable that the first substantial introductions were made by the Normans towards the end of the eleventh century. By the end of the sixteenth century pheasants appear to have been fairly well established over much of England. They were then taken to Scotland, Wales and Ireland but did not become common in much of Wales until the second half of the nineteenth century. It was not just a question of successful breeding and multiplying but also of adapting to a new environment which itself was entering a long period of major change, including felling of great tracts of woodland, the Agricultural Revolution and the Enclosure Acts, all of which helped the pheasant to become established.

Earliest introductions were of *P.c. colchicus* from the Caucasus which became known as old English pheasants but since the eighteenth century (first record 1785) stocks have been mostly of *P.c. torquatus* from China, their white neck rings earning them the common name 'ring-necked pheasant'. They are also commonly called 'Chinese pheasants'.

Several other races have been introduced, including the Japanese *P. versicolor* (1840), which was welcomed for its handsomeness, larger size, stronger flight, inclination to take wing more readily and disinclination to wander. The Mongolian (*P.c. mongolicus*) was introduced in the early nineteenth century. Thrown together, these subspecies have interbred freely to provide an amalgam of features and characteristics, the white neck ring remaining very common in feral cocks. The resultant range of hybrid plumages is spectacular.

The scale of introductions and rearing was influenced by rapid development of the gun in the nineteenth century, especially by the arrival of the breechloader which facilitated much bigger bags and stimulated demand for birds. The 'golden era' was 1880–1914, but the grey partridge was then still the most important game species.

On the debit side there is no doubt that in the past over-zealous keepers, desperate to keep their jobs and tied cottages, acted, often unnecessarily, to destroy great numbers of raptors such as owls and harriers before scientific field studies put everything into perspective. For example, research on the sparrowhawk, considered to be the worst avian predator on live pheasants, has revealed that sensible management can result in negligible losses. Thankfully, today most of the inflexible 'old school' keepers are gone and the new generation acts not only on evidence rather than emotion but also with genuine desire to enjoy all species on their beats, including the 'hook-beaks'.

RANGE AND DISTRIBUTION: The species is indigenous from the Caucasus and Caspian eastwards through central Siberia to China and Burma. It is present in Europe only as an introduced species but not northern Scandinavia or western Iberia, and distributed through eastern temperate to warm temperate zones but discontinuous in mainly dry areas through unsuitable habitat.

In Britain it is found everywhere except on the highest hills, even where the habitat is scarcely suitable, owing to the large numbers released. Indeed, management is carried out on such a scale that ornithologists tend to dismiss pheasants as an entirely unnatural part of the avifauna. Density is much lower away from areas of game preservation but local populations can sustain themselves well in isolation — eg about thirty pairs live on Brownsea Island, Hampshire after about forty years with no management whatsoever. The bird is more sparsely distributed in Ireland except where carefully preserved.

HABITAT: In its natural range the pheasant favours grassland or similar herbage near a source of water with some cover from scattered trees and shrubs. In Britain the original Asian habitat along the borders of river reed beds is used little except in the East Anglian fens but there is undoubtedly a general preference for well-watered country. On the other hand, largely treeless areas such as those frequented in the natural range are usually avoided here. Only a few occur on open blanket-bog and moorland, and high rocks are avoided. It is mainly a bird of wooded agricultural land, parkland and large estates.

The pheasant thrives best where woods contain thick undergrowth adjacent to feeding fields on light soil. Scrub, hedgerows and 'long-edged' woods are also important. It commonly visits gardens adjacent to open countryside and is not averse to foraging along roadsides, often leading to its downfall.

IDENTIFICATION: There is little danger of confusing the typical iridescent, mainly copper-coloured cock with his streaming tail taking up about 46cm (18in) of his 76-89cm (30-35in) length. The two central tail feathers vary considerably in length according to age and may reach 61cm (24in). There is so much colour variation that it is virtually pointless to describe it, but all birds have the large red wattle around the eye. The fairly common melanistic form resembles the different Japanese species. But beware confusion with feral birds of introduced species, especially golden, Reeves' and Lady Amherst's pheasants. The golden and Lady Amherst's are much more brightly coloured than our common pheas-

16

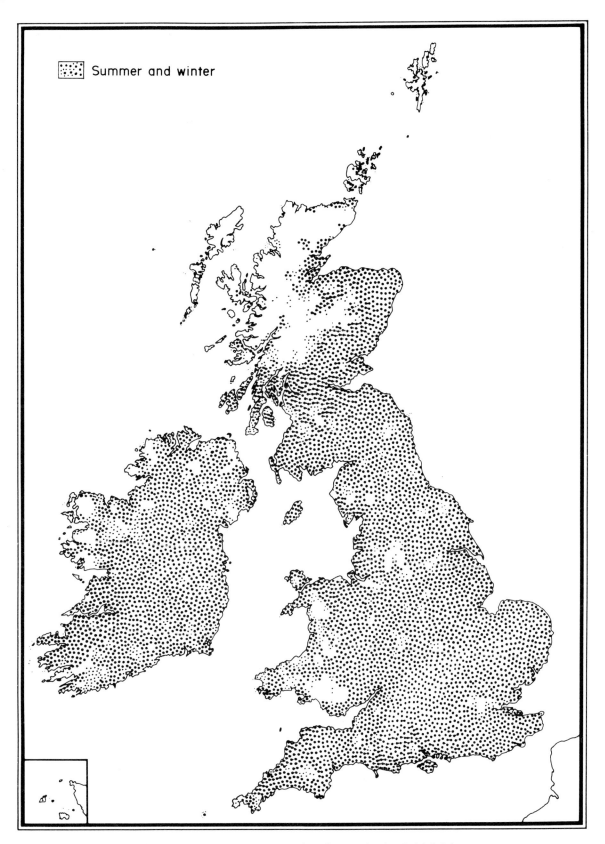

Pheasant — summer/winter distribution in the British Isles

ant while the Reeves', though more sombre, has a spectacularly long tail. The cream-coloured or Bohemian pheasant and melanistic forms have been about since 1927.

The hen is much browner and more uniform in colour but at 53-63cm (21-25in), including a tail of about 23cm (9in), is not likely to be confused with the considerably smaller partridge. Wild birds are generally smaller, especially in remote country. Sometimes birds show characteristic plumage of both sexes, notably with old hens assuming cock plumage and occasionally variations in young. Cocks moult in June and July and hens in July and August.

The average cock weighs 1,226g (2lb 7oz) within a range of 595-2,015g (1lb 5oz-4lb 7oz) and the average hen 1,027g (2lb 4oz) within a range of 737-1,617g (1lb 10oz-3lb 9oz).

VOICE: The cock's crow of *korr-kok* or *kok-kok* is one of the most familiar (and for the shooter most stimulating) sounds of our countryside. He is particularly noisy at dawn in spring and at nightfall just before going to roost when each crow is often followed by wing-flapping. Crowing occurs at any time of year, often in response to a shot or distant explosion, and the bird will 'reply' to imitation.

BREEDING: Where reared the usual practice is to catch adults in late winter or early spring so that they may breed in predator-proof enclosures, or else eggs may be bought from game farms. In any event, nowadays the eggs are normally collected and hatched artificially in incubators where exact control of temperature, humidity and hygiene means a very low failure rate. But the economics are harsh. Even with every modern aid, which might allow a single keeper to rear and release 2,000 birds a year, each bird released probably costs at least £10 to produce and even on an efficient shoot a 50 per cent kill would be good.

In their native lands the cocks are monogamous but in Britain at least they have become polygamous, with some exceptions. However, they do not appear to have been polygamous long enough to have recognised leks or pairing stations, though towards the end of March they crow more and fight over hens, gathering as many as they can. Cocks without territories crow much less.

A cock may establish a territory of about four acres but the hens wander about in groups behaving promiscuously; indeed a single hen's home range may include the territories of four or more cocks. A strong bond with an individual cock is formed for a short period only and there is no long-term pair bond. However, this semi-promiscuous mating system does permit a more even spacing of nests than true polygamy which would result in several hens crowding into the domain of the preferred cock.

With such a mixed background in Britain it is hardly surprising that the species has been known to hybridise with the black grouse, capercaillie, guinea fowl and domestic fowl. Where pheasants are at high density they may often spoil native wild partridge nests by laying in them.

The hen takes full charge of nesting duties, though there are records of cocks assisting in incubation and attempting to brood. She scrapes a ground hollow, frequently under thick vegetation such as bramble and mostly in an area of moderate shrub cover, and lines it scantily with leaves and grass. Occasional sites are in haystacks or rushes, beneath cut brushwood, or even in the old tree nest of another species.

Laying is from March to September, but mostly late April to June, the 7-15 eggs being mostly pale olive-brown. Occasionally there are as many as 20 eggs but instances of up to 26 probably involve two hens. When laying starts the hen

The cock pheasant will even crow in response to a shot or imitation of its call (*John Darling*)

settles down in a more defined range. Incubation takes 23-27 days and is generally by the hen only. If you find a nest the eggs will usually be uncovered because you will have frightened the close-sitting hen away, but when she leaves voluntarily to feed for a short time she may carefully cover her clutch with leaves before flying from the site and later returning in the same manner.

The chicks leave the nest area when only a few hours old and are tended by the hen, fledging after 12-14 days. The hen is not good in defence of her brood which is seldom fully grown before the end of July. Fox, stoat and rat are among the main predators. Generally there is a single brood but there are records of two and the clutch is often replaced following a disaster, after about two weeks at a different site. Re-laying may occasionally occur after a loss of the brood.

The introduced golden, Lady Amherst's and Reeves' pheasants are now breeding freely in the wild in Britain.

FEEDING: Feeding in captivity is not within the province of this book but it should be noted that in most areas artificial feeding will be necessary in severe weather in order to sustain the unnaturally high wild populations. Reared birds will hold well when there is a lack of hedge fruit and it is cold and damp in September and October. Holding crops are sown specially for food as well as cover. Of course, not all farmers are shooting men and may resent the pheasant in spring eating newly sown corn and peas (which might equal the damage of rooks and pigeons) but overall the species is probably beneficial to agriculture.

A wide variety of animal and vegetable foods is taken, ranging from fruits, seeds and leaves of wild plants to leatherjackets, wireworms, caterpillars, ants, grasshoppers, lizards, field voles, small birds, slugs, worms, snails and small snakes. Cultivated goodies such as grain, beans, potatoes, apples and plums are supplemented by acorns, hips, haws, hazel nuts, beechmast, holly berries, oak spangle-galls and even champignon fungus in the appropriate seasons. One wild female I found dead on a small island in July, 1960, with two dead chicks under her wings (one still had the egg tooth), had in her crop ant pupae, a small crab, sandhoppers and coltsfoot flower heads and leaves.

All food is taken on the ground, along with frequent drinks, and both chicks and adults require adequate supplies of grit to aid digestion and sometimes supplement the calcium intake. Consequently, population density is highest on calcareous soil and lowest on acid soil. Local habitat determines the nutritive value of available food and this in turn affects the breeding success. For at least the first two weeks insects form the bulk of the chicks' diet. Beetles are most important, followed by sawfly larvae, aphids, land-bugs and spring-tails. Sometimes adults die from eating yew leaf clippings.

MOVEMENTS: This is one of the most sedentary of birds, spending its entire life within a few square miles. There is some evidence of migration from extreme parts of the natural range in Manchuria. The range of the cock varies with the time of year — perhaps 50 per cent more in winter than in spring/summer, but the hen's changes little.

BEHAVIOUR: Though generally gregarious, forming small parties or 'nids', the pheasant is shy and wary despite semi-domestication and when seen in the open hurries to the nearest cover or, if in cover, crouches until any danger is passed. It is loath to fly, running swiftly ahead of men and dogs, and the faster it runs the more vertical the tail. If forced to fly it rockets explosively away, vertically if necessary to clear trees or thick cover.

In flight the neck is slightly extended and the tail spread but the pheasant rarely rises to any great height above ground in open country. The flight is the typical gamebird variety — short, rapid, strong and direct with short wings whirring noisily on rising but as soon as sufficient height is gained it glides silently on decurved wings, alternating flapping and gliding before dropping into cover at the earliest opportunity. Occasionally it may fly a few miles but it cannot be induced to fly strongly away from its home and will fly fast and far to get back to it.

The pheasant is most active towards sunset and early in the morning when it leaves cover to forage for food in the fields and clearings. The normal gait is a walk, rather more stately than the domestic fowl.

A typical gamebird, the pheasant is fond of dusting and bathing. Shooters are often surprised to discover that the pheasant will not only swim readily when injured or pressed hard but also when it is not necessary, reflecting its close association with water in its native haunts.

The species also has a strong preference for roosting over water. Generally it roosts in trees and the warmth of evergreens is favoured, especially in winter, but this depends on local cover. Occasionally it roosts on the ground in summer and generally prefers an eminence. Juveniles do not generally take to the trees before October. Unfortunately, at roost it loses its wariness and may be approached easily, making it vulnerable to poaching.

Quick to learn, by the end of the shooting season surviving pheasants (reputedly cocks more than hens) have become wily and it may pay shoot captains handsome dividends to reverse driving tactics for the day.

POPULATION: As the bird is so conspicuous it is relatively easy to monitor. There may be as many as 500,000 pairs in the British Isles. A bag variation of 200-400 per 400ha has been revealed by the National Game Census but this is largely due to yearly fluctuation in the wild population which comprises 65-75 per cent of national bags and about a third of the bag even in areas where rearing and release are carried out on a large scale.

While the feral population is long established and self-supporting it is interesting to speculate on how low it might become without regular, massive injections of reared stock. There were significant drops when keepering was suspended during the two world wars.

The Common Birds Census indices indicate that the breeding population has been increasing in recent years.

OPEN SEASON: England, Scotland, Wales (cocks and hens): 1 October to 1 February. Northern Ireland (cocks only): 1 October to 31 January, but a licence may be obtained fairly easily to shoot hens if the applicant can provide evidence of releasing birds. Applications to Department of the Environment (Conservation Branch), Stormont Castle. Irish Republic (cocks only): 1 November to 31 January, but a licence to shoot hens which have been released may be obtained from the Forest and Wildlife Service.

IN THE POT: The pheasant has long been established as a favourite table bird. As with all gamebirds length of hanging (by the neck) is a matter of personal taste. I prefer a hen hung for no more than a week (even in cool weather) and casseroled on top of the oven in a sauce of cream, cider and apples (Cox's). Some hang birds for several weeks for a really strong flavour. Also recommended is an oven casserole with the bird stuffed with mushrooms in a dry sherry sauce.

November birds are often best for they have fed well on autumn's natural harvest. Most birds will be of the year with short spurs but a very old cock is likely to have long, sharp spurs.

THE FUTURE: Even after nearly 1,000 years wild residence in Britain the pheasant has not really settled down. It is a pretty helpless bird, largely sustained by man's ingenuity and interest. It frequently deserts its nest, lays eggs in several places and often only a few of its chicks survive to the shooting season. Like so many birds and animals maintained at artificially high levels, it is subject to many diseases, though these are chiefly confined to the chicks or adults in the rearing field. Most are well known to the poultry farmer and include coccidiosis, gapes, favus and bacillary diarrhoea, though none is comparable with grouse disease. Wild birds are not attacked to anything like the same extent.

Annual mortality of reared and wild birds is high — 70–80 per cent irrespective of whether or not they are shot, but productivity is correspondingly high. On average two-thirds of the ordinary shoot's bag will consist of wild birds. However, habitat requirements are often ignored and there is great scope for concentration on this aspect in the future with the aid of specialist researchers such as those employed by the Game Conservancy.

The proportion of the bag taken by roughshooters may well increase in importance as economic recession accelerates growth in DIY shoots with a new emphasis on efficiency and habitat control.

In practice few people shoot pheasants before November when the leaf is off the trees and the birds are stronger on the wing, and recently it has been suggested that in many parts of the country shoots — especially 'cocks only' days — could continue to mid-February without damaging the stock. However, disturbance of other species would have to be borne in mind.

GREY PARTRIDGE
(Perdix perdix)

Though it remains widespread, the grey partridge population continues in general decline. Its fluctuating fortune this century has led to it being regarded as one of the chief indicators of the state of health of the countryside. And how that countryside has changed since William Turner wrote simply of 'the partridge' in 1544 when Britain harboured no other partridge species. His *Avium Historia* (in Latin) was the first printed bird book. In 1678 Willughby referred to the 'common partridge' in *The Ornithology* (first published in Latin in 1676). Macgillivray, in his *History of British Birds* (1837–52), introduced today's most widely used name, grey partridge, and the term 'English partridge' became more common after the redlegged or French partridge was introduced. Whatever the name the species has been replaced in scale by the pheasant as Britain's number one gamebird, yet for many sportsmen its fascination and sporting qualities are far greater.

HISTORY: As a major gamebird, indeed, one which has become the symbol of the Game Conservancy, the grey partridge has long been the subject of intensive study. Population decline began in the last century and by the 1920s had become so serious in Ireland that legislation prohibiting or restricting shooting was introduced. Without these measures and subsequent restocking the species might well have become extinct there. The situation has been relatively easy to monitor and has been based largely on spring pair counts. Causes of the decline are complex but it is almost certainly not, as sometimes supposed, anything to do with the coincidental ascendancy of the redlegged partridge.

Decrease in England became quite noticeable in the 1960s and the obvious thing to blame was the chemical revolution on the farm. But the greater application of herbicides, and fungicides as well as insecticides which kill the partridge's food is only partly responsible.

A decline in sheep has also meant fewer insects, especially on downland where the most valuable species are most common. The important sawfly larvae, *Collembola* and aphids have highest densities there, are at intermediate numbers on grassland and much reduced among cereals, especially after spraying.

Increasing urgency throughout the farming year in an attempt to maximise profits and production has seen wholesale disappearance of the 'marginal wastes' where partridge coveys used to forage. Fallow fields are rare, efficient new machines leave little spilt grain on stubbles and autumn ploughing has become the rule rather than the exception. Harvest is rapidly followed by stubble burning, reducing the food supply even further. Autumn ploughing has also, through soil disturbance, brought about a great reduction in one of the partridge's staple foods — tenthredinid sawfly larvae. The only redeeming feature of autumn ploughing is that it means reduced disturbance of the birds in spring.

Reduction in the area of tall grasses means far less winter cover. That offered by winter cereals, though welcome, is inferior. This results in the formation of larger territories because males can see their rivals at greater distances and thus the breeding population is necessarily reduced. There has also been decline in cereal crops undersown with clover and in the area of pure leys, in both of which sawfly pupae overwinter.

Insufficient food is bad enough in isolation but when coupled with frequent cold, late springs and cool, damp summers, as have been common over the last twenty-five years, then the chick survival rate is even lower.

RANGE AND DISTRIBUTION: The grey partridge is found from northern Spain across Europe to the head of the Gulf of Bothnia, to Turkey, Russia and central Asia.

It is widespread in Britain with almost continuous distribution in England despite the protracted decline. The species is rare or absent over large areas only in western Scotland, parts of Wales and in Ireland where decline started in the nineteenth century and there are none in much of the south; it is also absent from much of the Highlands and islands of Scotland.

HABITAT: Ideal surroundings are increasingly hard to find with the highest densities and greatest nesting success on farms with the 'patchwork quilt' of small fields in areas of mixed cultivation where hedgerows and rough ground re-main. The recent rapid removal of hedgerows in the trend towards larger fields is particularly detrimental, for plenty of cover is needed in early spring. Density is lowest in large areas under plough and on upland farms.

The partridge also breeds regularly on moorland to about 500m (1,625ft), rough pasture, heaths and commons, while sand-dunes, brecks, and even allot-ments and suburban wastes are frequented. It is very fond of coastal shingle and even feeds on the seashore below high water mark.

IDENTIFICATION: In flight the rufous tail is a good field mark. Generally brown and grey, and barred chestnut on the flanks, the sexes are not easy to identify but the hen is less boldly marked, her breast horseshoe is generally fainter than that of

the male and sometimes missing. The adult hen's crown is more grey-white whereas the cock's is usually grey-brown. The cock walks more upright. There are many colour variations; the juvenile has brown streaking where the adult is chestnut and is very similar to the juvenile redleg.

Grey partridge — summer/winter distribution in the British Isles

The cock measures 31cm (12in), averages 392g (nearly 14oz) within a range of 370-420g (approximately 13-15oz) and has no spurs. The hen measures 29cm (11½in) and averages 372g (13oz) within a range of 340-400g (approximately 12-14oz). As the bird runs frequently the hind toe is shortened to reduce the area of foot touching the ground.

VOICE: The partridge has possibly the largest vocabulary of our gamebirds and even whistles and hisses but is mostly known for the loud, harsh *kerric-kerric-kerric,* usually uttered at dusk or even well after dark by both sexes and particularly during the breeding season. In flight the covey will call *kar-wit, kar-wit* or *kirr-ie, kirrie,* but as they rise they make a harsh cackling.

BREEDING: On the opening of the shooting season partridges are still in family groups — coveys — but they break up into breeding pairs very early, late January or early February. In defence of territory cocks become very aggressive and in courtship birds chase one another, pairs often springing into the air. Pairing has been noted as early as the last week in December in exceptionally mild weather. Possession of territory ensures sufficient food at a difficult time of year and presence in March is a good indication that territory has been established.

The species is strictly monogamous and the cock is a devoted husband. The hen selects the nest site in thick vegetation in April and this is found quite easily by observing her in the early morning, as she returns to the nest after feeding, or by tracing the birds' tracks through vegetation. There are usually two of these runs, one on each side of the nest. The scrape is lined with dried grass and leaves. In site selection protection from the wind and being able to catch the sun appear to be important. Often the nest has a small branch or twig, frequently of blackberry, over it, apparently to offer protection, and concealment and shade when the leaves are out. Sometimes a haystack is used.

Young partridges are very reliant on suitable insect food so the eggs are mostly laid in late May so that peak hatching in June coincides with peak food availability. Laying can begin in late April and the average 12-18 pale olive or buff eggs are incubated for 24 days by the hen only. Clutch size is said to vary with the age of the female but larger clutches in the range 9-23 eggs probably involve two females. Eggs are laid on consecutive days, often between 10am and noon, and incubation starts on the day after the last egg is laid. The hen covers the eggs when she leaves the nest voluntarily and the cock escorts her to feed. She rarely deserts, will sit through torrential thunderstorms and may even be stroked on the nest.

The eggs all hatch within two or three hours and the cock shelters the first chicks out under his wings but the hen soon takes over. Both stoutly defend their young, feigning injury and even attacking dogs.

The family leaves the nest site a few hours after hatching and both adults tend the chicks which flutter at 10 days and fly after about 14 days. There is a single brood and Dixon noted: 'If birds continue to call into June and July it is a bad omen, and a sure sign that nests have been unfortunate.' Foxes, magpies and

Grey partridge covey in the stubble. The species continues to decline in a manicured countryside *(Roy Shaw)*

crows are among their main enemies and even in keepered areas most nest losses are due to predation.

Grey partridges are known to hybridise with redlegs.

FEEDING: Nearly 200 years ago Bewick wrote 'it is almost impossible to rear young partridges hatched under hens without a diet of ants' eggs'; but we have learned a lot since then.

Between January and March hedge bottoms are favourite haunts where many seeds may be gathered, and on downland the winter diet contains a high percentage of grass leaves. On farmland, growing wheat is favoured for its generally higher protein content and in this respect the increasing area of winter wheat is advantageous. Another good place to find partridges is in swede fields, for these harbour many insects.

Adults subsist on mainly grain and buds, flowers, leaves and seeds of low-growing plants, insects, spiders, slugs and small snails. The young are particularly dependent on sawfly larvae. After the harvest grain dominates.

MOVEMENTS: The species is resident with just a little local dispersal in autumn and winter.

BEHAVIOUR: There is probably no more difficult a driven target than a partridge, particularly in windy weather, for, though somewhat slower than grouse, it is smaller and has a more twisting flight. The quick changes in speed and course are quite deceptive. Surprisingly it is the slowest of our gamebirds on the wing.

27

For most shooters the familiar view of partridges is of them flying away low over the ground. When flushed they rise quickly and very suddenly, the small, broad, rounded, whirring wings carrying them away from danger, alternating with periods of gliding on stiff, bowed pinions. But they are reluctant to fly, and when in danger prefer to squat close to the earth or run quickly to cover with necks stretched up and backs straight. The normal gait is a stealthy walk with the neck drawn into the shoulders and the back rounded.

Busiest searching for food morning and evening, the partridge is very conservative in its habits, frequently seen doing the same things at the same time in the same place, day after day, unless food is scarce. During the hottest part of the day it will often lay up in cover and is fond of dust-bathing and basking. Only rarely do partridges perch on walls, fences or trees.

Today they are no longer found in very large gatherings but coveys continue to feed and sleep together, usually roosting on the ground facing outwards to watch for predators. It is only in rare places where they are not often pursued that coveys will still flock together. Each covey has a particular spot to which birds retire to 'jug' down for the night, usually in grass or other vegetation and not generally under a hedge or bush. Deliberate formation of a roosting circle is unlikely but droppings indicate that partridges usually jug in a rough arc facing the wind. In a high wind they seem to forsake the arc for a tight bunch facing the wind as is the normal practice of all resting birds other than the semi-domesticated pheasant. In my experience coveys roost towards the centres of fields.

In severe weather partridges may turn up in unexpected places such as rickyards in search of food but the responsible gunner would not then take advantage of weakened birds.

POPULATION: This appears to fluctuate considerably from year to year but recent estimates are in the region of 500,000 pairs for the British Isles. The Common Birds Census indices indicate continuing decline in recent years.

OPEN SEASON: England, Scotland, Wales: 1 September to 1 February. Northern Ireland: fully protected at all times. Irish Republic: only 1–15 November.

IN THE POT: The partridge is a great table favourite that needs no special treatment to enhance the flavour. Early season birds are often best. In September and early October the yellowish legs, dark beak and softer bones distinguish the young from the grey-legged, grey-beaked and hard-boned adults. Later in the season the young bird may be distinguished by the two outer primaries which are pointed, but round-ended in the adult. If these feathers are pointed but faded and worn then the bird is in its second year.

THE FUTURE: The partridge is subject to a number of diseases and is often heavily infested with lice, which explains the frequent dust baths. Salmonella pullorum (BWD), pneumonia and gapes occasionally cause serious local losses but the chief enemies are coccidiosis and strongylosis, the latter mainly the result of overstocking and in-breeding. It is estimated that between a half and one million partridges are released each year.

With such problems it is little wonder that the continuing trend is towards management through provision of suitable habitat for food, shelter and nesting in order to provide a shootable surplus. In 1983 the Game Conservancy launched an important new scheme aimed at educating farmers in the controlled use of herbicides and insecticides on cereals with a view to improving conditions for gamebirds. This enterprising research project is to be funded by the farmers themselves. The grey partridge stands to gain more than any other gamebird because of its great reliance on insects in the chicks' diet.

One alarming trend that appears to have slowed but is unlikely to halt in the near future is towards creating larger fields to gain economies of scale, so the outlook for the hedge-loving partridge is grim.

Today's maxim must be don't shoot your partridges unless you are certain that your stocks can take it. Many people gave up shooting them long ago but calls to suspend shooting entirely seem quite unjustified.

REDLEGGED PARTRIDGE
(*Alectoris rufa*)

The Guernsey, French or redlegged partridge has met with considerable antagonism from British sportsmen, who often assert that this species affords poor sport compared with the grey partridge, and in some areas attempts have been made to eliminate it. This probably has more to do with Britain's insular attitude towards 'foreigners' rather than sport, for the bird has some useful qualities and should not be seen as a competitor with the native grey.

HISTORY: The redleg is not indigenous to Britain, our population being derived entirely from liberated stock and their progeny. The first-recorded introduction attempt was in 1673, followed by several others in Surrey, Sussex and Essex before the Marquis of Hertford achieved success in Suffolk in 1790 with several thousand eggs imported from France for local hatching and rearing. Most subsequent colonisation stems from Hertford's efforts but over sixty further introductions are on record from 1830 to 1958. Most were in England's more favourable climate but some went to Scotland and Wales and one to Galway in Ireland.

As early as 1876 Booth reported that it was

. . . by no means a favourite with the generality of sportsmen. Its well-known shyness and constant habit of trusting to its legs rather than its wings as a means of escape from danger causes its rapid increase in some counties to be regarded as anything but acceptable.

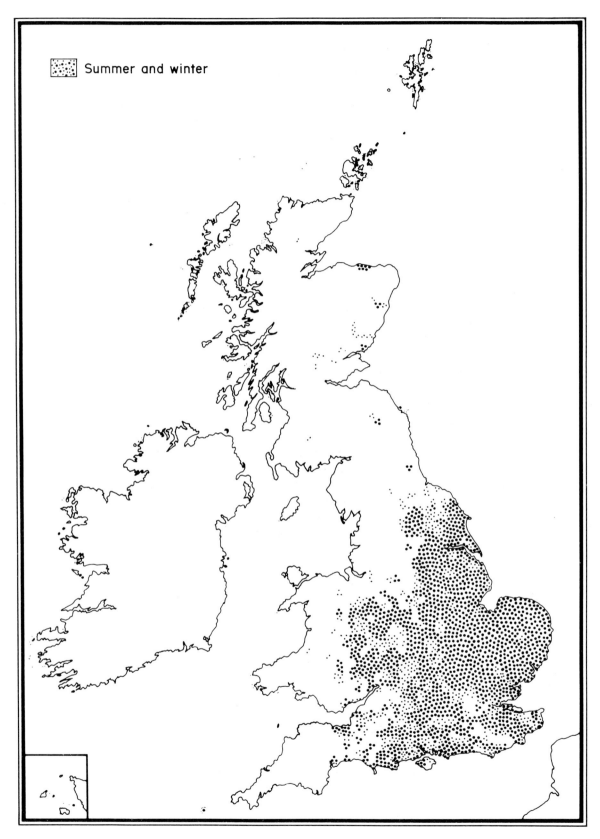

Redlegged partridge — summer/winter distribution in the British Isles

None the less numbers continued to rise and reached a maximum in about 1930, but decline and range contraction followed. However, there were some marked increases from the late 1950s, especially in north-west Norfolk, and by 1972 distribution was probably as wide as it has ever been.

Overall the redleg has been more successful than the grey partridge in recent years. Small-scale introductions outside the main range have always failed but it is still common to augment stocks from commercial game farms. Some releases have included the closely related chukar and rock partridges from south-east Europe. These are now well established and freely hybridise with redlegs. Hybrids have bred in the wild but produce fewer young than pure redlegs.

RANGE AND DISTRIBUTION: One of very few species endemic to Europe, the native population is restricted to south-west Europe. Its range in Spain, France, Corsica and north-west Italy has been extended by introductions to the Balearic Isles, Azores, Canaries and Madeira.

In Britain it is fairly widespread through south-east England. East Anglia is a stronghold. Howells (1963) concluded that distribution coincided with annual rainfall under 89cm (35in), lower precipitation in the breeding season being favourable to chick survival. So generally there is an aversion to the north and west, and it is absent from Cornwall, Devon, most of Wales, Lancashire, the Pennines and the North Yorkshire Moors northwards. It was introduced to the Irish Republic in 1979.

It is now more numerous than the native grey in parts of eastern England.

HABITAT: Generally the preference is for drier land than that favoured by the grey partridge and East Anglia probably provides the optimum conditions with intensive agriculture in a continental-type climate, low rainfall and a light soil. Redlegs also occur on sandy heaths, coastal shingle and dunes, chalk down-land and occasionally in woods with wide rides or large glades. It likes rougher ground than the grey, with more bush. The heavy, wet soils of the Weald are avoided.

IDENTIFICATION: It is not easy to distinguish from the grey partridge at long distances for it flies and runs with the same action as the grey, but within shooting range look for the black-and-white eye stripes and barred flanks. It has the same rufous tail as the grey but no dark horseshoe on the breast.

In the field the sexes are indistinguishable but in the hand look for the cock's knob-like spurs. Legs, feet and bill are coral red and the bird is slightly larger than the grey.

The young resemble young greys before they acquire adult markings in November, except that the plumage is rather more spotted than striped. They lack the distinctive head pattern and barred flanks.

The male's length is 34cm (13½in) and average weight 516g (1lb 2oz) within a range 500-547g (1lb 1½oz-1lb 3oz). The female's length is 33cm (13in) and average weight 439g (15½oz) within a range 391-477g (14oz-1lb 1oz).

VOICE: The cock's calling is long and varied with a distinctive, loud and challenging *chucka chucka* or *chuck-chuck-ar,* frequently delivered from a low perch. When put up, both sexes cry *kuk kuk* and occasionally they give a shrill, treble *crik-ik-ik.*

BREEDING: When pairing in February the cocks become rather pugnacious with frequent combats. The covey breaks up later and starts breeding later and over a longer period than the grey, small coveys being found even into April.

The nest is generally hard to find, in a hedge bottom, nettlebed or other thick cover, and for once it is the cock that makes the scantily lined scrape. Sometimes the site is in crops or even a haystack. Redlegs are more inclined to nest off the ground than greys.

The redleg is unique among British birds in that one female may lay two clutches in separate nests — one for her mate to incubate and one for herself so that each will raise a brood. The 10-15 buffish, spotted red-brown eggs are laid from late April to May and up to 28 have been recorded, the larger clutches perhaps having something to do with our climate. But this high rate of egg pro-duction is offset by increased losses, for, unlike the grey partridge the redleg never covers its eggs when left and many are destroyed by rats, stoats etc. Eggs are not laid on consecutive days. Sometimes they are left for thirty-six or even forty-eight hours. Yet, surprisingly, clutches left uncovered for weeks and even-tually incubated by the male are hatched as successfully as those incubated immediately.

Incubation takes 23-25 days by either or both parents. The chicks leave the nest and run almost as soon as hatched, are tended by both parents and fly after about 14 days.

FEEDING: The redleg's diet is predominantly vegetable, including leaves, cereals and seeds, but also insects and spiders in summer. The young are dependent on animal food (mainly arthropods) for their first few weeks but are better at ranging than young grey partridges, and sometimes seem to get by on certain plant foods without insects.

They feed haphazardly throughout the day but there is a strong preference for

Cock and hen pheasant

evening meals. The cock and hen usually feed alone off the nest. Where they occur on the beach they will feed well below high water mark, even to the ebb.

MOVEMENTS: The redleg is a sedentary resident.

BEHAVIOUR: Like the grey partridge, this is a bird of fairly regular habits and usually visits some places at certain times each day. But it is quite different in its sporting qualities. Flight is easy and strong with the rapidly beating, noisy, whirring wings typical of gamebirds, generally taking a low line with no change of direction. However, there is change in pace as with the grey, and being faster than the latter the redleg is more of a sporting target.

Again, like the grey it is skulking and loath to fly but prefers to run, often with amazing speed, rather than squat. Therefore it is not suitable for walking-up — hence the unpopularity in the old days when most partridge shooting was over dogs. It is also blamed for scaring greys and making them run too. It is restless and nervous and remains in cover more than the grey, being ever alert and watchful, craning its neck to see out of cover, looking all around even as it runs to hide.

Some shooters say it offers poor sport because the coveys form into flocks which soon scatter when alarmed. Because of its incessant running, driving is necessary to get a reasonable bag. Yet the tendency to scatter when shot at may help to break up coveys of greys and offer more steady sport.

Reluctant to fly, its feet often get so clogged with mud on wet days that it *cannot* fly. It tends to run uphill and fly down, and the walk is round-backed.

Unlike the grey it favours a perch with a commanding view — haystacks, hedges, fences, walls and even trees, and often takes no notice of passing cars. It is easy to see when crops are short in the spring, and its noisiness often brings it to attention. It roosts on the ground but seems to prefer off-ground sites and will roost in a close bunch in a tree. The roost site is changed frequently.

POPULATION: There are probably around 100,000-200,000 pairs.

OPEN SEASON: England, Scotland, Wales: 1 September to 1 February. Northern Ireland: may be shot under licence from the Department of the Environment (Conservation Branch), Stormont, on production of evidence that birds have been put down. Irish Republic: fully protected.

IN THE POT: The rather dark flesh has been unpopular in some areas but, though not so fine as that of the grey partridge, this is a worthy table bird. Young have the tips of the two outer primaries coloured cream.

THE FUTURE: The redleg is generally underrated as a reared quarry species. It frequently brings off large broods and of these a large proportion reach maturity

Redlegged partridge *(top)* and *(below)* grey partridge cock *(left)* and hen

Redlegged partridge with newly hatched chicks. Male and female often raise separate broods *(Eric Hosking)*

despite high predation. Winter losses are low and it can withstand heavy shooting pressure. It should figure more in future bags but not, it is hoped, to the extent that the grey partridge is neglected.

Stricter legislation on introductions should prevent stock becoming even more mixed.

RED GROUSE
(*Lagopus lagopus scoticus*)

The red grouse, gorcock, moorcock or moorfowl has long been associated with the most exclusive shooting in Britain and certainly today this remains so as far as driven shooting is limited by high costs. The species offers some of our most exciting shooting within a spectacular landscape, and increasingly the guns come from richer countries such as the USA and Germany to enjoy this uniquely British sport. However, some walked-up grouse shooting is available in remote areas abroad, such as in Scandinavia.

The impact of the grouse on our environment is enormous. Until recently grouse moors covered 3 million acres in Scotland, 1 million acres in Ireland and 1 million acres in England and Wales, but they are decreasing rapidly in some areas.

HISTORY: Whatever is said of decline we are always talking only relatively and the fact is that this species remains at an artificially high population level in a country that was originally well-wooded. As forests were cleared, man settled down to a sedentary existence and gathered his crops and domesticated animals about him, with sheep in hilly districts. But with the railways and easier access in the nineteenth century came a decline in sheep farming and crofters were moved out as landowners realised that grouse brought more income than did sheep. The process was stimulated by the introduction of the breechloader in 1853, for this gun's increased firepower made driving a practical proposition.

Being of great economic importance, the grouse became the subject of considerable study and concern at an early date. Subsequent decline eventually led to a parliamentary Committee of Enquiry being set up under the chairmanship of Lord Lovat in 1904, the outcome of which was publication of the massive, two-volume report *The Grouse in Health and Disease*.

Early concern was over disease, the two most deadly forms being coccidiosis and strongylosis. Coccidiosis is carried in food and water and attacks other creatures but strongylosis is grouse disease proper, all grouse carrying the parasitic threadworm. The disease has been recorded for 200 years and is quite natural, but under intense grouse management when the moor stock is too high epidemics occur. Shooting reduces the disease by reducing the stock.

Although attempts at introduction to Exmoor in the early 1820s failed, further introductions there and on Dartmoor in 1915–16 succeeded. Ireland's decline became marked from about 1920 and throughout Britain in the 1930s many moor stocks dwindled and did not recover. Of course, rents plunged with the bags. In some areas the inter-war period was productive but even there decline returned from 1940, especially with keepering in abeyance.

The Scottish Landowners' Federation decided to support a three-year research programme supported by voluntary subscription from 1956. Later the Nature Conservancy took over and set up the Unit of Grouse and Moorland Ecology. In 1968 the specialist staff were embodied in the Game Conservancy. Findings revealed that disease and predation generally affect only the non-breeding surplus which remains after the shooting season; they were not responsible for the big drop in bags. While grazing by sheep and cattle has had a deleterious effect on the habitat it has been demonstrated conclusively that the major reason for decline is deterioration of heather quality brought about by a reduction in the number of keepers.

Suspicions that the Irish stock's (formerly regarded as a separate race — *Lagopus lagopus hibernicus*) decline was due to an inherent loss of vigour, despite frequent introductions of Scottish birds, were disproved experimentally.

RANGE AND DISTRIBUTION: Famous for being formerly regarded as the only bird

37

species entirely restricted to the British Isles, it is now regarded merely as a well-marked island subspecies (race), *Lagopus lagopus scoticus,* of the willow grouse (*Lagopus lagopus*) which ranges across America and Eurasia. Whereas the willow grouse has white wings all year, our red grouse has had no need to change to winter white in a milder climate.

Grouse moors are mostly between 300 and 600m (975–1,950ft) but can range from sea level to 800m (2,600ft), for heather occurs at different heights in different areas and altitudinally the red grouse's range may overlap with that of the ptarmigan. The Scottish Highlands are the stronghold and there are good populations on Orkney, the Outer Hebrides, the Border hills, parts of the Lake District, the Yorkshire Moors and the Pennines. Wales has some good moors, but in southern England only small populations are found on Dartmoor and Exmoor.

HABITAT: Heather dominates the open, treeless moorland frequented by the red grouse but crowberry and bilberry are desirable as alternative foods. In west Ireland, west Scotland and locally in Wales the species occurs in wetter parts, sometimes also on blanket-bog with sparse heather and among patches of heather on chiefly grassy areas. Conifer plantations are abandoned when the trees are about 3m (9ft 9in) high.

Moor management is the key to high population density. This involves control of predators, especially foxes and crows, application of fertilisers, drainage where waterlogging exists, and above all rotational burning to ensure a continuous succession of young heather shoots for food. Burning also keeps down the tick population which spreads coccidiosis, but some old heather must be left for shelter and nesting. Heather and grass burning is strictly controlled and landowners should check with the Ministry of Agriculture Fisheries and Food on the latest regulations. Burning is restricted to certain times of year except under licence and there is some regional variation. In 1983 a review was initiated as the regulations had remained virtually unchanged since 1949.

Disturbance from hill walkers, tourism and so on appears to have had little impact and recent climatic changes do not appear to have significantly affected the food supply. The heather beetle is a problem in that it attacks the plant, and the sheep tick, which weakens and even kills grouse, is also carried by deer, hares and rabbits.

IDENTIFICATION: The red grouse is subject to considerable plumage variation, especially regionally; for example, Irish birds are generally paler. In addition, both male and female have two distinct moults each year, but the male's are in autumn and winter whereas the female's are in summer and autumn. The male is in summer plumage from the end of May or the beginning of June to the beginning of October and in winter plumage from mid-October to mid-May. The female is in summer plumage from April to August and winter plumage from August to March. The male is in eclipse from the end of May into June.

The cock's comb is large and red whereas the hen's is smaller and pinker. She is

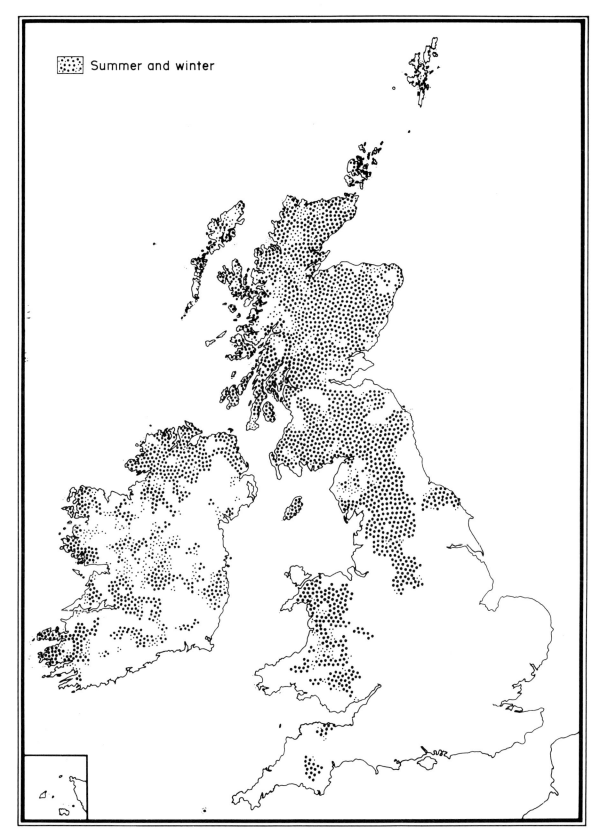

Red grouse — summer/winter distribution in the British Isles

paler and more heavily barred with lighter pigment whereas he has thinner, more wavy lines and spots. The hen usually has more brown and yellow mottling on the wings and dark tail. Adults appear greyer in winter with white underwing-coverts, and occasionally show white on the flanks and belly. The legs are feathered down to the claws.

The juvenile is like the hen. The comb is less distinctive but cocks have chestnut under the chin and on the throat with little or no black barring, while in the hen these feathers are generally yellower and the black barring is more pronounced.

The cock's length is 36-39cm (14-15½in) and average weight 680g (1lb 8oz) within a range 600-690g (1lb 5oz-1lb 8½oz) and the hen's length 33-36cm (13-14in) and average weight 586g (1lb 4½oz) within a range 550-670g (1lb 3½oz-1lb 7½oz).

VOICE: The distinctive *go-back, go-back* and repeated *kow-ok-ok-ok* are synonymous with wild moorland. The cock's crow is especially noticeable during courtship and early in the morning — a loud, clear *cok-ok-ok*. The hen utters a low croak.

BREEDING: It is hardly surprising that the breeding success of the red grouse should attract considerable media publicity every year for there are great fluctuations in an utterly unpredictable climate and everyone is interested in a 'sport of kings'.

The species is generally monogamous but a few males with large territories hold two hens which both nest within his patch. The cock marks his territory in dramatic display, leaping skyward with wings spread to descend again steeply, extending his neck and feet and fanning his tail. There is always some autumn sparring and in a mild winter pairing occurs in December or January. Some territories are taken as early as October.

The hen makes a simple scrape in the ground, lining it with grass and heather. Though nesting occasionally takes place as early as the end of February, usually the 6-11 (occasionally 4-17) creamy-white eggs, almost obscured by chocolate-red blotches, are laid from late April into May. The warmer and drier the season the larger the number of eggs. Laying takes place every 24-48 hours and the 22-24 day incubation by the hen commences with the arrival of the last egg. Favourite sites are in the safety of deep, old heather but with recently burnt ground producing young heather shoots for food nearby. The cock is attentive and escorts the hen to and from feeding.

A mild winter followed by late snow will cause great havoc but eggs can stand a surprising amount of cold and hens will continue sitting in fairly deep snow. Even badly frosted eggs rarely fail to hatch. Frost and snow *after* hatching are much more serious.

The downy chicks leave the nest soon after hatching and the single brood is tended by both sexes. They can flutter at 7 days and fly at 12–18 days but they remain together as a family into the autumn, even as late as November. If the clutch is lost it is usually replaced by another, but smaller, one. Grouse are very bold in defence of their young, not only mounting distraction displays but also even physically attacking human and animal intruders.

FEEDING: The red grouse relies almost entirely on ling heather, especially in winter, eating the shoots, flowers and seed heads. Adults prefer to eat the current year's growth from heather aged about three years. In fact biologists do not know any moor where there are plenty of grouse and no heather or bilberry (*Vaccinium myrtillus*).

Other favourite foods are shoots and fruits of cranberry, stalks and leaves of bilberry, flowers and shoots of *Eriophorum* (cotton grass, drawmoss or moss crop), bog myrtle, dwarf willow, grass, rushes, clover and bracken. In autumn evidence of ground fruits in the diet can be seen by the purple-stained droppings on rocks. Also eaten are birch buds and catkins, sheep sorrel, chickweed, bell heather, whinflowers, pine buds, heath rush and grass seeds.

There is naturally considerable regional variation in the plant foods but insects are especially important to the chicks in their first two weeks. Wet summers are not so disastrous as they are for partridges as young grouse eat far less insect food, and heather dries very quickly. Young chicks also eat heather tips, moss capsules and various flowers from the first day. After ten days plant food dominates and at three weeks the diet is entirely adult. In severe weather and during harvest they will visit the oat stubbles and even stack-yards.

Grouse have been known to live for years without heather but in the end it is vital for their well-being. As with other gamebirds, grit is essential for digestion of food. Quartz grit is especially favoured and grouse may travel considerable distances to get it. Grit can be retained in the gizzard for weeks but generally there is no shortage.

The young seem to drink less but certainly the adults drink every day from dewdrops, pools, streams and frost or snow.

MOVEMENTS: The 'disappearance' and possible migration of grouse has long stimulated the interest and imagination, but there does not appear to be any significant seasonal or regular movement. Exceptionally severe weather may cause birds to leave the highest ground and move possibly several miles onto farmland. In this instance mortality is often very high, and when the birds do not

Cock grouse deep in the heather, upon which the species is so utterly dependent *(Roy Shaw)*

return to the moor it is sometimes wrongfully assumed that they have migrated. Surprisingly though, some may move to *higher* ground during periods of heavy snowfall, for on the tops the wind is more likely to have drifted the snow and thus exposed the important heather.

Notwithstanding this basically sedentary behaviour, packs have been known to move a dozen or so miles and there have been mass movements which have not been accounted for. Some movements of a mile or so are ahead of eagles, others of several miles may be ahead of beaters, and they may even move a mile or more to feed or drink.

BEHAVIOUR: A casual ramble on the moor may not reveal many grouse for the bird is loath to fly, preferring to remain inconspicuous in the heather, trusting to its camouflage colouring. It is forever vigilant for danger, peering out of cover, craning in all directions, and will run off if necessary. The main predators are foxes, hen harriers and golden eagles but wildcats, peregrines, buzzards and stoats take some. Crows and shepherds' collies take young and eggs. Predation is highest when there are packs of 'surplus' grouse, from September, tails off in March and April, and is infrequent from May to August.

Occasionally a grouse is seen on a rock, stunted willow, dry-stone wall or birch. During courtship grouse are surprisingly easy to approach, but in July and August moulting birds spend much time in very rank heather for then they are more vulnerable to eagle and fox.

They flush at the last moment when disturbed, beating away low over the heather with whirring flight, the broad wings bowed for occasional glides before they alight again several hundred yards away. Sometimes a winter flock may fly off for a mile ahead of the line.

After a few days shooting in an early season the coveys start to pack, some-times one sex together, though that is not the general rule. By the end of August they are already more wary and wild and in September and October getting good bags becomes more difficult with so many holding together and tending to pass the butts as one. Young tend to pack earlier than adults and hens more readily than cocks because it is the territory holders which sit tight. A few old males never pack. Sometimes the packs are driven from the moors by territory holders and must resort to stubble fields, grassland, bog and scrub to feed. Yet they do not usually move far and by the afternoon the repleted territory holders may allow them to return. It certainly is survival of the fittest and most unshot birds which fail to secure territory by the end of October will die anyway.

Cocks become more noisy and aggressive in August. Watch for them on a boulder or wall in the early morning for later in the day they may rejoin their families. In the critical month of October many pairs and territories change around. As winter progresses the cocks become increasingly territorial and from January to March will allow no afternoon feeding, so the 'homeless' remain in packs.

During periods of heavy snow on high, bleak moors the birds may have to keep treading to avoid being buried, but they will also deliberately burrow into snow. They roost in the heather but never so tightly as partridges, usually a metre or so apart and sometimes in an arc facing the wind.

POPULATION: There are probably about 500,000 breeding pairs. A moor's popu-lation is determined by the underlying substratum, densities being highest over base-rich rocks such as diorite, epidiorite and all limestones which increase soil fertility and therefore the nutritional value of the heather. The best ground may hold 50-60 pairs per square kilometre — as high as achieved on managed moors. Lowest natural densities are over granite or thick peat.

On average the grouse is short-lived. Nearly two out of three alive in August die within a year, irrespective of shooting. Annual mortality averages 65 per cent so that most nest just once. Some may live for eight years.

The breeding population of a moor is determined by the number of cocks holding territories. Birds without territories are driven into marginal areas where, progressively weakened through hunger and exposed to predators, they soon die. Grouse are non-dispersive (80-90 per cent die within about a mile of where ringed) so the surplus fails to move to other moors and is eliminated by April. In all years the maxim is to shoot hard and early to bag as many of the surplus grouse as possible before packing makes them more difficult to shoot: they will die anyway.

OPEN SEASON: England, Scotland, Wales: 12 August to 10 December. Northern Ireland: 12 August to 30 November. Irish Republic: 1–30 September. September shooting is often best because the late young are able to fly greater distances but are not yet too wild.

IN THE POT: Each year the race to put the first grouse on the restaurant table becomes more competitive, with helicopters and planes in liaison with expert shots, for the bird has long been associated with top cuisine. The excellent meat is fine plain-roasted but lends itself well to exotic experimentation.

Determination of age is always important for that very special occasion and perhaps the simplest and most reasonably accurate way to do this is to examine the shape of the two outer primaries (flight feathers). In an old bird these have rounded ends whereas in a young bird they are pointed in comparison with the other primaries. However, a second-year bird that has not yet moulted has these two feathers pointed but faded and tattered.

THE FUTURE: Grouse shooting is in an almost imperceptibly slow decline. Whether so much land will remain devoted to grouse production is doubtful, even if remaining in private ownership. The economic value of grouse to Scotland is important but no single species should be the be-all and end-all of life anywhere. Surely there must be room for sheep too. However, over-grazing by sheep and red deer is often ignored, especially with the ewe subsidy. This lets in rough grasses which are of little use to grouse. Whatever the outlook, disease will remain a limiting factor in population density. Sheep unfortunately carry the important louping-ill, which is transmitted by ticks.

To date there has been negligible success with methods used with pheasants and other gamebirds in stocking moors with hand-reared or caught-up grouse. The chief problem is adjustment from an artificial to a natural diet. Thus concentration will remain on management of the habitat. But there too are problems. For example, in Ireland the grouse is going through a very hard time because of tremendous bog development and afforestation with the financial aid of government and profit stimulus. Also, there is a major problem there with the heather; and we cannot expect the weather to remain generally favourable indefinitely.

The whole future of our uplands became the focus of attention with the introduction of the Countryside Commission's review in 1983. Not only are we concerned widely with afforestation and other factors with changing economic values, but also increasingly with tourism, public access and the rights of a predominantly urban-based population to enjoy Britain's remaining 'wilderness' areas. In the last decade alone twenty-eight of the thirty-four major Welsh grouse moors have been lost to forestry.

BLACK GROUSE
(Lyrurus tetrix)

Traditionally regarded by sportsmen as a disappointment because its behaviour is not conducive to 'organised' shooting, the black grouse is none the less an exciting and very worthy quarry, a bird of strong will and as wild as its favourite haunts.

HISTORY: The species has suffered great range contraction over the last 200 years as much of its favoured marginal habitat has disappeared. It did occur east to Norfolk and Lincolnshire and south to Cornwall, Dorset, Hampshire and Surrey. Many English counties lost it in the late nineteenth and early twentieth centuries. It has been suggested that the widespread distribution of the nineteenth century may have been partly an artificial result of local introductions and planting of hawthorns to provide winter food. Perhaps some apparently suitable areas remain vacant because the species just cannot take the increased disturbance.

Scotland enjoyed a period of increase and abundance at the end of the nineteenth century but there too decline returned this century. No doubt egg collecting and shooting for skins and, to a lesser degree, for the pot, hastened the decline.

Hampshire's indigenous stock probably died out in 1909, though some were reported there in 1918–19 and 1954, and there was an apparently successful release in the 1930s. But the whole picture is confusing because of the large number of local introductions and reintroductions, many of which have failed. The species is not indigenous to Ireland and repeated attempts to introduce it there in the eighteenth and nineteenth centuries always failed. There have also been introductions of blackgame to Surrey, Sussex, Berkshire, Buckinghamshire, Norfolk, Suffolk, the Orkneys and North Wales, but generally they were unsuccessful. It is probable that the small, isolated population in Devon and Somerset, on Exmoor, is no longer viable without regular reinforcements of hand-reared birds such as in 1969 and 1971.

Yet there are bright spots, most of which are probably nurtured by releases. There have been increases in Wales since the late 1940s and in Scotland since the 1950s. Greatly increased young afforestation has attracted blackgame into areas regarded as long deserted. Some observers have attributed this merely to more efficient recording through increased forester and birdwatcher visits. Dartmoor's population was thought to have gone by the 1950s but a nest was found in 1968. Perhaps the birds wandered from Exmoor?

RANGE AND DISTRIBUTION: The species occurs chiefly in the boreal zone — from England, Wales, Scotland and Scandinavia through eastern Europe to central and western Asia — and has been successfully introduced to Russia and Poland;

45

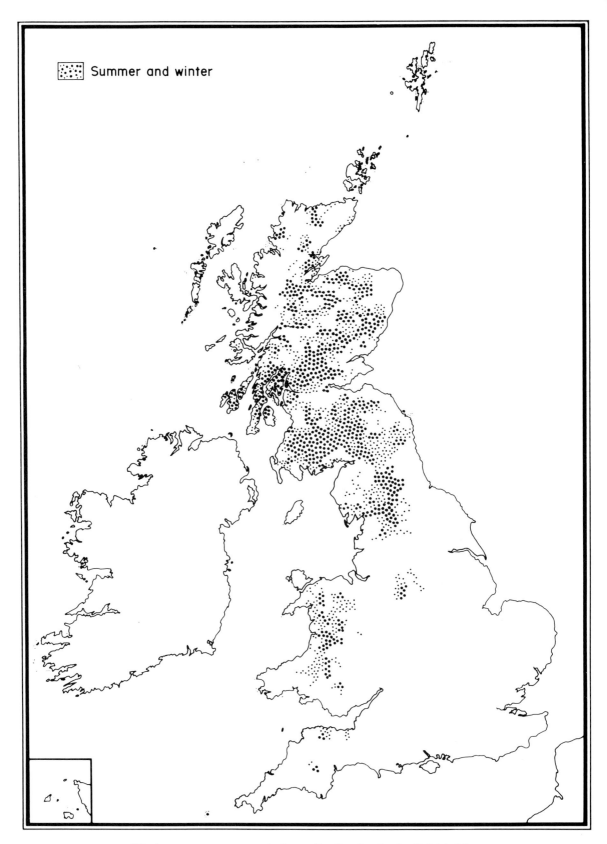

Black grouse — summer/winter distribution in the British Isles

introductions to Ireland, North America and New Zealand have failed. It is declining in most countries except in Britain (northern), the German Alps, some Bavarian forests, Norway and Sweden.

Apart from a few pairs on the Quantocks and Exmoor it does not breed south of Staffordshire in England. More common in Wales and most common in Scotland, it is generally confined to hilly districts of the west and north. Among the islands only Islay has a really good population.

HABITAT: Blackgame are most common along woodland fringes, being not nearly so much a forest bird as the capercaillie. They are found on open moorland dominated by heather but there are generally some trees and scrub nearby, and the species is partial to water, either swampy land with bogs and rushes or areas with streams and ponds. Conifer plantations, up to twenty or so years old, are frequented but mature, open pine forest with heavy undergrowth is also used along with open birch woods. High, rocky ground above the moors also offers shelter.

The birds venture from these rough areas to feed on adjoining marginal agricultural land and in autumn tall bracken is favoured, especially when adjacent to stubbles.

IDENTIFICATION: There is little danger of confusing the handsome male (blackcock) with any other species in his glossy black garb with lyre-shaped tail, white undertail-coverts, white wing-bar, large red wattle over the eye and white shoulder patch. In autumn eclipse he is dingy and without the lyre-shaped tail. Cocks take on their winter plumage when only half-grown (from about mid-August) when they show patches of black and white, but the tail is only slightly curled and altogether there is not the full glory of the old cock.

The female (greyhen) is more difficult to identify but the only likely confusion is with the female capercaillie or red grouse. She is about a third smaller than the blackcock and is generally rust-red and brown with the head, neck and tail barred black. Although she is the only British gamebird with a forked tail this is not easy to see at a distance, and the pale wing-bar is probably more noticeable. She is larger and greyer than the red grouse but smaller and less barred than the capercaillie. The juvenile is like a small, dull female. Watch out for confusing blackgame hybrids with capercaillie, red grouse and pheasant.

The blackcock's length is 53cm (21in) and average weight 1,269g (2lb 13oz) within a range 1,050-1,750g (2lb 5oz-3lb 14oz). The greyhen's length is 41-43cm (16-17in) and average weight 945g (2lb 1oz) within a range 750-1,100g (1lb 10½oz-2lb 7oz).

VOICE: The 'crowing' may be heard as early as January and the 'rookooing' of the cocks at the lek is reminiscent of the pigeon. The soft crooning may be heard over a quarter of a mile away on a still day. Away from the lek the cock is mostly quiet but he does utter a sneezing *tchu-wai*. The greyhen has a pheasant-like *kok-kok* or *tchuk*.

BREEDING: The black grouse is famous for its remarkable courtship ceremony at favoured sites called leks, which are not true territories. Cocks arrive there in March, quite a month before the hens, to joust. Later, hens may confront hens. Most fighting is sham with a great deal of hopping up and down and tails spread. Sometimes confrontations become serious as individuals try to reach the lek centre which is the best place to secure matings. Lek displays are chiefly confined to two or three hours after dawn and one hour or so in the evening. Occasionally old blackcocks resume lek displays in autumn. Contrary to popular belief the species is not truly polygamous, but rather promiscuous, for the blackcock does not leave the lek with a harem. All he does is mate there. Sometimes traditional leks have held such attraction for the birds that modern development on or around them, such as buildings, has been ignored.

The cock takes no part in nesting duties. The hen selects a site — rarely above 400m (1,300ft), though the upper limit is 600m (1,950ft) — beneath a bush or among rushes or other vegetation to make a scrape which she lines sparsely with grass and leaves. Occasionally this may be on the open moor or exceptionally in a tree nest of another species. The 6-10 (5-16 recorded) buff, sparsely spotted red-brown eggs are laid from late April into June and incubated by the greyhen for 24-27 days. Taking no part in incubation, the cock retains his bold plumage.

Blackgame chicks leave the nest soon after hatching, are tended by the greyhen only, can fly after about 21 days but are not fully grown until much later. They stay with the hen until autumn approaches but young cocks often form packs by mid-August. There is but a single brood so productivity may be extremely low in a wet season for nests are frequently washed away in favoured habitat.

Old greyhens can be troublesome in that, barren themselves, they appear to harass younger greyhens unduly, interrupting their breeding schedule and even bullying their young. Perhaps for this reason alone old birds should always be shot, but they are very cunning. A policy of not shooting any hens appears to make no difference in attempts to increase local stocks of blackgame.

FEEDING: Almost entirely vegetarian, the species is of sufficient interest to the Forestry Commission to warrant publication of their booklet *Forest Record No 66*. Heather is important, especially in winter, but the bird is more omnivorous than the red grouse, taking birch buds, shoots and buds of Scots pine, bilberry,

The female black grouse (greyhen) returns to her nest *(Eric Hosking)*

bog myrtle and elder catkins in winter, and in summer and autumn much more, including berries, grasses, grain, potato and turnip tops, seeds, herbs, flowers and insects, including many heather beetles. Grit and water are also taken.

The bird's infamy among foresters is through its eating young tree shoots to cause the development of 'stag heads', but on the whole conifer feed forms only a small part of the diet and significant economic loss occurs only locally. The most important thing is for tree nurseries to be sited well away from concentrations of blackgame. Most damage occurs when heavy snow denies the birds their usual diet and they are forced into plantations for shelter and food. Late winter and early spring are the danger times for young conifers, before they are too high for the grouse to reach.

MOVEMENTS: Blackgame are sedentary birds, with just local seasonal movements.

BEHAVIOUR: Whichever sportsmen said this bird is a disappointment must have been of the sedentary ilk, preferring sport to come to them. Like most gamebirds, blackgame prefer to hide or run but they rise silently into powerful, rapid flight. Their bulk makes this appear deceptively laboured, the quick wing-beats alternating with gliding, but they are hard targets, often flying faster than the red grouse.

49

Whereas red grouse do not appear to mind flying downwind, blackgame have an aversion to it. Dixon suggested that the unusual shape of the tail may account for this. Driving them is almost impossible for when put up their direction is uncertain. Flushed birds will often circle and return whence they came, or even double back over beaters. Little seems to deter these wilful birds and if they decide to fly out the side of a drive no flanker will stop them. They also seem reluctant to fly uphill and when flushed on a slope will generally sweep away to a lower level. If you do manage to get a shot off they usually rise high and fly right away to far cover, sometimes for quite long distances and involving more 'sailing' than with the red grouse. All this may make commercial shooting by the day unpredictable, but surely to bag one of these fine birds is worth more than a hundred reared pheasants.

Their walk is slow and sedate, with a distinct roll, and because in the record bags the number of cocks far exceeds the hens some writers have concluded that the greyhen is much less inclined to fly than the cock. This may also be linked to the packing by sexes and most observers are of the opinion that sexes do not mix — the fact that they come over the guns together does not imply mixing! By autumn birds are in packs of 10-20, and today 30 would be notable, whereas packs of several hundreds were once reported. Old birds tend to lead solitary lives and at low density the species is particularly shy and retiring.

For roosting, the ground is generally preferred by the hen in summer but the cock spends much time in trees and always prefers to roost there except during his moulting eclipse in July and August.

As with red grouse and many other species, mist bewilders blackgame and then they allow a much closer approach. During a severe snowstorm they may huddle together in trees or even burrow into a drift for shelter.

POPULATION: There are probably under 50,000 pairs but numbers are increasing.

OPEN SEASON: England, Scotland, Wales: 20 August to 10 December. None in Ireland. For over a century sportsmen have commented that August blackgame are so tame and weak on the wing as to be unfit for shooting. Some have suggested starting on 1 October but others want to shoot them when they visit the moors earlier for red grouse. In 1876 Booth noted: 'By November, however, when they have gained both strength and experience, it will, on most moors, need hard work to fill a bag without recourse to driving.'

IN THE POT: The meat is excellent, especially that of young birds, but do not hang them for more than a few days unless you like a strong flavour.

THE FUTURE: Given sufficient sanctuary, such as is being afforded by continued coniferous reafforestation, there is little reason why this fine, sporting bird

Black grouse *(top)* — blackcock *(right)* and greyhen; red grouse *(bottom)* — cock *(right)* and hen

R. McPhail

should not become re-established in some of its former strongholds, especially with a little help from and tolerance by tree growers. Indeed, in 1983 it was announced that the Northern Ireland Grouse Council had been given permission to attempt an introduction there in parallel with the Republic of Ireland.

Abroad, the practice of spring shooting with barking dogs and shotguns or rifles is declining but trophy taking is still the prime motive and concentrates on the cock. International pressure should soon check this practice.

PTARMIGAN
(*Lagopus mutus*)

It has been suggested that when the sun's fire burns low and ice creeps further across the earth the ptarmigan will be the last bird left alive, and indeed there is a great deal in this for the species has evolved to live at inhospitable altitudes which would soon kill most creatures.

HISTORY: Despite its remoteness, even the ptarmigan's habitat has suffered man's encroachment and its range has contracted. In 1797 Bewick noted that it was 'sometimes, but rarely, found on the lofty hills of Cumberland and Wales'. Not now though. It bred on the hills of south-west Scotland until 1830 and on the Isles of Arran and Rhum. At that time an increase in sheep grazing may have had some effect, reducing food plants below the level to sustain viable groups. It ceased to breed in the Outer Hebrides in 1938. There was further range contraction following climatic amelioration in the first half of this century, but since the 1950s the weather has become colder and the ptarmigan's numbers have increased.

The only recent range contraction on the Scottish mainland has been in the extreme south but any generalisations must take account of the species' considerable natural population fluctuations. Reintroductions have failed.

RANGE AND DISTRIBUTION: This 'white grouse' or 'whitegame' has within its main range a particularly favourable habitat in Scotland. Density is much lower in subarctic and arctic regions. It is circumpolar from Iceland and Scandinavia across northern Eurasia to the Bering Strait and across North America (where it is called the rock ptarmigan) to the coasts of Greenland. Outside this northern range it occurs only on the higher parts of the Pyrenees, Alps, central Asia and Japan.

In Britain, as elsewhere, the height at which the ptarmigan is found varies according to the latitude of the ground. The essential arctic-alpine heath de-

Ptarmigan: a pair in winter plumage *(top)* and autumn plumage *(bottom)*. The cock is standing

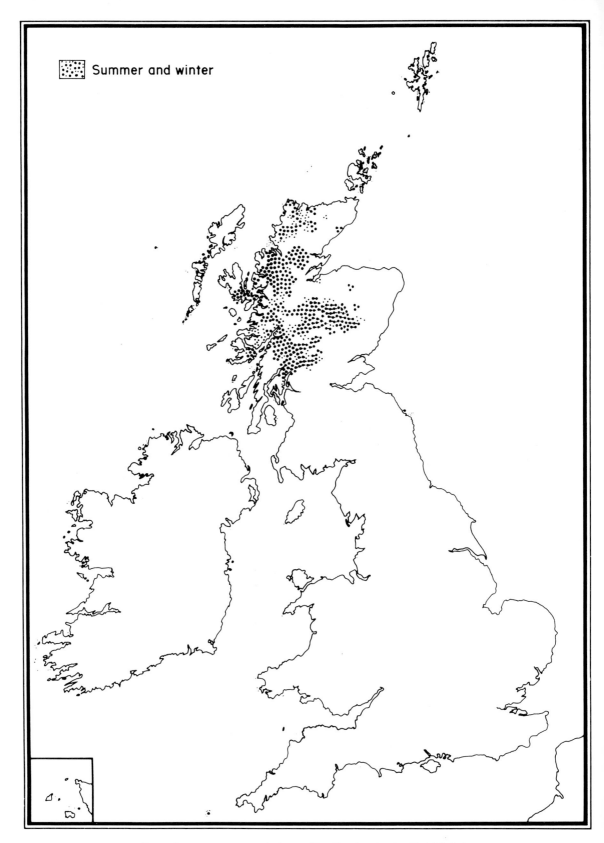

Ptarmigan — summer/winter distribution in the British Isles

scends to lower levels in north and north-west Scotland than in the Cairngorms and Grampians of the central Highlands. For example, near Cape Wrath in Sutherland it occurs as low as 180-300m (585-975ft) but in the Cairngorms the height is 760-1,240m (2,470-4,030ft).

In recent years the most southerly outpost has been around Ben Lomond in Stirlingshire. Ptarmigan can be seen quite easily on the Inner Hebrides, at Wester Ross around Torridon, Skye and Mull but the areas around the ski-lifts at Cairngorm and Cairnwell offer particularly good ptarmigan watching.

HABITAT: Evolution in appearance, diet and behaviour has confined this hand-some bird in Britain to the arctic-alpine heath of Scotland.

IDENTIFICATION: Sometimes looking just like another dark stone in the scree or a shadowy bump in the snow, the ptarmigan is famous for camouflage and has a coat to match every season. To find some for shooting you will certainly need a dog that ranges close ahead. There is little danger of confusion for this is often the only bird species present and where they do overlap with grouse they can always be distinguished by their permanently white wings and underparts.

It is almost fair to say that the ptarmigan is always changing its plumage and each change is acquired by a complete moult. In breeding dress from April to July the male is dark grey and the female buff, mottled and barred orange-brown. From August to October the male is pale grey and the female sandy-grey. The third moult into winter dress (November to March), in which both sexes are all white, is triggered by temperature change. Only the tail remains black but, being tipped white, is hardly visible. The male may be distinguished from the female by the black mark between beak and eye. Both have the red wattle.

The juvenile is like the autumn female but with pale brown wings, and tail the same colour as the back. Booth (1876) noted that

. . . only the oldest birds assume the pure white dress so early as the end of the shooting season, the young occasionally retaining several grey feathers a month or even six weeks later. Some of the more backward birds do not become thoroughly white till their second winter.

Certainly the changes are subject to considerable time variation.

Between early June and the end of September the leg feathers in both sexes are moulted and renewed and the claws are also shed (as in red grouse). The thick feathering on the feet and legs is said to facilitate walking in the snow.

Both male and female have an average length of 33-36cm (13-14in) and weigh a little less than a red grouse.

VOICE: The ptarmigan's calls are as unusual as its life-style with a low croaking or grunting which is quieter than the cry of the red grouse and is sometimes described as *kuh-kuh-kurrrrrrr*. There is cackling, a repeated grating alarm and a crow from the male in the breeding season.

BREEDING: With fox, raven, crow and stoat ready to take chicks and eggs, and eagle and peregrine poised to seize any unsuspecting adult, concealment is essential in breeding in such a barren environment. The species is monogamous and there is time to raise only one brood in the short summer of the tops.

As soon as the ground is free of snow (generally in March but sometimes considerably later) males occupy territories. Typical gamebird displays involve threats, fights, aerial chases and boundary patrols, sometimes flying steeply upwards before descending on rapidly beating wings, croaking at the same time. Successful males secure large territories for breeding while less vigorous ones remain unmated in small territories.

The nest hollow is often concealed among dwarf vegetation and lined with a few grasses and feathers; it is extremely hard to find for the female sits very tight. In an advanced year laying of the 5-10 (occasionally 3-12) eggs begins in early May, but not until late May or June in an inclement season. They are creamy-white with dark-brown markings and are incubated for about 25 days by the female only. A replacement clutch may be found as late as July. During incubation the species rarely calls and is reluctant to fly and draw attention to itself on the open hill. The male keeps watch and leads away intruders. The female too may feign injury.

The chicks leave the nest soon after hatching and are tended by both parents for a few days only for then the male usually deserts, though he may rejoin the family before the young fledge at only 10 days old. They often remain with the female and join winter flocks from November on but some broods disperse between August and October.

Breeding success is no better at low than high densities or in good rather than bad summers despite larger clutches. Our unpredictable weather, with snowstorms and torrential rain even in June, causes high chick mortality.

FEEDING: The sparse vegetation above the treeline does not offer a large variety of foods but there is usually an abundance of bilberry, crowberry and heather which form the bulk. As well as other mountain plants a few insects, mainly crane-flies, are also taken. The birds move down the mountainsides to feed early in the morning.

They take grit, usually large quantities of quartz, and do drink. Even in a severe winter it is rare for them to abandon the tops and they will even burrow into the snow for food.

MOVEMENTS: Sedentary birds, ptarmigan make just some local movements to lower ground in winter.

BEHAVIOUR: Probably the wildest of our gamebirds, the ptarmigan is a thorough ground bird and is always reluctant to fly. But the whirring flight is fast with rapid wing-beats, skimming over brows with stiff, arched pinions, often taking the covey right away to the next mountain top.

The ptarmigan walks like a grouse with the back rounded and tail depressed. In a family group the male is more upright and struts importantly while the female rolls, but in winter packs they all roll. They are very fond of dusting on their sides.

In the shooting season reaching the ground is usually more of a problem than locating the birds for snow and ice set in early in the Highlands, often from the end of October, and even before that mist-shrouded tops frequently prevent safe shooting. It is always best to have at least several days available. Once you are there, look for them in the sheltered lower corries if it is stormy, and if there is any sunshine remember that they are fond of basking in the lee of the wind.

Summer packs of unmated males may be joined by a few mated males later on but winter packing rarely commences before the end of November and then it is not by sex.

Ptarmigan on the nest, surrounded by snow. The species is well adapted to Scotland's 'high life' (Dennis Green)

POPULATION: Various estimates have suggested 10,000-100,000 pairs but the number in autumn may be ten times that by spring. In 1965 Watson estimated that the spring breeding population in the Cairngorms massif may vary from 1,300 birds in a poor year to 5,000 in a good one, with about 15,000 in a peak autumn.

Highest recorded density is on the high ground of Aberdeenshire, but Inverness-shire, Ross-shire, Sutherland, Banffshire and Perthshire also have good numbers.

OPEN SEASON: Scotland only: 12 August to 10 December. August birds are easy targets compared with the weathered birds of December.

IN THE POT: Bewick noted that 'they feed on the wild productions of the hills, which sometimes give the flesh a bitter, but not unpalatable taste; it is dark-coloured, and has somewhat the flavour of the hare.' Others cannot tell the difference between ptarmigan and the favoured red grouse on the plate!

THE FUTURE: Growth in tourism has brought skiers, climbers and armies of ramblers to the high tops yet ptarmigan not only remain confiding but also have actually become tamer in some areas. There is no evidence that human pressure is now having an adverse effect. The sheer remoteness of the remaining habitat should protect the ptarmigan but we must avoid despoliation through mining and make sure that the atmosphere remains relatively pure. Acid rain is unlikely to reach these areas but an occasional check certainly would not hurt.

Shooting appears to have little impact on the overall population for this is not a bird of big bags, most local sportsmen being content with a few brace here and there. Visiting sportsmen are quite content and generally thrilled to get just one bird which is usually taken back and preserved as a trophy. What must be guarded against is undue local pressure on a ground through excessive commercial shooting, for even if the birds are not bagged those few present may suffer harassment from which they will not recover.

CAPERCAILLIE
(*Tetrao urogallus*)

Although clearly regarded as such, the capercaillie is not legally a gamebird because when the Game Act of 1831 was passed the species was extinct in the British Isles. But this 'wood grouse', 'cock of the wood' or capercailzie, by far the largest of our quarry birds, is indigenous to Britain, where bones have been found in prehistoric kitchen middens.

Capercaillie is pronounced capp-er-kail-yee and is probably derived from the Gaelic *caball coille* from *caball,* a horse, and *coille,* a wood — 'horse of the woods'.

58

HISTORY: The species became extinct in England around 1660–70. It was still widespread and common in Scotland and Ireland at the end of the seventeenth century but large-scale felling of natural pine forest, even in the wilder areas, soon brought the bird to the verge of extinction. In 1797 Bewick described the species as 'very rare' but it was then probably already extinct in Scotland where some had lingered at least to 1771 in the Abernethy and Glenmoriston Forests (Inverness-shire) and the last-known indigenous stock was shot on Deeside (Aberdeenshire) in 1785. Strath Glass and the adjacent glens had also been last refuges. The Irish population became extinct in about 1790.

Being so large and conspicuous in what were then some of the poorest parts of the British Isles, the capercaillie was certainly reduced in numbers by shooting and snaring. Yet it was not very long before concerned sporting landowners decided to attempt reintroduction to Scotland, with the result that all the British population today is descended from introduced stock. The way these birds settled down is remarkable considering the species was extinct here. Obviously the habitat was still suitable in many areas and it was chiefly a matter of protection. The largest introduction (fifty-five Swedish birds) was made by Lord Breadalbane at Taymouth Castle, Aberfeldy (Perthshire) in 1837–8. With further introductions much of the former range has been recolonised.

The two world wars brought major setbacks with huge demands for wood, at a time when imports were difficult if not impossible, resulting in extensive felling. The period 1929–45 was particularly disastrous for forest birds.

But there was one bright spot this century — the formation of the Forestry Commission in 1919 with the aim to make Britain as near as possible self-sufficient in wood. There is no doubt that maturation of the early plantings and subsequent new woodlands have encouraged the spread of the capercaillie along with other woodland species.

Sadly, efforts at reintroduction to England and Ireland have generally failed rapidly. Following one attempt with thirty-five birds at Grizedale Forest (north Lancashire) in 1971 nesting was reported in 1973.

RANGE AND DISTRIBUTION: The 'great grouse' is found in the Pyrenees and Alps and ranges across Scandinavia and northern Europe through Russia to central Siberia. Unlike other British members of the grouse family, the capercaillie has not achieved subspecific status — our bird is the same as those abroad. Only in Britain are increasing numbers recorded, though Yugoslavia's population is said to be stable.

In the British Isles it is found only in Scotland, chiefly east central areas, but also throughout the Highlands. It seems unable to establish permanent breeding haunts in the maritime climate zone of the western Highlands. Yet there are groups in some forests near sea level. Some areas north of the Great Glen in the east also hold birds. Found from the Moray Firth to the upper reaches of the Forth, it is abundant in the valleys of the Spey, Dee, Don and Tay and favourite haunts include Rothiemurchus, Glenmore, Balmoral, Mar, Culbin and the Black Wood of Rannoch.

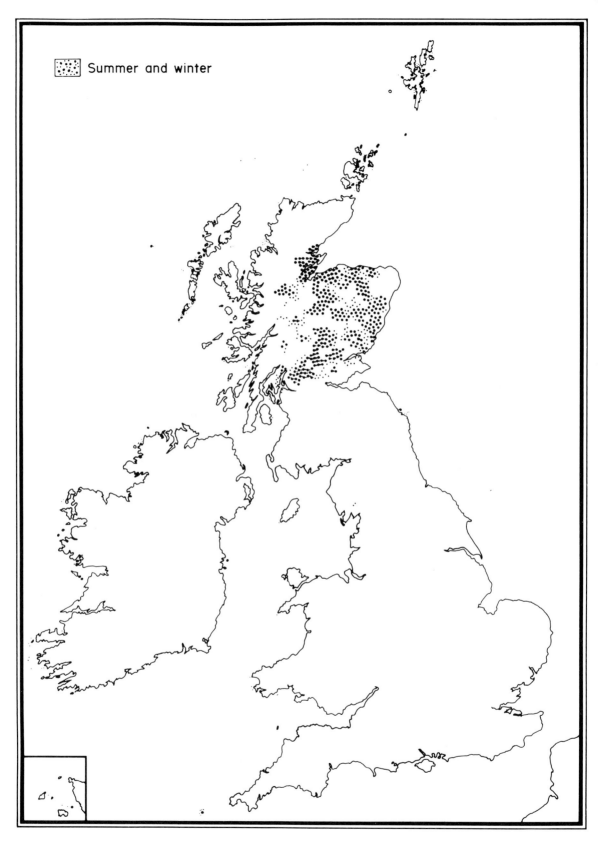

Capercaillie — summer/winter distribution in the British Isles

HABITAT: This is one of a small number of uncommon species which bring some importance to the northern coniferous forests but it is also at home in deciduous woods, especially in winter. Favourite haunts are in old, natural woods of Scots pine with open glades. Pine plantations are first colonised when fifteen to twenty years old and larch and spruce plantations from twenty to thirty years old, especially when mixed with Scots pine. Hillside woods are preferred.

Birds are occasionally found in heather well away from woods and in the autumn will visit stubble fields.

IDENTIFICATION: There is nothing in Britain with which the huge, black male of turkey-like proportions may be confused. Close inspection reveals the dark-green breast, brown-tinged wings, red wattle above the eye, touch of white at the bend of the wing, feathered legs and shaggy 'beard'. His wings are long and broad and when fanned the nearly square tail makes the bird appear even larger.

The smaller, mottled ruddy-brown female could be confused with the greyhen at a glance but the reddish patch on the breast of the capercaillie should distinguish. Juveniles of both sexes resemble the hen but the males adopt a dull adult plumage by the end of September.

The male's average length is 84-90cm (33-35½in) and he weighs an average 3,920g (8lb 10oz) within a range of 3,400-4,400g (7lb 8oz-9lb 11oz), but birds up to 7,710g (17lb) are said to have occurred. The female's average length is 58-64cm (23-25in) and weight 1,755g (3lb 14oz) within a range 1,500-1,950g (3lb 5oz-4lb 5oz). Some females are said to reach 2,720g (6lb).

VOICE: This bird's curious mixture of vocal surprises could convince the stranger that goblins live in the remnants of the ancient Caledonian pine forest. With distended throat feathers, drooping wings and widely fanned tail the cock delivers weird, brittle notes, cork-popping and gobbling, usually beginning with a rattle and ending with knife-grinding. At the lek cocks may be visited by croaking females with a *kok-kok* like that of the pheasant. Outside the breeding season the cock is mostly silent.

BREEDING: The male's extraordinary displays take place on special grounds called leks, as with blackgame. There mock battles involve leaping into the air and much tail fanning, but again the species is promiscuous rather than polygamous. Some males defend their territories exceptionally boldly, even attacking men and dogs as well as birds.

The hen makes a scrape in the ground, often at the foot of a pine tree, and lines it with vegetation. This is often between exposed roots but sometimes one may be situated in the open in heather, bilberry or juniper. An exceptional site is in the tree nest of another species.

The single clutch of 5–8 (up to 18 recorded) pale-yellow, speckled-brown eggs is laid from late April into May and incubated by the hen alone for 26–29 days. The chicks leave the nest on the day after hatching, are tended by the hen only and can flutter after 14–21 days, though they are not fully grown until much later. Dixon suggested that the smaller clutches are the produce of younger hens.

Many hybrids between blackcock and female capercaillie and between pheasant and capercaillie have been recorded. In areas of range expansion it is usually the hens which arrive first and in the absence of cocks of their own species they mate with blackcock or pheasant.

FEEDING: Like the black grouse, this species is of sufficient interest to the Forestry Commission to warrant publication of a booklet — *Forest Record No 109* (HMSO, 1976) — for in winter and early spring almost the entire diet consists of the needles, and to a lesser extent the buds, shoots, cones and seeds, of Scots pine, Douglas fir and larch, and to a much lesser extent those of spruce and other conifers. The birds concentrate on pines after the first snows have fallen, generally in November. Most browsing damage is done when the bursting buds and new shoots are eaten, and recovery depends on the vigour of the trees. Actively growing stands may show little damage after five or six years but thin, struggling plantations may suffer serious check.

Not only do capercaillie prefer certain trees but also certain needles, probably in relation to their nutritive value. Mostly sparse needle clusters are taken; possibly because they are easier to manipulate but also because they come from stunted plants. Trees which have stopped growing in height are favoured because their rounded tops facilitate perching. Pines on the edge of or in rides are favoured.

Severe damage can occur where succulent, young nursery stock is adjacent to established forest. Not only are these planted trees more conspicuous but also they may have increased nutritive value through the addition of fertilisers.

Females begin to restrict themselves to winter food earlier than the males in autumn, but in spring they increase their range of food earlier because they must build reserves for egg laying. In addition the marked differences in size and structure between the sexes lead them to have different preferences in winter feeding habits, so much so that flocks of males and females remain completely segregated. Females prefer lower branches where they have more protection from predators whereas males generally feed in crowns of trees. Despite all their appa-

Female capercaillie at the nest. Shooting concentrates on the cock, as a trophy *(Eric Hosking)*

rent cunning, these birds lose weight between December and January as the feeding day is not long enough to sustain their great bulk with relatively low energy foods.

Spring adds young blackberry shoots and leaves to the diet. Summer brings fruits and berries, some insects, leaves and buds of alder, birch and hazel, flowers of heather and hawkweed, clover leaves, bracken shoots, grass, ants and their eggs, beetles and worms; and autumn yields grain, seed pods of flowers and acorns. The young eat more animal matter to get sufficient protein for growth. A considerable amount of grit is taken and there is much drinking from the open-topped water tanks as used in forest fire prevention.

MOVEMENTS: The capercaillie is a sedentary resident with some local movements and dispersal. Dixon noted: 'given much to wandering up and down the countryside aimlessly, females and young males especially so'.

BEHAVIOUR: The British practice of driving capercaillie to guns is not a common method of shooting throughout the bird's range. However, this is a fine sporting bird for its pace is extremely deceptive and it might well be the most difficult shot of all our birds. This is despite the fact that the bird gets up noisily from the ground and gives plenty of warning of its approach. When launching from trees the bird's approach is quieter. The flight is very quiet and typical gamebird style with a series of rapid wing-beats alternating with long glides. The capercaillie flies with the neck extended and is probably much faster even than the blackcock, weaving easily through the trees. In moulting eclipse it is scarcely able to fly and it never flies very far unless crossing a valley from wood to wood, but sometimes when put up it will rise to a great height and cover a long distance. The walk is typically gamebird but with little nautical rolling.

In the breeding season the bird is very shy and elusive, especially at low densities, but keepers, foresters and landowners are usually aware of its presence and are responsible for most records. At that time the females move and feed in parties but cocks are generally seen singly. In the shooting season they are occasionally caught unawares but mostly seen breaking from conifers. Males commonly pack in winter.

Capercaillie spend most of the winter in trees, feeding, sitting to digest meals and roosting. Summer roosts are also mostly in trees, the same being used night after night. They are also said to burrow into snow for shelter and to roost in open areas.

POPULATION: Probably less than 10,000 pairs occur in the British Isles. In remnants of old Caledonian forest density has been recorded at 17-20 birds per square kilometre.

OPEN SEASON: Scotland only: 1 October to 31 January.

IN THE POT: The capercaillie is not a table favourite. Dixon noted that in winter as the male feeds more on trees it acquires the flavour of turpentine or resin but the female, which feeds more on the ground, is more palatable. Bewick said 'it feeds on the cones of the fir trees, which at some seasons give an unpleasant flavour to the flesh, so as to render it unfit for the table'. It is none the less good eating.

THE FUTURE: Abroad, specimens are still stalked with barking dogs during the display season and shot with a rifle or shotgun for trophies, though this is decreasing and I hope will never take off in Britain, whether legal or not. However, in Scotland there is already a considerable amount of trophy hunting involved in the shooting of this magnificent bird, with continental guns taking the lead in paying perhaps £100 to £150 for one bird. This places an undue emphasis on cocks. Consequently there is hardly a forest that is not shot. This is a delicate problem and the right balance must be found for on the one hand there could be unscrupulous commercial shoot operators over-exploiting an area but on the other reasonable financial return has often contributed to the preservation of a species. Certainly odd birds which turn up in plantations should not be shot as they are the potential colonisers. They are likely to be females, which, being smaller, can exist under less favourable conditions.

Densities are higher in natural stands of pine than in planted, structurally uniform woods. Therefore much more consideration must be given to preservation of ideal habitat to provide breeding reservoirs from which birds may spread. Their presence in commercial stands is usually tolerated for even if no allowance is made for shooting revenue the sight of these magnificent creatures is ample reward. Even with the present forestry system there is considerable scope for improved capercaillie conservation in Scotland. In addition there is no reason why sensible long-term plans should not provide for the reintroduction of the species to wilder parts of England, Ireland and Wales, though the Wildlife and Countryside Act 1981 decreed that each release into the wild (including simply moving birds) now requires a special licence from the Department of the Environment.

WOODCOCK
(*Scolopax rusticola*)

Whichever aspect of this bird is considered, for the shooter it spells one thing — excitement. The cry 'woodcock forward' during the course of a shoot never fails to make the adrenalin flow more freely.

Superbly adapted to its environment, the woodcock has long been associated with mystery. As late as the eighteenth century it was thought that the woodcock's months of absence were spent on the moon, and even today a great deal of lore remains.

HISTORY: When pot hunting was more important than sport the woodcock was taken by whatever means were at hand. It was easily captured in nets, traps and 'springes' placed in its regular runs or paths, for at night it is not in the habit of flying or leaping over obstacles. It was also guided simply by low fences into nooses. In common with other birds which are easily trapped the woodcock was branded as stupid and its name became synonymous with slow-wittedness.

Shooting records help to pinpoint where woodcock have traditionally concentrated in winter, the big bags coming from the west of Ireland, the best in England from Norfolk and south-west Cornwall, and in Scotland from the Hebrides. However, the history of the resident population is not so well documented.

In Britain, until the late 1820s the woodcock had been noted breeding regularly only in England. But the remainder of the nineteenth century witnessed a marked increase and spread, and by the mid-1930s breeding had occurred in every mainland county of Britain and Ireland. The reason for this is not known but the cessation of shooting during the breeding season must have helped.

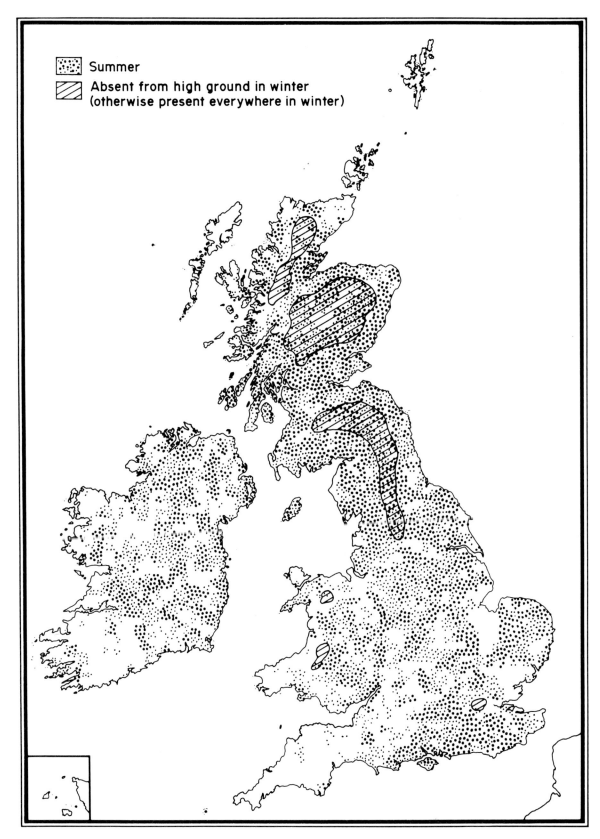

Woodcock — summer/winter distribution in the British Isles

Management of estates for pheasants helped too in the provision of suitable habitat and 'safe' areas.

Since World War II little change in distribution or numbers has been recorded. Some local decrease through felling of old woodlands has been more than offset by a continuing increase in young forestry plantations. Overall the trend appears to be upwards.

RANGE AND DISTRIBUTION: The species breeds from northern Spain across Europe and Siberia to Japan. It is mostly absent from the Mediterranean except Corsica. There are outposts in the Caucasus and Himalayas and on some Atlantic islands.

Although the woodcock has bred in every county in the British Isles records are few from areas such as Cornwall, Devon, Cork, Kerry and the fens of eastern England. Some areas have insufficient woodland or woods that are too damp. One inexplicable gap is south Suffolk and north Essex. The gaps are generally thought to be uncolonised areas rather than range contractions. Woodcock are also absent from the Outer Hebrides, Shetlands and Orkneys. In winter, however, the species is much more widespread and immigrants tend to concentrate in the mild, wet areas of the south and west — the very places where breeding is sparse.

HABITAT: Resident birds require open deciduous woodland with dry ground for nesting but nearby wet or damp areas for feeding. In the south this may include large, broad-leaved woods and in the north thin birch woods and scrub. Favoured woods are generally free from the cold and draught associated with old beech woods, and have a good understory of bracken, rhododendron, bramble, laurel and holly. Larch woods with patches of scrub oak are regular haunts and, while woods must have damp areas, they should not have continually dripping trees and wet cover. Open bracken will also attract woodcock. Coniferous woods are mostly avoided, but young plantations, especially those with wide, grassy rides or other open spaces, are used increasingly.

While generally choosy, the woodcock may turn up almost anywhere and is about as unpredictable as the weather.

IDENTIFICATION: The broad, rounded wings and dumpy appearance remind one of an owl, especially as the species is crepuscular, but the stout, long bill held downwards in flight will always identify the woodcock, even in silhouette. The sexes are alike and the juvenile is much like the adult. This is the only wader with a long bill and short legs, probably the result of loss of wading habitat.

There is considerable variation in colour and pure white, all buff, and cream and brown have been recorded. However, there are two main types — one basically rufous-brown patterned black, buff, chestnut and grey, and the other darker and greyer. Some observers hold that the darker birds, which are also generally larger, are English while the others are foreigners. Others suggest the reverse! Nearly all summer birds I have seen in southern England have been of the lighter variety.

The woodcock is also subject to considerable variation in size and weight. Average length is 34cm (13½in). The male's average weight is 315g (11oz) within a range 269-350g (9½-12½oz) and the female's 336g (12oz) within a range 280-430g (10-15oz). In recent years there has been an increasing number of records of 'short-billed' woodcock with bills averaging around 45mm (1¾in) against the normal length of 70-75mm (2¾-3in), but their very wide incidence leaves little room for speculation. One suggestion is that this is an evolutionary response to changes in feeding areas and the rapid drainage of bogs and wetlands would tend to make one support this theory. Perhaps the bill will steadily shorten as the legs appear to have done? On the other hand the sudden appearance of short bills lends support to the comparatively new 'jump theory' of evolution.

Altogether the woodcock's anatomy justifies close examination. The head is obtusely triangular rather than round, with the full black eyes near the top and the ears slightly to the front and below the eyes because there is no room for them elsewhere. There is, as usual, a good reason for this adaptation with which the woodcock can literally see out of the back of its head with full 360° visual field. With the bill almost continually probing in the ground for food such eye arrangement means that the bird is better able to watch out for predators, and because the bill tip is so sensitive the eyes are hardly needed forward to look for food. The only disadvantage appears to be that the overlap between the eyes is reduced and this cuts binocular vision and range judging. The binocular field is actually slightly wider at the back.

That remarkable bill is furrowed along its entire length, and the upper mandible, full of sensitive nerve endings, overhangs the lower with a kind of knob which may well aid extraction of worms from the soil in conjunction with the sharp-pointed tongue. The bill is also prehensile and used like forceps to extract prey.

Even the plumage is noteworthy. In the eighteenth century Bewick wrote: 'At the root of the first quill in each wing is a small, pointed, narrow feather, very elastic, and much sought after by painters, by whom it is used as a pencil.' Today these are still prized but we now call them 'pin feathers' rather than pen feathers and wear them in our hat bands as symbols of sporting prowess. Lord Margadale's grandmother is reputed to have had a fan made from 10,000 pin feathers.

Capercaillie — cock *(above)* and hen

VOICE: The woodcock is usually only heard to call when 'roding', uttering a few grunting croaks followed by a sharp *tsiwick* repeated several times and audible for considerable distances. The high-pitched part of the call sounds as though it comes from a much smaller bird. There is also an eerie croaking heard only at close range.

BREEDING: The woodcock's breeding season is marked by the strange 'roding' flights, mainly at dusk and dawn from March to early July. The word roding is derived from the old Scandinavian word *rode* which means foray or excursion, and in the case of the woodcock this involves a regular flight-path with a slow, owl-like wing-beat and the uttering of weird squeaking and groaning calls, usually over tree-tops. This is probably only undertaken by the male and is an invitation for the female to call him down to copulate rather than an advertisement of territory. Vesey-Fitzgerald said that he had seen roding during late September and in early January and suggested that from the sporting point of view it is unwise to shoot woodcock after the end of December. However, it is worth noting that the main exodus of immigrants does not begin until March. On the other hand the breeding season of resident birds is long, with eggs being found from early March to mid-July. The male is promiscuous, sometimes mating with several females during a season, and does not hold a territory.

The nest is a mere hollow lined with dead leaves, frequently at the foot of a tree, among dead bracken or with a light covering of bramble. The 4 eggs (sometimes 3 or 5) are grey-white to brown heavily marked with chestnut and ash-grey blotches, with peak laying mid-March to mid-April. The sitting bird is superbly camouflaged.

Incubation is by the female only and lasts for 20-23 days commencing with the laying of the last egg. The interval between the laying of each egg may be 2-4 days. When flushed from the nest the female will often produce an elaborate and convincing injury-feigning display. The chicks hatch in warm, brown down, leave the nest immediately and, unusually for a wader, are probably fed by the parent for a few days after hatching. There are usually two broods.

Incredible as it may seem, woodcock do carry their young in flight and there are many accredited eye-witness accounts. Other waders, including snipe, sandpiper and redshank have also been seen doing so. The debate is perennial. As early as the eighteenth century Gilbert White doubted Scopoli's assertion that woodcock carry their young in the bill when fleeing. In fact the chicks are carried singly between the thighs away from danger but there are also reliable accounts of lifting over obstacles. Generally the flight is only for a few metres or so and is laboured. Carried chicks are anything from new-born to about three-quarters grown and appear to be partly supported by the parent's depressed, fanned tail.

FEEDING: Generally the woodcock roosts by day and feeds at night, but it will

Woodcock

feed by day in exceptionally severe weather, visiting the unfrozen saltings if really pressed. Also, as breeding gets under way, it will feed more by day and roost at night. Lunar rhythm is also said to influence feeding, the prey being more active at the full moon, but the extra light appears to be unimportant.

Drought during spring may be more serious than hard weather for the diet is fairly restricted. Earthworms always predominate (90 per cent of the diet in winter). Beetles, millipedes, centipedes, spiders, insects and their larvae, small freshwater molluscs, and some seeds and grass are also taken and much food is brought to the surface for swallowing. In more temperate parts of its range the woodcock also commonly takes blackberries.

Flight to the feeding ground usually follows a regular route but if the site is close the woodcock prefers to walk to it. The species is rarely seen feeding but I have witnessed this several times when standing hidden and very still as darkness fell and woodcock settled about six feet away. The bill is often thrust into the ground up to the 'hilt' and will probe through soft snow into mud. Recent research indicates that smell may also be important in prey location.

MOVEMENTS: Resident, summer visitor, winter visitor and passage migrant — the comings and goings of the woodcock have been the subject of great debate among sportsmen for centuries.

Most British and Irish birds are thought to be sedentary but even with these there is a lot of movement related to weather, though mostly only locally. Of those that do migrate from Scotland and northern England about two-thirds are thought to go to Ireland, half the remainder to southern England and the rest to France, Spain and Portugal.

Winter visitors and passage migrants start to arrive on the east coast from Scandinavia, Russia and Germany in September. The peak influx is at the end of October and the beginning of November and the tail end in early December. These large numbers of birds usually arrive singly rather than in flocks, many passing on to western Britain and Ireland where the greatest numbers are shot.

At the height of the influx birds may come in waves and in some areas these are remarkably punctual. There has been widespread belief that major arrivals coincide with the full moon but this is most likely to be coincidence. Sudden 'rushes' are usually due to bad weather delaying them on the Continent where they accumulate before departure. When they do come after the weather has cleared then obviously the moon is likely to be *clear* but not necessarily *full*. Memory then exaggerates.

Other observers have noted that woodcock only ever seem to arrive in the night or in dark, misty weather. This is not necessarily so for time of arrival depends on length of journey, wind etc but there is undoubtedly a greater influx during very cold weather and this is often preceded by murky conditions. Indeed, like most migrants, they seem to have an uncanny knack of sensing when rough weather is due and they always appear to keep ahead of it.

They are said to migrate upwind at considerable elevation until over the land but at the time of their main arrival Britain's prevailing winds are westerly and,

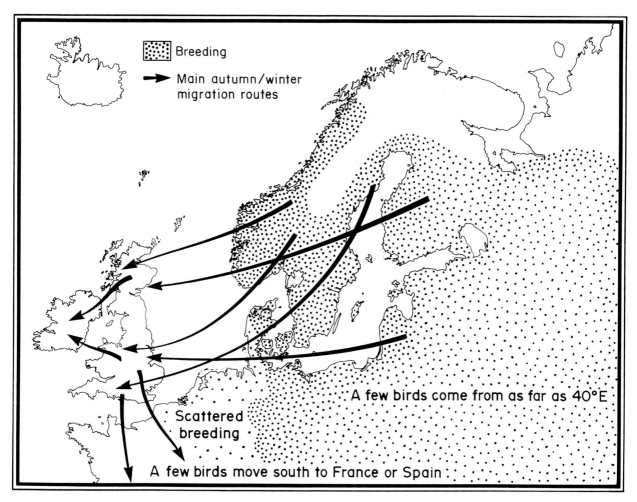

Legend:
- Breeding
- → Main autumn/winter migration routes

A few birds come from as far as 40°E

Scattered breeding

A few birds move south to France or Spain

Woodcock — main autumn/winter migration routes of British-involved populations

thus, in approaching from points east, they would travel upwind anyway. Immediately after their arrival they are often found exhausted in coastal ditches and dykes and are not worth shooting for they are mostly tame and thin, but they soon disperse inland.

With the onset of severe and prolonged frost they seek out lower, warmer ground with marshes and springs which usually remain unfrozen and if necessary will return to brackish marsh. Then they are likely to be emaciated and should not be shot irrespective of whether or not a cold weather ban has been imposed.

From the beginning of March to the end of April the visitors keep drawing towards the coasts and, as Bewick recorded, they 'avail themselves of the first fair wind to return to their native woods'. Peak return is not until the end of March, for these northern and eastern birds generally breed later than our residents in milder Britain.

BEHAVIOUR: The species is so highly regarded as a testing mark that anyone

Woodcock and newly hatched chick. The species' ability to carry its young in flight has been debated for centuries *(Dennis Green)*

achieving a right and left at them could apply, with statements from two witnesses, to join the famous Bols Woodcock Club. In 1983 the Club was terminated, but in 1984 the Shooting Times Woodcock Club was launched.

During the day woodcock love to skulk under hollies or other evergreens but when flushed they rise with a great swish of wings. The flight is indeed quite fast but what makes the woodcock such a hard mark is that it will usually be twisting away among trees where its wide, rather short wings give excellent manoeuvrability. It is much easier to shoot in open country. Undisturbed flight is slow and somewhat wavering, undecided and bat-like and best seen along rides at dusk.

Many woodcock are shot on driven pheasant shoots. They walk like snipe, with necks drawn in and bills inclined downwards, but do not walk so far or so easily as the smaller bird. As beaters approach they will run but when they do take wing their flight is often very predictable with paths between certain trees favoured in old haunts. Because of this woodcock driving is possible where numbers permit.

There is an old saying that 'woodcock shooting should never be put off till to-morrow'. Dixon said: 'If plenty of birds chance to be in the covers they should be looked after at once, for very often if a night is allowed them they have taken their departure.' There is a lot of truth in this, especially in areas which are not great woodcock haunts. When pursued, though they make off rapidly, they do not usually fly far, dropping so suddenly into cover and sometimes running off to hide that one is left wondering whether it was an apparition.

The species is very unsociable and it is exceptional to see them together outside courtship. Even though they may use communal feeding grounds they will fly to them independently.

Reports suggest occasional roosting in trees to avoid foxes. It is said that after a stormy night it is profitable to look for them in the more sheltered hollows and roosts.

POPULATION: The resident population has been estimated at 50,000 pairs but bag returns indicate that the winter population must be at least several times that. The species' secretive, crepuscular and nocturnal habits make observation very difficult. Annual adult mortality is estimated at 37 per cent of the population (perhaps 70 per cent in a severe winter), the average life expectancy is 2.2 years and the maximum age recorded in the wild is 12 years.

OPEN SEASON: Scotland: 1 September to 31 January. England, Wales, Northern Ireland: 1 October to 31 January. Irish Republic: 1 November to 31 January. To end on 1 February might be more sensible as that is the end of the pheasant shooting season and very many woodcock are shot on pheasant drives, some probably illegally on 1 February because of this disparity. In Eire it is not permitted to shoot woodcock between sunset and sunrise.

IN THE POT: 'Usually the entrails are not drawn but roasted within the bird whence they drop out with the gravy upon slices of toasted bread and are relished as a delicious kind of sauce' (Bewick). Even without this bizarre treatment the flesh is held in very high esteem and it is probably one of the most delicious gamebirds. Young birds have the tips of the primaries ragged and worn whereas in old birds they are intact.

THE FUTURE: Woodcock shooting may be suspended by law during severe weather but there is much disagreement on this. After the bans of 1980/81 emotive opinion suggested that a longer-term ban should be enforced. Scientific comment was that it might be better to continue shooting in hard winters when numbers are often very high in the British Isles and many birds will die later anyway, but then shoot less hard in the following winter to enable breeding stocks to recover.

Irrespective of these ups and downs the trend in the woodcock population appears to be upwards, for increasing forestry is providing more and more acceptable habitat. Being largely coniferous, this new woodland is not ideal but the young trees are attractive to woodcock and provide virtually unshootable areas which act as great reservoirs for further colonisation.

Much more study is needed, especially internationally, and a good start was made in 1975 with the Woodcock Production Survey — a joint BASC/Game Conservancy project in which shooters send in for study one wing from each bird shot. The first six years revealed a young to adult ratio of 1.2:1.

The woodcock's future now appears very bright for public opinion will increasingly demand more of the mixed, broad-leaved woodland, which is first-choice habitat, in the reafforestation programme.

COMMON SNIPE
(Gallinago gallinago)

In many areas this little bird is passed over by pot-hunters because in these inflationary days the lean body offers little in return for the price of a cartridge, and in some instances a shot at snipe may spoil the chance of a shot at duck. Personally I would never ignore the opportunity to shoot a snipe under average conditions, for the bird offers one of the most exciting and testing of marks and one of the finest table dishes.

HISTORY: As a marsh bird the snipe has suffered through continuing drainage over hundreds of years, probably reaching a peak rate of decline in the early nineteenth century. But at the turn of this century there was increase and colonisation of counties in southern England, perhaps related to climatic change.

Marked decline returned to some areas, especially in southern England, after World War II when the drive to revitalise the economy, partly through maximising agricultural yields and accelerated by the desire for national self-sufficiency, resulted in the drainage of thousands of swampy lowland fields. Upland strongholds have not suffered nearly so much because of their inaccessibility, difficult terrain and resistance to economic development.

The species probably evolved from the same stock as the woodcock.

RANGE AND DISTRIBUTION: The common snipe is virtually cosmopolitan, being replaced by similar species or subspecies in Africa or South America. It breeds from Iceland right across temperate and northern Europe through Siberia to northern Japan and the Bering Strait, from Alaska over most of Canada, much of the USA and in India.

Widespread in Britain, it is most common on the damp moors of Ireland and northern Scotland, and has bred on the Isle of Wight since 1967 after previously being recorded there in 1919.

HABITAT: The ideal is clear, boggy patches for feeding next to sufficient cover

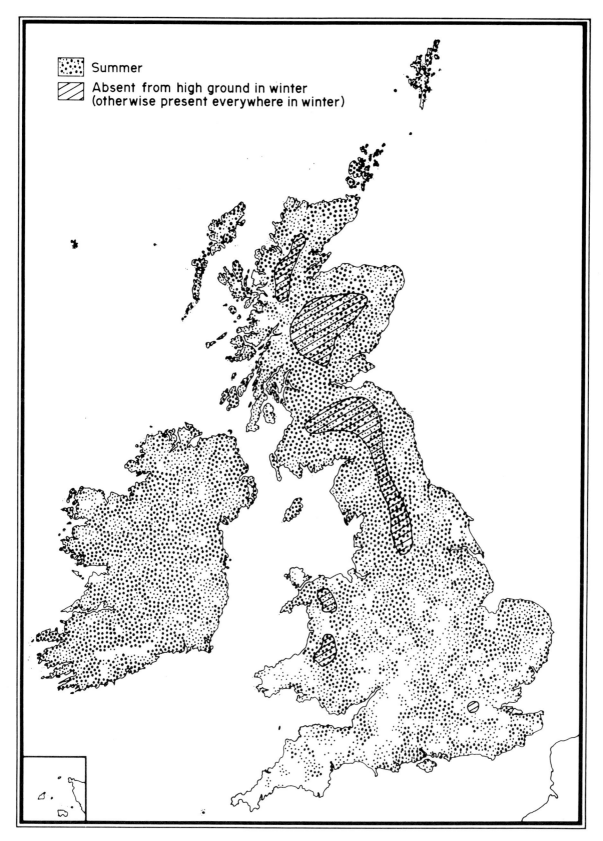

Common snipe — summer/winter distribution in the British Isles

for hiding. It needs wet ground such as rushy fields, blanket-bogs, water meadows, washes, saltmarsh, river valleys and lake edge. Most farms with a marshy field bottom hold a few snipe but these wet pockets survive only as long as their development is uneconomic. In Ireland renting a marsh virtually guarantees snipe shooting, but in England some apparently suitable marshes are strangely empty much of the time. This may be related to food preference.

Snipe sometimes breed on dry, stony moorland or in dry meadows.

IDENTIFICATION: The best field marks are the very long, straight bill (over two-and-a-half times the length of the head) and the white of the outer tail feathers. Coupled with the fast, zig-zag flight and distinctive call, these features spell snipe. The sexes are alike, well camouflaged with stripes and bars of buff and brown, the creamy double V shape on the back and striped head being most noticeable. The young, among the most attractive of all young waders, are downy, silver-spangled russet chicks. The juvenile resembles the adult.

Watch for the protected (not Ireland) jack snipe which is scarce in many areas and much smaller with a far shorter bill (about the same length as the head) and no white on the tail. Its flight is less erratic, low and direct, and it does not tower when flushed. It is reluctant to fly and springs with amazing suddenness but rarely travels far when flushed, frequently dropping within shot.

The woodcock is much larger and heavier than the common snipe but the much rarer great snipe has been shot by mistake. This protected species shows more white on the outer tail feathers when flushed, is more rotund — even woodcock-like — has a shorter, thicker-based bill (held near the horizontal), flies more directly on bowed wings and occurs in all months outside the breeding season.

The snipe's eyes are like those of the woodcock in being set far back on the head (it actually has binocular vision backwards to help spot predators). This facilitates probing with the bill which has a bulbous, fairly smooth end which dries and shrinks quickly after death. This knob is pitted and a section reveals a honeycomb of hexagonal cells with nerves linked to the main face nerve.

Average length of both sexes is 26cm (10½in) including the 7cm (2¾in) bill, and average weight 118g (4oz) within a range 100-130g (3½-4½oz).

VOICE: The snipe is sometimes called the 'heather bleater', but this has nothing to do with voice. A resonant, quavering humming is produced mechanically by the two outer tail feathers vibrating in the wind as the bird plunges through the air at 45° with the tail spread out. The note's undulation is caused by the wing-beats. This is heard at any time of year, but mostly during courtship and regularly from late March to mid-June.

Generally a silent bird, when flushed it rises with a loud, harsh *scaap*. The spring call is an insistent, repeated *chipp-er chipp-er chipp-er*.

BREEDING: The nest is a simple hollow lined with grasses among sedges, rushes or grasses or frequently in a tussock and usually near water. There is usually a well-beaten path along which the birds walk to and from the nest. The snipe enjoys a long breeding season with hatching almost continuous from May to mid-August. Peak laying is in April. There are usually 4 (sometimes 3) pear-shaped, olive-grey or olive-brown eggs heavily blotched with dark sepia. Incubation takes 18-20 days by the female only.

The chicks leave the nest within a few hours, are tended by both parents and fly at about 21 days, though about seven weeks pass before they attain the weight and wing-length of the adult. In common with some other lowland waders the parents frequently divide the brood soon after hatching and go separate ways, the two halves feeding and roosting perhaps 100m (325ft) apart. This reduces the risk of total brood loss to predators.

Parents sometimes produce an injury-feigning flight and they have been seen carrying young. The species is occasionally double-brooded.

FEEDING: The flexibly tipped, long bill probes mud for worms, nerve endings sensing the vibrations. Snipe feed vigorously but this is essential for the frail bodies rapidly lose condition when food is short. They commonly feed in almost liquid mud, swallowing without withdrawing the bill. Apart from the main course of worms they also take water beetles, caddis larvae, fly grubs, woodlice, snails, molluscs, crustaceans, berries and some seeds of marsh plants. During breeding they tend to feed away from the nest area to conserve food for later in the season.

Most feeding is at night, for they generally roost by day, but there is a period of intense activity at dusk. In winter, especially in cold weather, they feed more freely in the open and in daylight. You might catch one feeding quietly at the edge of a pool. At inland roosts when there is a full moon they will often sleep more by day and feed more solidly at night. This appears to have nothing to do with light for they also feed when the moon is overcast. Lunar 'rhythm' appears to affect prey activity.

MOVEMENTS: The snipe is a resident, passage migrant and winter visitor. Most British and Irish birds make only local weather movements from their damp, inland haunts to feed along the shore but in exceptional frost some may emigrate to western Europe.

Winter visitors and passage migrants arrive from September to November throughout the country, except in northern Scotland, from Iceland, Scandinavia,

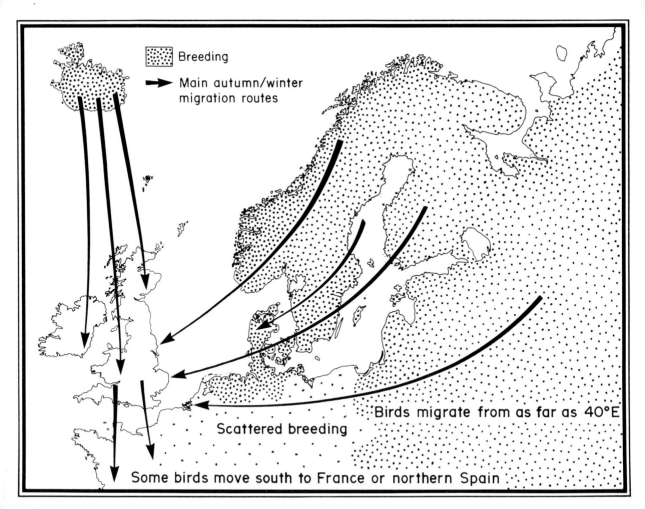

Common snipe — main autumn/winter migration routes of British-involved populations

the Baltic states, western Europe and the western USSR. Many of the Icelandic and Faeroese birds winter in Ireland. Most northern birds winter further south than Britain, in southern Europe and Africa.

Visitors return in March and April. Migration is often by night.

BEHAVIOUR: The snipe is seen in the open much less frequently than other waders. In walking it has the horizontal carriage and deliberate movement of its tribe, the neck drawn in and bill pointed downwards. When approached it usually crouches and will not fly until the last possible moment, but when flushed it makes off rapidly with characteristic evasive flight. It is usually flushed singly but sometimes in small 'wisps'. Large parties are uncommon.

Snipe have good eyesight and hearing so the best way to approach them is a perennial topic among sportsmen. Some prefer to walk-up snipe downwind because the snipe, like most birds, will rise into the wind if possible and may pass the gun. On the other hand an approach into the wind often thwarts the snipe's keen hearing and allows one to approach within shot. But perhaps it is best to ignore the wind altogether and pay more attention to the nature of the ground. However, it is worth remembering that snipe prefer to feed and rest out of the wind. A very difficult target when driven, it is mostly shot walked-up so that most birds are going away.

When flighting at dusk, snipe are difficult to kill, for in alighting they are fond of dropping from considerable height, at the last moment raising their wings high above their backs in typical wader fashion, and they do not move much before it is very gloomy.

Occasionally they perch on fences or in trees, particularly in summer. The normal roost is in a 'form', a simple depression in long grass or other vegetation, where much of the day is spent.

The snipe has been associated with weather-forecasting for it tends to display at low levels before rain but goes much higher at the approach of high pressure.

POPULATION: There are probably at least 100,000 pairs but many more in winter. Largest estuary concentrations are in Hampshire and Sussex. Despite loss of habitat they may well have increased as a result of encouragement by sportsmen.

OPEN SEASON: England, Scotland, Wales: 12 August to 31 January. Northern Ireland: 1 October to 31 January. Irish Republic: 1 September to 31 January. Watch out for late young in August. Let them go to strengthen their pinions.

Snipe against a Lancashire sunset *(Dennis Green)*

IN THE POT: Bewick wrote: 'A very fat bird, but its fat does not cloy, and very rarely disagrees even with the weakest stomach. It is much esteemed as a delicious and well-flavoured dish, and is cooked in the same manner as the woodcock.' Some say it is ill-flavoured at the start of the shooting season, perhaps because of the summer insect diet. I like it enormously (drawn) whatever the season but it is almost always skinny during prolonged frost.

THE FUTURE: As already mentioned, the traditional enemy of the snipe is land drainage, and with the position rapidly deteriorating in the Irish stronghold overall prospects look bleak. At least the new legislation concerned with notification of Sites of Special Scientific Interest and the associated scheme to compensate farmers forbidden to develop land should save some important snipe bogs. The Farming and Wildlife Advisory Group and other bodies should be given greater assistance in encouraging farmers to preserve odd wet corners as reserves rather than drain them for minimal returns.

GOLDEN PLOVER
(*Pluvialis apricaria*)

Other than the snipe and woodcock, for which a game licence is needed to shoot in the UK, the golden plover remains the only wader on the quarry list throughout Britain after the implementation of the Wildlife and Countryside Act 1981. It seemed to be purely a matter of whim and favouritism that retained the delicious 'goldie' while politicians ignored scientific logic to protect other numerous species such as curlew and redshank. None the less, the golden plover is among our most sporting birds and is one of the most abundant waders wintering in the British Isles.

HISTORY: Golden plover have become less widespread this century throughout their breeding range in central and southern Europe. Their range has retreated northwards. It is thought that this is probably a recent phenomenon due to climatic amelioration and large-scale afforestation in upland areas.

Although still our most important stronghold, northern Scotland too has suffered decline. The range in Wales has contracted and suitable parts of Exmoor (Somerset) and south-west Ireland (Cork, Kerry and Tipperary) have been evacuated for thirty to sixty years. Dartmoor has provided the only notable gain, with breeding first confirmed in 1950.

RANGE AND DISTRIBUTION: The species breeds in arctic/alpine and subarctic to arctic zones including Iceland, Scandinavia, British Isles, northern Russia, southern Baltic states and Denmark. It winters in temperate to warm temperate zones including southern and western Europe and North Africa.

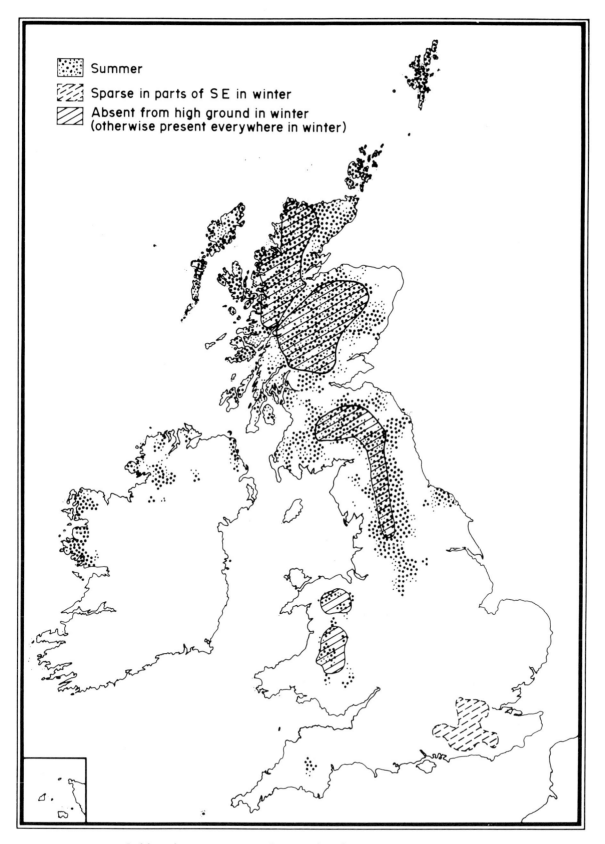

Golden plover — summer/winter distribution in the British Isles

In Britain it breeds on flat or gently sloping moorland in the north and west, and also in Ireland. In the south it breeds generally only on land above 1,300m (4,225ft) but in northern Scotland and western Ireland it may breed down to sea level.

Overall the largest midwinter populations are in northern England, south-west England, East Anglia, southern Scotland and Northern Ireland. Most large flocks gather on or close to the coast.

HABITAT: In summer grassy upland moors are preferred and in winter grassy and other lowland fields and coasts.

IDENTIFICATION: In summer the golden plover is a very handsome bird indeed with black face and underparts and spangled black and gold upperparts. In winter the black breeding dress disappears but the bird is still fairly easy to iden-tify for the largely white underparts and pale underwing contrast well with the yellow brown upperparts which still look as though flecked with luminous yel-low paint. The shape is compact, the bill short and the head large and rounded. The sexes are alike.

Usually they are in full summer plumage by the time they arrive at the breed-ing grounds in April or May. As soon as nesting commences white feathers show among the black and by the time the young are strong enough to leave the hills the old birds have mostly assumed their autumn dress. However, specimens may appear in mid-September still in almost full summer plumage.

Juveniles are more uniform than adults, darker below and paler above. Beware of confusion with the grey plover which is now protected except in Northern Ireland (where protection is imminent). In spring Icelandic and continental birds can be distinguished from British breeding birds by their much more extensively black underparts.

The average length is 28cm (11in). The foot is noteworthy in having only three toes, with no hind toe whatsoever.

VOICE: Throughout the year the species is a delight to listen to, whether it is the mournful ripple on the wild breeding grounds or the clear *hu-i* or *klee-wee* uttered as a flight call at night when the flocks migrate overhead. The alarm note is a plaintive *kö*.

84

Golden plover — a very sporting mark, and a delicious meal *(Robin Williams)*

BREEDING: They arrive at the Highland breeding grounds in April or early May, depending on the weather. Courtship ceremonies are communal. Both sexes make scrapes before the female chooses one to line with twigs, lichen and grass. Several pairs are often found nesting together.

The 4 (occasionally 3) creamy, green-tinged or buff eggs are spotted and blotched dark brown and laid mid-April to June. The nest is very hard to find but the birds' distraction behaviour is a good pointer.

Incubation is shared by both parents (mostly the female) and takes 28-30 days. Hatching is more simultaneous than with other wader clutches and the downy young leave the nest after a couple of days. Like the snipe, the parents often divide the brood between them to minimise the risk of total loss to predators. The single brood flies at about four weeks. Because of the very unpredictable weather in the northern stronghold it is not unusual to find both eggs and young near snowdrifts.

The beautiful aerial display is the best guide to territories, each pair having a prominent, mossy hummock on which the off-duty bird stands guard.

FEEDING: As the bill shape indicates, golden plovers are omnivorous and take worms, insects and their larvae, spiders, small shellfish, grass and weed seeds, berries, algae, moss etc. Farmland gives them rich pickings where they concen-

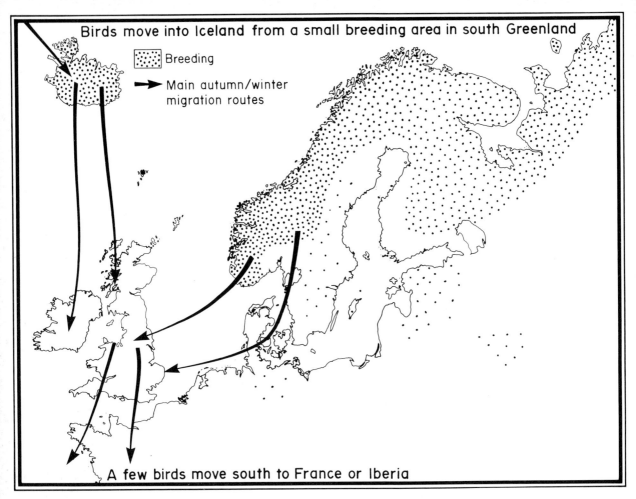

Golden plover — main autumn/winter migration routes of British-involved populations

trate on permanent pasture, taking soil invertebrates on or very near the surface. In some areas, such as East Anglia, cultivated land (especially winter-sown cereals) is used extensively, and in southern Britain there is a tendency to use arable farmland more heavily in late winter.

Much of their food is taken at night, especially by moonlight. In winter most feeding is on the mudflats and saltings but they frequently retire inland between tides to rest or sleep until the mudflats are exposed again. Food is located visually so strong wind may temporarily spoil feeding by obscuring visual clues.

MOVEMENTS: The breeding grounds seem remarkably empty after the young leave the nests in July and the families leave together. If June brings severe weather and high chick mortality then the moors may be deserted several weeks earlier. These resident birds move from the hills to winter on lowland farms, estuaries and coasts. Young may reach the Sussex coast as early as September but

Golden plover (above) in winter plumage and common snipe

R. McPhail

R. McPhail

they are very tame and should not be shot. They are easily enticed even by a bad execution of their call note.

In September and October there is a large influx of passage migrants and winter visitors and on the east coast numbers can be remarkable. They come from Iceland, Scandinavia and the Continent. Many pass on to south-west Europe or north-west Africa but Britain is a main winter base. Ireland is a particularly important wintering area for Icelandic golden plovers.

Hard winters may push British birds south to milder parts of Europe, including Ireland. Their movements are certainly erratic and some say that their departure foretells bad weather but there is no real evidence for this. They are probably mostly influenced by local frost which sends worms and insects deeper into the soil. Under such conditions large gatherings may assemble in mild areas such as the south-west or on the coast where the intertidal zone normally remains free of ice.

The return migration begins in March and ends in May according to latitude.

BEHAVIOUR: The golden plover walks with an upright stance and rapid steps but it is the flight which makes the species so sporting. This is always rapid and often steady, especially on migration or when changing location, and the wing-beats are regular and quick. Typically wader-like, the flight is graceful, generally low and with the wings slightly depressed. However, the species frequently indulges in aerial evolutions, flocks assuming a V or W shape.

The most difficult shooting is usually at evening flight when the birds seem to fall out of the sky from compact groups to skim along scarcely above the shoreline. Where there are defined flights morning offers better chances. The birds go inland soon after dawn and return to the saltings soon after dusk. On moonlit nights they usually stay inland.

As the birds move south in autumn and winter large flocks may form on splashy meadows. They often associate with lapwings but the species separate in flight. In the nineteenth century Booth wrote

> During severe weather they may be found congregated to the number of several thousands, generally frequenting tidal mudbanks, and retiring at high water to the adjoining marshes. It is at this season, while feeding on the mud, that they occasionally offer chances of which the puntgunners in the neighbourhood are not slow to avail themselves — as many as 50, 60 and 70 being frequently obtained at a shot.

Today numbers would not permit this but even if they did there is no market for the birds in an increasingly fastidious society and in any case the modern sportsman would not behave so.

Roosting flocks are tight, compact gatherings with the birds virtually motionless and all facing the same way. In southern Britain most roosts are on cultivated

Mallard drake *(above)* and duck

land, especially plough. In the north grassland and coastal roosts are more popular.

POPULATION: There are an estimated 30,000 pairs breeding and 250,000 birds wintering in Britain plus a probable further 200,000 in Ireland.

OPEN SEASON: 1 September to 31 January throughout the British Isles.

IN THE POT: A very palatable bird, especially when feeding mainly on fresh marshes.

THE FUTURE: There is serious decline throughout the whole of western Europe but the species remains very common and in the short term there is no logical reason to fear its loss from the quarry list.

The Birds of Estuaries Enquiry January indices (the base set at 100 in 1973) showed the proportionate large reduction in numbers since 1978: 1978 – 99, 1979 – 34, 1980 – 36, 1981 – 73, 1982 – 22. Yet knowing how erratic the species' movements are it is dangerous to draw conclusions. It is worth noting that the curlew's index remained at exactly 100 in 1982 yet that species was taken off the quarry list.

Murton noted that the golden plover's breeding distribution in Europe is surprisingly restricted and has the characteristics of a relict species which was probably at its peak during the immediate post-glacial periods. Thus in the long term we must heed the climate, in the medium term the afforestation of upland breeding grounds and in the short term irrational moves by 'antis'. The small number shot is unlikely to have any significant effect on the population.

MALLARD
(Anas platyrhynchos)

The ubiquitous 'bread and butter' quarry duck. It is hard to believe that the squabbling birds which boldly take bread with the sparrows in town parks and along riverbanks are of the same species which provides such excellent sport in very wild places.

HISTORY: This is the ancestor of most domestic duck breeds and crossbreeds throughout western Europe, the tuft of curled-up feathers on the upper tail often being present on domestic forms to show their origins. In the nineteenth and early twentieth centuries only the male was called mallard, the name deriving from the Latin *masculus* for male and *ard* from the Old High German *hart* for hardy or bold. It was generally called the wild-duck even though the species name mallard had been used in the Middle Ages.

There is a long tradition of rearing and releasing mallard but this really got under way with the establishment of many wildfowling clubs in the 1950s and 1960s under the guidance of WAGBI (now BASC). Originally this generally had the short-term objective of improving local sport with 90 per cent or more being shot during their first winter. Gradually clubs became more conservation-conscious and aware of the need to project a responsible image to the public and increasingly birds were released into no-shooting zones specifically to increase the wild population. With such protection first-year survival is high and many live on to colonise new areas so there is no doubt that wildfowlers have done much to increase the distribution of this already very successful species.

The Common Birds Census revealed a steady increase on farmland during the seven years following the remarkably severe winter of 1962/63, reaching more than three-and-a-half times the 1963 level by 1970.

RANGE AND DISTRIBUTION: The mallard is circumpolar in northern and temperate zones, extending southward into Morocco and northward to western Greenland. In Europe it is absent only from the highest mountains and Sicily. It winters south to North Africa, northern India and the east coast of China.

Found all over Britain and Ireland, except for the highest and most barren hills, this is our most widely distributed species of wildfowl, summer and winter. Densities vary considerably.

HABITAT: Virtually every type of lowland wetland is used throughout the year, and also maritime areas outside the breeding season. Deep water is usually visited only when the bird is alarmed. It is found on all types of urban and suburban water where its ability to live with man has been helped by free interbreeding with captive stock.

IDENTIFICATION: In good light the handsome drake is easily identified with his dark neck and breast and white-bordered blue speculum, but watch out for the protected red-breasted merganser in flight. The female resembles the female gadwall, pintail, wigeon and shoveler, though slightly larger, but in good light

Mallard — summer/winter distribution in the British Isles

the blue speculum will identify. In bad light the frequent quacking in flight will identify. The juvenile is similar to the female.

Obviously the boldly marked drake needs to become less conspicuous when he is moulting and unable to fly away from danger so he assumes a special dull eclipse plumage in July and August, regaining full glory in September. The female also has an eclipse.

The bird's length is 58cm (23in); the average male weighs 1,216g (2lb 11oz) within a range 1,017-1,442g (2lb 4oz-3lb 3oz) and the average female 1,084g (2lb 6oz) within a range 921-1,320g (2lb 0½oz-2lb 14½oz).

The late young bird, the 'flapper', should not be shot but left to provide better sport when stronger on the wing.

VOICE: Only the female makes the loud quacking like a farmyard duck, the male's call being softer, less raucous and higher-pitched — *quork* or *quek* or *queek*. These flight contact notes often announce the birds' presence before they are seen, help to confirm identification in poor light and prepare the sportsman for a shot. The male also makes a high whistle. The mallard is easily called within range.

BREEDING: Mate selection begins in autumn with several drakes chasing one duck through the air. Display develops with the drake swimming around the duck with neck outstretched along the surface of the water. Sometimes drakes chase ducks late in the breeding season and in areas where nests are crowded together commonly attempt 'rape' without the courtship ritual. Pairing proper may begin in November but December is usual and they are thought to pair for life. Early in the year pairs fly off to the breeding grounds.

The nest of leaves and grass lined with down and vegetation may be located in a great variety of freshwater and brackish habitats — small ponds to large lakes and reservoirs, riverbanks, stream margins and even just marshy fields. It is usually on the ground in dense undergrowth such as brambles, nettles, grass, bracken and heather. Islands are preferred for their greater security but sites may even be on hillsides several miles from water. I have found them in open, dry woodland. Other sites are fairly exposed, perhaps at the foot of a fence, and sometimes they choose the inside of a tree stump, the crown of a pollarded willow or a hole in a tree as much as 10m (33ft) high. Exceptional town sites have included flower boxes, roof gardens, building ledges, bridge supports, static water tanks and moored boats. Mallard also readily accept artificial sites such as wooden boxes and woven baskets, especially on floating islands.

Eggs and small ducklings have been found in October and November but some of these are from young females reared earlier the same year and breeding at only six months old. The date of nesting varies with the area and an exceptionally early mild spell may start the mallard off, sometimes only a week after the ground temperature has risen above freezing point — perhaps the second half of February. Unfortunately these early nests are prone to predation because of lack of cover, even if they survive a return to severe conditions. In 1983, for example,

February was bitterly cold and snowy after a mild December had started many birds breeding. Luckily many of the early eggs could be saved because the Department of the Environment issued an open general licence for the collection of mallard eggs before 31 March for the purpose of incubation and release.

Most eggs are laid from March to May — usually 10-12 (sometimes 7-16) and pale grey-green or olive-buff — but may be found as late as September. Incubation is by the duck only and takes about 28 days. Fertility and hatching rates are high in the wild — about 90 per cent. The downy, brown ducklings are usually tended by the mother only. They leave the nest soon after hatching and are led to water. They fly at about six-and-a-half weeks but may be tended for up to two weeks beyond that. Unfortunately the mortality rate is very high and from a clutch of 8-10 an average of only 2 chicks fledge.

Although only one brood is usual on the Continent, two are common in Britain, probably because of our milder climate, especially with park or pond birds whose food supply is more reliable. Hybridisation with farmyard ducks is common.

FEEDING: The mallard is a dabbling duck which likes shallow water where it can reach the bottom to take aquatic vegetation by up-ending, comically keeping its tail up by continual paddling as though swimming. It never dives for food and is chiefly a night feeder.

The species' great flexibility in feeding has contributed to its success, the proportion of animal food varying according to its availability. The staple foods of seeds, buds and stems of water plants are supplemented by animal food ranging from insects to fish. On the farm they take exposed potato tubers which have been softened by frost and will visit fields a long way from water to take grain on stubbles or occasionally by pulling down stems, but usually only causing very slight damage. However, they may cause considerable damage in watercress beds by pulling up and eating the plants. Earthworms, acorns and chestnuts are also taken. Some town birds are reputed to drown and swallow sparrows. I have seen them beak swimming rats and voles.

MOVEMENTS: The breeding population is mainly resident but there is some movement southwards and towards the coast when pressed by hard weather.

Winter visitors and passage migrants arrive from September and October and leave as late as April and May. They come from the North Sea countries, Iceland, Scandinavia and eastern Europe.

BEHAVIOUR: Like the other dabbling ducks the mallard swims well and lightly, and generally dives only if wounded or courting. When flushed it rises easily and almost vertically from the water but when a flock is put up it almost always splits up, sometimes into pairs. It is highly gregarious in winter and even in the breeding season males flock. As the bird rises it often flies obliquely for some distance. The flight is fast but the shallow wing-beats are less rapid than those of most duck, though faster than those of geese. The whistling of the wings helps to identify the bird in poor light.

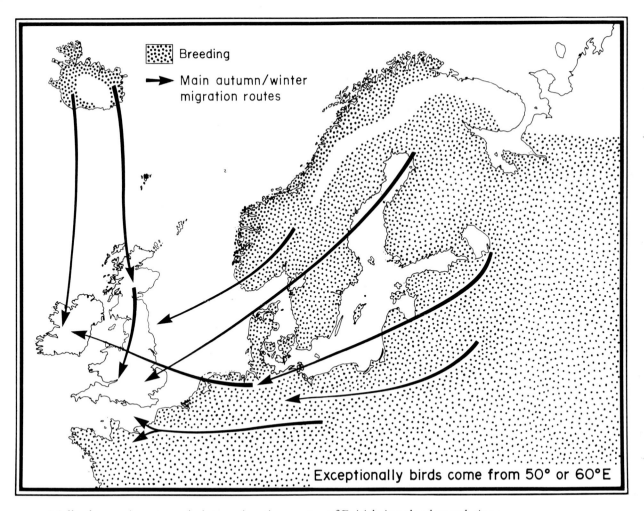

Breeding

→ Main autumn/winter
migration routes

Exceptionally birds come from 50° or 60°E

Mallard — main autumn/winter migration routes of British-involved populations

There is no regular flock formation on the wing. Birds are also encountered singly or in pairs during the shooting season. They are always wary in regularly shot areas.

Except in the breeding season mallard generally rest by day on or near water and flight to feed at dusk, returning at dawn. In many areas there are regular dusk flights inland to marshes and rivers for natural foods or to farmland, often well away from water, to feed on grain and weeds. Although flight times and lines are on the whole regular they may take surprising directions, perhaps related to the weather, moon, tide or amount of local disturbance. For example, they may rest on inland waters by day and flight to the coast at dusk. As with all wildfowl, the sportsman must study his patch to get best results. This is the easiest duck to decoy.

POPULATION: Mallard have apparently recovered from a decrease in the 1970s, the Common Birds Census indices indicating an increase in the breeding population in recent years. The resident population alone is thought to number 100,000

Somerset mallard taking off *(Robin Williams)*

to 150,000 pairs. The 1981/82 UK Wildfowl Count was 149,900 for January (165,920 for 1980/81 when the highest single count was 6,430 on the Humber Estuary), and the average winter maximum for 1976/77 to 1980/81 was 147,450.

The West European population is numbered in many millions and the British Isles form an important refuge. Huge numbers are released. Some observers put our winter population at 250,000–350,000 or more.

Average annual mortality is estimated at 65 per cent of the population; the adult's life expectancy is 1.2 years and the maximum recorded age in the wild is 16 years.

OPEN SEASON: Throughout the British Isles: 1 September to 31 January, but in England, Scotland and Wales extended to 20 February in or over any area below high water mark of ordinary spring tides.

IN THE POT: A mallard shot over stubble in September is best for the table but

96

even those birds taken from the coast are good. Some say they are scarcely worth eating when they have been feeding on marine weeds but I have yet to dislike one.

Early in the season young birds may be distinguished by the tips of their tail feathers which end with a notch where the downy tip has broken off, whereas the adult's are pointed.

A roasted mallard stuffed with apples, oranges and onions takes some beating but perhaps the one I enjoyed most was a whole bird eaten cold in the back of a Land-Rover in Yorkshire half-way through a very wet driven partridge shoot. The only accompaniments needed were plenty of pepper and salt and a doorstep of bread and butter.

Generally wildfowl do not require hanging unless a very strong flavour is preferred. Hanging does little to tenderise. It is best to pluck and draw them *before* freezing.

THE FUTURE: Interest in rearing and release is waning as sportsmen, especially wildfowling clubs, increasingly concentrate on habitat management — either through excavating new ponds and lakes or sending regular work parties to existing waters to prevent silting up, to provide the optimum vegetation for food and cover, and to control predators. This is an excellent trend for not only does this improve the sportsman's image but also benefits a host of other wetland birds, animals and plants.

Except for some unforeseen disease or great climatic change, a bird so adaptable as the mallard should fill our bags for ever.

WIGEON
(*Anas penelope*)

Those simple words 'the wigeon are in' never fail to excite the true wildfowler for this is *the* sportsman's duck that evokes wild places, wild weather and memorable flights.

HISTORY: For centuries wigeon were sold extensively in markets all over Europe. John Latham (1740–1837) records two names — 'easterling' and 'lady fowl' — for young male and female wigeon respectively on sale in the London market. Perhaps easterling was associated with the bird's prominence in cold, easterly weather. The word 'wigeon' was also used to denote a fool, probably because this duck's gregariousness led to its downfall with puntgunners.

The first recorded finding of a British nest was in Sutherland in 1834, the wigeon being one of several subarctic duck species which appear to have colonised Britain during the cooler climatic phase of the nineteenth century. Breeding birds spread down central Scotland but lateral expansion was slower. The

Tweed was reached in the 1890s, Yorkshire in 1897, Cumberland in 1903, Galloway in 1906, Northumberland in 1913 and the Outer Hebrides in the 1920s. This rapid expansion appears to have ended by 1950 and was followed by some contraction.

Nesting was reported in Ireland in 1933 and 1953. In southern England and Wales breeding attempts have been few and probably involved escapees or birds with slight shot wounds that could not return to their native haunts. The species has not been taken seriously by wildfowlers as one for rearing and release.

RANGE AND DISTRIBUTION: The wigeon breeds mainly in subarctic to boreal zones across northern Eurasia from Iceland and Scandinavia to the Bering Strait. It winters south in Britain, south-west Europe, the Mediterranean, Caspian, Persian Gulf, north and west Africa, Iran, India, Thailand and the east coast of China.

Most British nesting pairs are found along the upland spine of England and Scotland from Yorkshire and Cumbria to the Pentland Firth, much as they were fifty years ago but with a little shift to the east in the central Scottish Highlands. Main breeding centres are on the north Pennines, in the Ettrick Forest in Selkirkshire, central and east Perthshire into Kinross, upper Speyside, central and east Sutherland, Caithness, the Outer Hebrides and Orkney.

Winter concentrations are in south-west and north-east Scotland and east and south-east England where huge flocks gather on estuaries, such as the 35,000 on the Ouse Washes. Guns on the south coast usually enjoy moderate sport but generally the further west the more one is dependent on very cold weather.

HABITAT: For breeding, moorland tarns, lochs and streams are preferred and horseshoe lakes along meandering rivers are ideal. Bogs and even damp woodlands are also used.

In winter wigeon gather mainly on coastal saltings and muddy shorelines, especially where their favourite food abounds, but as disturbance from many sources increases and weather fluctuates, adaptability is paramount and they tend increasingly to frequent floods, large lakes and reservoirs.

IDENTIFICATION: The white patch on the male's forewing is an excellent field mark in flight — it is the only British duck to have this. Seen from below, the dark head of the male contrasts with the white underparts. The female is slimmer than the female mallard and has a small, steel-blue bill. Both sexes have a distinctive rounded head, pointed tail and green speculum. The wings are long and narrow and come down well below the body in flight. The colour of the legs and feet varies considerably but is mostly dark grey.

Both sexes go into moulting eclipse and the first eclipse is recognisable in the drake through the retention of drab wing-coverts rather than white shoulder patches. Eclipse may begin in June and continue to November, but is mostly from the end of July with full plumage resumed from August. In eclipse the male looks like a dark female.

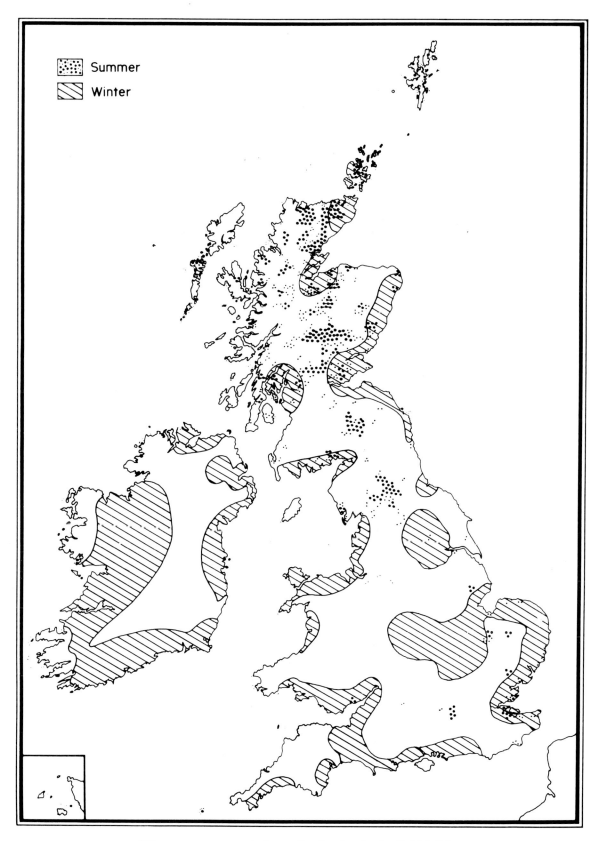

Wigeon — summer/winter distribution in the British Isles

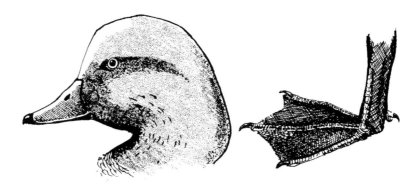

The adult female has two colour types, one chiefly brown and the other grey — possibly through maturity. The juvenile resembles the predominantly grey duck but is duller, particularly the speculum, until February when the plumage of the male assumes its rich colourings.

When moonflighting watch out for the larger, protected shelduck which often associates with wigeon, but a little practice should soon help to distinguish the distinctive sound of wigeon wings.

The length is 46cm (18in). The male weighs an average 872g (1lb 15oz) within a range 670-1,090g (1lb 7½oz-2lb 6oz) and the female 777g (1lb 11oz) within a range 600-910g (1lb 5oz-2lb).

VOICE: The characteristic high-pitched whistling *whee-oo* of the drake maintains flight contact between birds, usually announces the arrival of a flock even at considerable distance and is one of the most stirring sounds in nature. The female has a low, growling purr.

BREEDING: Islands are favoured for their security and on them wigeon may nest close together, such as on St Serf's on Loch Leven, the largest British concentration. Irregular nesting in southern England is on brackish coastal marsh or inland pools near rough ground. However, the site may be 200m (655ft) from water, perhaps on a bracken-clad hill overlooking a loch or tarn.

The nest, always on the ground, is made by the female and is just a hollow lined with dead leaves, stems and down, well hidden in bracken, rushes, long heather or tussocks. The single clutch of 7 or 8 (occasionally 6-10) creamy-buff eggs is laid from the end of April into May and incubated by the female only for 22-25 days during which the drake stands guard. The ducklings leave the nest soon after hatching, are tended by the female and become independent when they can fly at about six weeks.

FEEDING: The wigeon is a dabbling duck whose preferred food has been the subject of considerable debate in recent years. It feeds mainly by grazing, mostly marine *Zostera* (eelgrass, which has become known as wigeon grass) which it takes on land at low tide or, if the tides are wrong, by pulling up by the roots while paddling in the shallows or by up-ending, which it is not too good at. It is

100

Duck wigeon at nest. This is one of several subarctic duck species which appear to have colonised Britain during the cooler climatic phase of the nineteenth century *(Eric Hosking)*

the *Zostera* beds which attract large numbers of wigeon but in some major haunts these have declined as *Spartina* grass has spread and disease has occurred. Sea pollution too may be a contributory factor. In addition some areas blame the great increase in numbers of brent geese for these birds also concentrate on *Zostera*. However, Vesey-Fitzgerald suggested that wigeon benefit in sharing their food with brent as they feed on the brent's leavings. But he was writing in 1946 and could not foresee the state of the *Zostera* beds today or envisage the success of the brent.

Where there is little *Zostera* on the coast, wigeon flight inland to marshes and flooded meadows to graze like geese but will also feed there from the water surface. Some seeds, grain and animal foods are also taken.

Time of feeding varies. September and October arrivals usually feed by day because they are mostly immature birds which are unfamiliar with man and easy to approach. In the past these birds were a focus of attention for the puntgunner (hence the term 'wigeon' for fool). Yet they soon learn and later in the season in disturbed areas they are as nocturnal as mallard. Where they are undisturbed they also feed by day at low tide. In heavily shot areas they swim about offshore until night. The sportsman must study the local pressures in conjunction with tide and weather when planning an outing.

MOVEMENTS: The British population is mostly resident, moving to the coast in autumn with some drifting towards the south-west and Ireland.

Britain is fortunate in having such a mild climate for this latitude and this

101

attracts great numbers of winter visitors. About half the total wigeon population of north-west Europe winters in the British Isles. We get most of the Icelandic group and others come chiefly from Russia, Siberia and Scandinavia. The immigration commences at the end of September and continues through October into the first half of November. As the cold weather intensifies the birds move further south, even beyond Britain, so the most productive shooting in the far north is usually at the beginning of the season.

The Wildfowl Counts 1981/82 revealed that for the second year running the main arrival of Scandinavian and Siberian immigrants into southern England was in early November and winter distribution was governed by expansive floods. The return migration is in March and April.

BEHAVIOUR: Like most dabblers, wigeon walk easily and run quickly. They are highly gregarious and on estuaries and in harbours large flocks resting on sandbars, mudflats or the sea are a familiar sight. When disturbed they can rise together out of the water almost as well as teal and keep tight formation with swift, powerful flight, twisting and turning. They are shy and wary and some say their senses of smell and hearing are so acute it is best to heed wind direction in ap-

Wigeon — main autumn/winter migration routes of British-involved populations

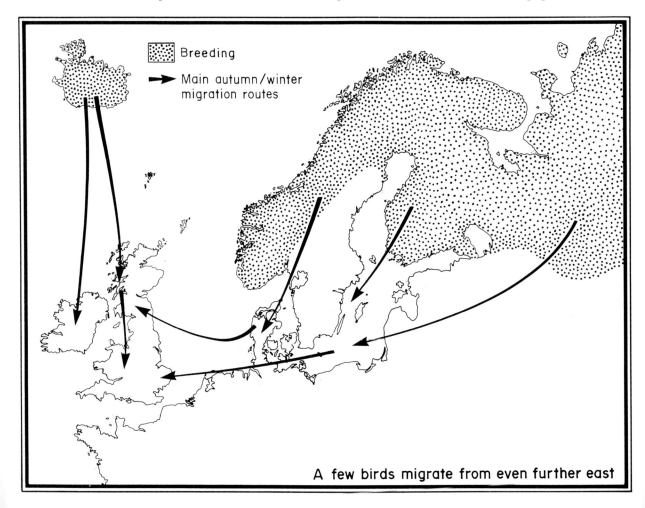

Breeding

Main autumn/winter migration routes

A few birds migrate from even further east

proaching them. Nevertheless they respond well to decoys, not necessarily resembling their own species. When they come in they often glide from considerable height on arched, motionless wings, beating them rapidly, as though to brake, just prior to alighting. They are good swimmers, and when wounded dive well and repeatedly to avoid capture by retrievers.

At night they are more likely to move about in small flocks and in most areas this is the species of fowl most frequently shot under the moon.

POPULATION: The wigeon is only holding its own as a scarce breeding species — probably 300–500 pairs.

The UK Wildfowl Count for January 1982 was 209,770 (183,310 for December) and the average maximum for 1976/77 to 1980/81 was 175,560. In October 1981 (when the Icelandic breeders had arrived) a quarter of those counted were on the coast between Littleferry, Sutherland and Findhorn, Moray; 7,000 were in Nigg Bay and on the Cromarty Firth.

OPEN SEASON: Throughout the British Isles: 1 September to 31 January but in England, Scotland and Wales extended to 20 February in or over any area below high water mark of ordinary spring tides.

IN THE POT: Flavour varies considerably according to what the bird has been eating. Hanging is not recommended. Plain roast is often rewarding but birds which are expected to have a strong flavour can be delicious when the breast is sliced thinly and fried with onions in the manner of liver.

THE FUTURE: Thankfully the species has enjoyed recent increase and is successful enough to withstand occasional runs of poor breeding seasons resulting from inclement weather. Britain is never likely to be wild enough to sustain much of a breeding population even in a favourable weather pattern, and increased tourism and rambling is likely to aggravate the situation. As the bulk of their sport is from foreign-bred birds British shooters must be active in international co-operation to safeguard prime breeding grounds abroad.

In addition the wintering population can be encouraged by maintaining healthy *Zostera* beds and generally avoiding oil or other pollution.

TEAL
(*Anas crecca*)

This is the only species of wildfowl to have a regular clay pigeon shooting stand (admittedly in exaggerated form) named after it — 'Springing Teal' — so immediately it is obvious that the bird's flight is remarkable and its position can be confirmed as a truly sporting species. After the mallard it is the one species of duck widespread enough to be likely to pop up almost anywhere and add variety to the inland shooter's bag.

HISTORY: Records show that the species has been common in Britain in winter for centuries, but recent history suggests a slight decrease as a breeder. Some strongholds in Scotland have been abandoned since World War II but in most places it has only ever been a sporadic breeder. Although the bird will take to any size of water, peripheral aquatic vegetation is essential but the trend has been to clear out for fishing or water sports many of the waters which have escaped drainage. The general lowering of the water table on much agricultural land, and coastal reclamation, have taken many good sites.

Because it will not breed freely in captivity the teal has never been a favourite with wildfowling clubs operating rearing and release schemes.

RANGE AND DISTRIBUTION: Circumpolar in range, the teal breeds in subarctic to temperate zones, wintering in warm temperate to subtropical zones and the edges of the boreal zone in western Europe. Despite its vast Palearctic breeding range nowhere does it occur at high densities. It is replaced by the green-winged teal in North America and in Europe it is absent from the south-east and south-west.

It is widespread as a breeder in the British Isles but very scarce in the south-west. Most of Scotland and Ireland have good populations but it is scarce in north-west Scotland where the vegetation is poor and wetter summers may affect brood survival. It breeds in most counties in north and east England, thinning out further south.

In winter it is widely distributed inland and around the coast. Most estuaries and harbours have at least a few.

HABITAT: In upland breeding strongholds the teal favours rushy moorland, bogs, heath pools, peat mosses and lochans. Lowland nest sites are less common but include freshwater and brackish marshes, lakes, rivers and streams, but only those where emergent and peripheral vegetation provide adequate cover.

In winter this is our most widely distributed duck. It takes to the smallest pond or even drainage dykes where cover occurs. While estuaries and mudflats are used extensively, fresh water is preferred, including reservoirs, lakes, streams, sewage farms and floods.

IDENTIFICATION: The tiny size of this duck should always identify, the only other similarly-sized duck being the protected garganey which is mostly a summer visitor leaving in August (sometimes staying until October) and only rarely occurring in mid-winter.

At long range the drake appears greyish with a dark head. Both sexes have the metallic green and black speculum and in flight the two white wing-bars may

Goldeneye *(above)* — drake *(right)* and duck; wigeon *(below)* — cock *(left)* and hen

R.McPh

show. The sound of the wings and rapid flight are distinctive. Complete or partial eclipse occurs in both male and female from July to October but full plumage is mostly resumed by the end of September. Eclipse and juvenile drakes resemble the female but with darker, more uniform upperparts. The juvenile's underparts are more spotted.

The average length of both sexes is 36cm (14in). The average male weighs 350g (12oz) and the female 280g (10oz).

VOICE: The drake's low, musical *crrick-crrick* is a familiar marshland sound but not at all duck-like, though the female utters a short, high-pitched quack of alarm almost like a bark. In flight flocks call continuously, the *krit-krit* carrying a long way.

BREEDING: In courtship the male dips his bill in the water, rises from the surface and arches his neck to draw the bill in again. The folded wings are lifted over the back and the tail is cocked.

The duck alone lines a ground hollow in thick undergrowth with dead leaves, bracken and down. Although generally the nest is more closely associated with water than that of the mallard it may be 150m (500ft) or more from the nearest pool or stream, hidden among gorse or heather on dry ground or even in bracken-covered woodland glades. Nesting is so sporadic in much of England and Wales that in some areas teal may nest in only two years out of ten.

The 8-12 (occasionally up to 15) pale buff (sometimes tinged green) eggs are laid from late March to mid-May according to how far north. Incubation takes about 21 days by the female only, the male, as is usual among *Anas* species, having deserted and dispersed prior to moulting. The ducklings leave soon after hatching, are tended mainly by the duck and fly at about 23 days. Broods seldom swim in open water but prefer to hide among marginal vegetation or under banks. The parents will feign injury to distract predators from the young. There is just one brood but eggs have been found as late as September, probably replacing earlier losses. Pairs appear devoted and probably pair for life.

FEEDING: This dabbler feeds mainly on the surface in the shallows and also up-

Tufted duck *(above)* — drake *(right)* and duck; teal *(below)* — cock *(right)* and hen

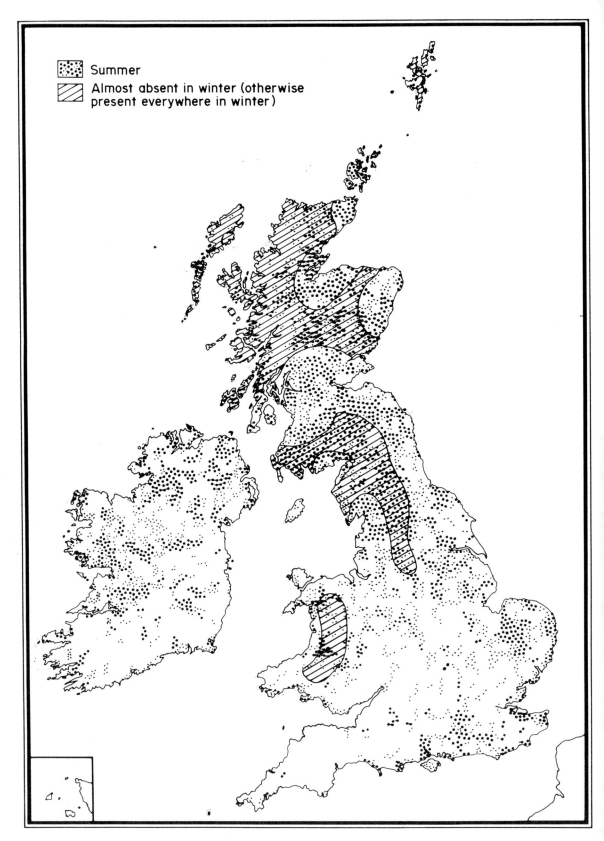

Teal — summer/winter distribution in the British Isles

ends. Water weeds and their seeds, insects, worms and molluscs are taken with a stronger emphasis on animal food in summer and aquatic seeds in winter. In autumn teal frequently flight several miles to feed on stubbles.

Teal are chiefly night feeders but will feed by day where there is very little disturbance. In most cases they spend the day resting on large waters or on coastal marshes and flight out to small inland waters at dusk. Then, as they tend to follow regular routes, they may offer good sport as they flash low over the gloomy fields, twisting and dipping to evade all but the best shots.

MOVEMENTS: The teal is a resident, winter visitor and passage migrant. The British breeding population is chiefly resident but they do tend to move south or south-west in autumn. A few even emigrate from southern counties to western Europe or the Mediterranean, especially in severe weather. Although on the Continent large scale moult migrations occur, most British teal drakes appear to moult alone or in small groups near the breeding ground.

Large numbers of passage migrants and winter visitors arrive as early as August but chiefly in September and October with a tailing off in the first half of November. They come from Iceland, Scandinavia and adjacent parts of the Soviet Union, Poland, the Baltic and North Sea countries, and soon disperse.

Flashlight reveals the nocturnal feeding habits of teal in the shallows of a pond (Dennis Green)

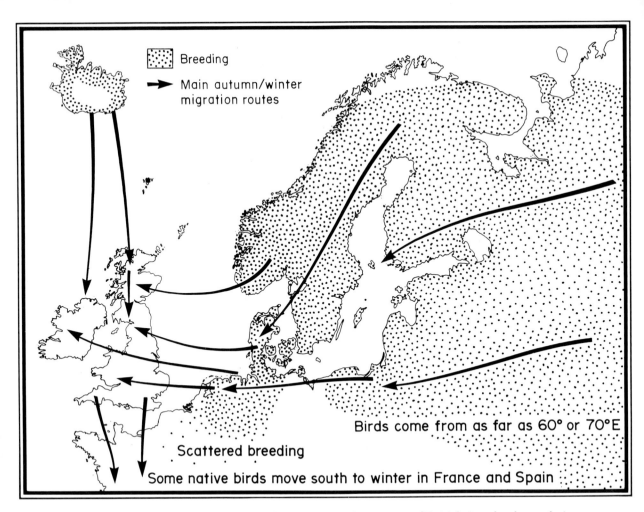

Legend within figure:

Breeding

→ Main autumn/winter migration routes

Birds come from as far as 60° or 70°E

Scattered breeding

Some native birds move south to winter in France and Spain

Teal — main autumn/winter migration routes of British-involved populations

The main concentrations are in south-east England. Some large flocks occur. The return migration lasts from March to early May, eastern and northern locations being vacated last.

BEHAVIOUR: The teal is often seen standing on one leg with its head drawn in or tucked under its scapulars. But it walks poorly with a waddling gait and is most frequently seen on water. It swims well and lightly but dives only when wounded, and then with difficulty.

However, this little bundle of energy is by no means shy and holds fast in cover (sometimes just a few tussocks in a marshy field) until flushed. Its rapid reaction to danger is its claim to fame, catapulting almost vertically into the air with rapid wing-beats, rocketing away with twists, dips and swerves. Such a response is essential for teal frequently live in well-wooded areas where generally thick cover gives little warning of a predator's approach.

There is no regular formation in low flight but the tight bunch will fly as one in the manner of waders, turning swiftly in unison. They are highly gregarious and even large flocks fly like this. Many a shot misses behind or is confused by the sudden multiplicity of targets but one straight shot is quite likely to bag several birds. Like snipe, they often suddenly drop down again into cover after being flushed. Long-distance flights are much higher and often in lines or V formation.

POPULATION: The breeding population is estimated at 3,500–6,000 pairs. A record high was recorded by the winter UK Wildfowl Counts 1981/82 with 102,190 in December, and of these about 35 per cent were in the Mersey Estuary. The average maximum for 1976/77 to 1980/81 was 72,510; 1980/81 was also a record at 89,030 so the population is thankfully in the ascendancy. However, it has been suggested that Britain harbours about half the December and January European population.

OPEN SEASON: Throughout the British Isles: 1 September to 31 January, but in England, Scotland and Wales extended to 20 February in or over any area below high water mark of ordinary spring tides.

IN THE POT: One of the most delicious duck at all times, though one per person is necessary for a good meal.

THE FUTURE: The major threat to this species is drainage, not just reclamation of large marshes adjacent to the coast but also the continual filling in of ponds and bogs which carries on year in year out in every county. Not only must there be greater effort to save all the little waters but also there must be less manicuring of aquatic vegetation for man's use, and more awareness of habitat. The teal is a resilient species and will prosper with little encouragement. It will never be threatened by over-shooting for it is simply too fast for most guns on most occasions.

PINTAIL
(*Anas acuta*)

Though pintail numbers in the British Isles are good they never approach those in Asia and North America and it will come as a surprise to most people that this is possibly the most abundant duck in the world. The drake of this predominantly maritime species is one of our most handsome quarry birds and the respect and admiration with which it is viewed by the shoregunner have earned it many intriguing names. My favourites are 'sea pheasant', 'cracker' and 'winter duck'.

HISTORY: In the eighteenth century the species was seldom numerous in England but flocks were sometimes abundantly spread along the shores of Scotland and Ireland and on some lakes. However, as a British breeder it appears to have been a nineteenth century colonist with the first proved breeding record in

Inverness-shire in 1869. England's first was in Kent in 1910 and Ireland's in County Roscommon in 1917.

Although a slow expansion into the 1950s followed, sites remained curiously scattered and not many were occupied for more than a few years in succession. There may have been some decline in breeding since the 1950s. A number of wildfowling clubs have successfully released captive-bred pintail.

RANGE AND DISTRIBUTION: This species breeds in subarctic to cooler temperate zones — northern Eurasia, the British Isles and North America. It is very locally distributed in parts of Europe but much more numerous in Scandinavia and northern Russia. In winter most birds move south-west (apart from Icelandic birds to Britain and Ireland) and large numbers occur in West Africa.

Breeding is patchy in Britain with the chief centres being the North Kent marshes and the Fens. Sites in Scotland, several Irish counties and northern England appear to be less reliable. However, there are large winter concentrations, especially at the Dee, Ouse Washes, Martin Mere, Ribble and Medway. Smaller numbers occur at many other estuaries and waters near the coast.

HABITAT: Breeding sites occupy diverse habitats including moorland pools, lochs, freshwater marshes and lowland lakes. In the Highlands upland lochs are used but so too are low-lying waters on the large outer islands. The two regularly used English sites are sea-level fen and marsh where rough grazing is crossed by numerous drainage dykes. These dabbling duck require fairly shallow water, at least at the margins.

Winter haunts are mainly sheltered estuaries and shallow coasts, and only those floods and waters near the sea will be visited because the species is almost entirely maritime in this season.

IDENTIFICATION: In silhouette or at a distance the male's two sharply pointed central tail feathers which form the 'pin' provide the best field mark. The female's tail too is long and pointed, though not to the extent of the male's. She is

Pintail — summer/winter distribution in the British Isles

greyer and more delicate than the female mallard, with a slender bill and no distinct speculum. Both sexes have a long neck and are graceful birds. The male's chocolate hood contrasts well with the white breast and belly. In flight watch for the pale trailing edge to the female's wing.

The juvenile is like the female but darker and more uniform, the young drake being greyer and the central tail feathers not markedly elongated. Both sexes go into eclipse generally between early July and early September, during which the male resembles the duck but with darker upperparts. Full plumage is usually regained by the end of October.

The average length of the male is 66cm (26in), with tail up to 20cm (8in), and of the female 56cm (22in). Both weigh about 680g (24oz).

VOICE: In display the male utters a low double whistle. His other calls are a low *kah* or *kruck* and a nasal, wheezing *gzeee*. The female's subdued quack is often uttered when alarmed; although much less strident than that of the mallard, it is audible for a long distance. She also produces a growl reminiscent of the female wigeon.

Generally this is a quiet species, especially by day, but a feeding flock may voice a low chattering.

BREEDING: This single-brooded species is semi-colonial, with nests often more exposed than those of other ducks. Frequently they are on open ground in short grass but may be hidden among long grass, rushes and heather, sometimes 50-200m (160-650ft) from water. An exceptional site is in marram grass on coastal dunes. Location is often made easier by the male's tendency to remain nearby.

The female lines the nest hollow with leaves, stems, grass and down and lays the 7-9 (occasionally 6-12) eggs from mid-April in the south to mid-June in the north. They vary greatly in colour but are mainly olive-green and sometimes pale blue. The incubation of 21-23 days is by the female only.

Pintail ducklings leave the nest shortly after hatching and are soon led to water. They fly after about four weeks but the female tends them for seven weeks. The species' distraction display involves flight just above the ground with the legs dangling as though the bird is in difficulties.

FEEDING: A dabbling, surface feeder that up-ends, the pintail eats mainly water plants, some freshwater insects, molluscs and worms. It also resorts to stubbles and grass fields and may unearth roots and stems. Most food is taken from bottom mud and in shallow water. This species is mainly a nocturnal feeder even where disturbance is minimal.

MOVEMENTS: British breeding birds move south but probably remain in the country in winter.

Most Eurasian birds migrate south in winter, some as far as central Africa, Sri Lanka and Borneo, but many birds come to the British Isles as winter visitors and

114

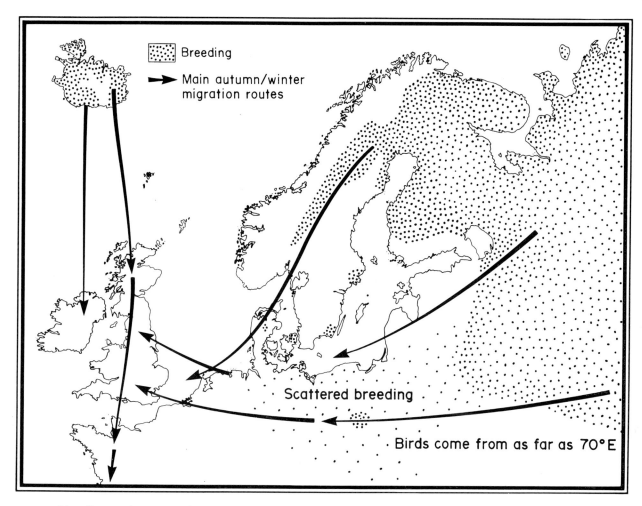

Legend on map:

Breeding

→ Main autumn/winter migration routes

Scattered breeding

Birds come from as far as 70°E

Pintail — main autumn/winter migration routes of British-involved populations

passage migrants from Iceland, Scandinavia and northern Russia. They arrive from September and are gone by the end of April.

BEHAVIOUR: Because pintail swim well and sit high and close on the water they have been a favourite target of the puntgunner and up to about forty years ago probably more were shot by the puntgunner than by the shoregunner. But the shot had to be good for this very wary duck, often found in association with wigeon and other fowl, is usually the first to take wing at any sign of danger and once fired at a flock will invariably fly right away. If present they are often in very large flocks.

Pintail walk well and gracefully, usually with the long neck outstretched and the tail raised. They can also run well. Some of the old books say they post sentinels but I do not subscribe to this. Being wary birds and generally in large flocks there are bound to be at least a few looking up from feeding at any one time. Mutual protection is one of the main reasons why flock feeding has evolved, but it is not planned.

115

A pair of pintail; the long central tail feathers give the bird its name (Brian Gadsby)

The flight is direct and rapid, with very fast wing-beats, especially when disturbed, and it is by far the fastest of our duck. The wings make a strange swishing sound, a hissing unlike all other British duck and this is a useful aid to identification in poor light. They often fly in long lines or V formation.

Generally in winter pintail rest offshore in large parties or small groups and flight inshore only after dark, leaving before dawn.

POPULATION: This is Britain's rarest breeding dabbling duck and the resident population is put at a mere 50-100 pairs.

The Wildfowl Counts gave winter maxima of 23,090 for 1980/81 and 19,180 for 1981/82 (January). The average maximum for 1976/77 to 1980/81 was 19,880. Top site was the Mersey Estuary with 18,450 in 1980/81 and 11,440 the following November.

OPEN SEASON: Throughout the British Isles: 1 September to 31 January, but in England, Scotland and Wales extended to 20 February in or over any area below high water mark of ordinary spring tides. The pintail is protected by special penalties during the close season in England, Scotland and Wales.

IN THE POT: This bird is very good eating despite its predominantly maritime habitat, for much of the feeding is on fresh water.

THE FUTURE: Predictions are difficult for a species which is known throughout its breeding and winter range for random movements and population fluctuations. One has only to compare the 1980/81 and 1981/82 Wildfowl Counts given above. It does favour inland waters very near the coast and these have tended to disappear at a faster rate than most lakes and marshes in the wake of drainage for farming and, in the south-east particularly, through the sprawl of towns, tourism and industry. However, the pintail can be encouraged easily. I know of one completely new lake near the South Coast where good numbers of pintail flighted regularly in the first winter. Again, the future of the species is dependent on the preservation and provision of suitable inland waters and a clean coast with quiet roosting areas.

SHOVELER
(*Anas clypeata*)

This brightly-coloured duck is chiefly known for its amazing bill which has earned local names such as 'broad-bill'. Bewick described this neatly in 1804:

> Bill 3 inches, rounded like a spoon at the end. The insides of the mandibles are remarkably well furnished with thin pectinated rows which fit into each other like a weaver's brake, and through which no dirt can pass.

HISTORY: Bewick noted that it was 'not ascertained' as to whether the shoveler breeds in England 'where indeed it is a scarce bird'. In earlier days it should have done well in eastern England before the great swamplands of the Fens were largely drained but the ups and downs of our climate may not have always been favourable. It appears to have been a rare breeder of long standing.

Ireland too would appear to be a traditionally good haunt and at the end of the nineteenth century the shoveler was thought to be breeding in eighteen Irish counties, with five further counties added up to 1950. Since then the 'kertlutock' has probably declined there in the face of bog development.

However, in Britain as a whole, the shoveler has done well this century with major increase and expansion, mainly 1900–50, matching that throughout western Europe. This may have been related to climatic amelioration. Scotland too shared this increase, though it is not known to have been colonised before the 1840s, and even by 1900 breeding sites were few there.

Since 1950 continued drainage has reduced the already very restricted, favoured marshy habitat. Rearing in captivity is extremely difficult because of the very specialised feeding so the species has never been the subject of a significant release programme.

RANGE AND DISTRIBUTION: The shoveler breeds right across Eurasia but avoids the northernmost tundra zone. In Europe it is sporadic and absent from large areas of the south and west. In North America it breeds from Alaska to the Great Lakes south to about 40°N.

The species is resident only in the south-west of Europe. Migratory birds

Shoveler — summer/winter distribution in the British Isles

winter in warm temperate to subtropical zones — south to North Africa, parts of East Africa, Asia Minor and east through India to the east coasts of China and Japan.

The range of British breeding birds is firmly restricted by the specialised habitat requirements, shallow, muddy waters being found only in the lowlands, and nowhere do they breed above 120m (400ft). Hence the largest numbers are in the south-east between the Wash and the Thames Estuary. Other sites are grouped locally as in Northumberland, east Yorkshire, the Lancashire mosses and the meres of the west Midlands. Some breed on Anglesey and the lower Severn but very few in the south-west. Scotland's stronghold is the south-east lowlands but some occur further north and west as far as the lochs of Caithness and Orkney and the famous Machair of the Outer Hebrides. Most of Scotland is unsuitable.

There is considerable variation in numbers at many sites from year to year. Despite the habitat requirements our winter distribution is wide, though necessarily local.

HABITAT: As the huge spatulate bill is suitable only for shallow, eutrophic waters shoveler are generally found only on brackish and fresh water throughout the year. For breeding, lakes and reservoirs with shallow edges and an abundance of water weeds, marshland pools, drainage dykes and well-watered grazing marshes are favoured. In winter, floods, chiefly on meadowland bordering lakes, and estuaries on low-lying coasts are used.

IDENTIFICATION: The broad bill — longer than the head, narrow at the base and with a spatulate tip — is one of the best field marks, especially in flight. The male's chestnut belly contrasts well with the dark head and white chest. The prominence of the sky-blue forewings is emphasised by one of the species' old names — 'blue-wing shoveler'. In the female the blue is duller and much less noticeable. However, her bill, smaller size, shorter neck, heavier build and different carriage should distinguish her from the female mallard.

The juvenile resembles a dull female. Both sexes go into eclipse, during which the male assumes the bill colour of the female. His eclipse is long, commencing about May or June, and often the full plumage is not regained until December or even January. Mid-July to the end of September is more usual. During this quiet period he resembles the female but his back is darker and more uniform and he has more colour to the wing.

In flight the wings appear well set-back on the body but this is partly due to the disproportionate effect of the huge bill.

The length is about 51cm (20in), and average weight 624g (1lb 6oz).

VOICE: The shoveler is generally a rather silent bird outside the breeding season. The male has a throaty *took-took* and the female a loud, creaking, mallard-like double quack, sometimes in decrescendo. The male also utters a loud, nasal *paay*.

BREEDING: The nest hollow is usually well hidden among tall grass, nettles,

The remarkable bill which gives the shoveler its name. Both mandibles are edged with fine, intermeshing lamellae which are used to filter food from shallow waters *(Eric Hosking)*

heather, reeds or gorse on dry ground, often with protection against the prevailing wind. It is found in some open situations too, on grazed marshland, bog and grass banks around reservoirs, lakes and large ponds. The female lines the deep cup with grass and down, sometimes with surrounding grass stems forming a kind of tent.

The 8-12 (sometimes 7-14) buff or green eggs are laid late April to May and incubated by the female only for about 23-24 days. The ducklings leave soon after hatching when they are very shapeless and ugly, largely because of the huge beaks. They fly after about six weeks but are often tended by the female for a further week. There is only one brood and the male sometimes joins the family for brief periods, though he does not help.

FEEDING: The species' huge bill — like a shovel — gives the bird its name. It is specially adapted for feeding on the surface of ponds or lakes. Both mandibles are edged with fine, intermeshing lamellae which superficially resemble the teeth of a small comb and are used as a filter.

This dabbling duck paddles quickly through the shallows, mostly with the head and neck submerged and thrusting the spoon-like bill forwards and from side to side. From the thin mud and water it filters out tiny plants and animals and sieves out the water. It rarely up-ends to pick up food from beneath the water because there is no need to. But it does dive more than our other surface feeders, especially when alarmed.

A wide variety of foods is taken — animal and vegetable in roughly equal amounts, including freshwater crustaceans, molluscs and insects, seeds, buds and leaves of water plants. Feeding is undertaken alone, in pairs or small flocks, by day and by night, but especially after dusk in disturbed areas.

MOVEMENTS: It is a summer resident, passage migrant and winter visitor. British and Irish breeding birds migrate south for the winter to France, Spain, Portugal and North Africa. Other birds winter just south of their breeding range but some reach South Africa and Central America. Some observers are of the opinion that a few British breeders remain for the winter and this would seem quite likely in mild years.

There is a large influx of birds from Iceland, Scandinavia, northern and eastern Europe and Russia between September and November. Migration appears to be mostly at night and shoveler are not known to congregate specially for the purpose. Home birds are mostly gone by the end of October.

The return migration begins fairly early. Movement in February and March is quite noticeable but the passage trickles on even into May for some have much further to go than others and Britain is an important staging post on many routes.

BEHAVIOUR: On land the shoveler is awkward, waddling with the body carried somewhat erect. It is only moderately gregarious in winter, feeding mostly in small flocks, but it may gather in large numbers at favoured roosts. It is always

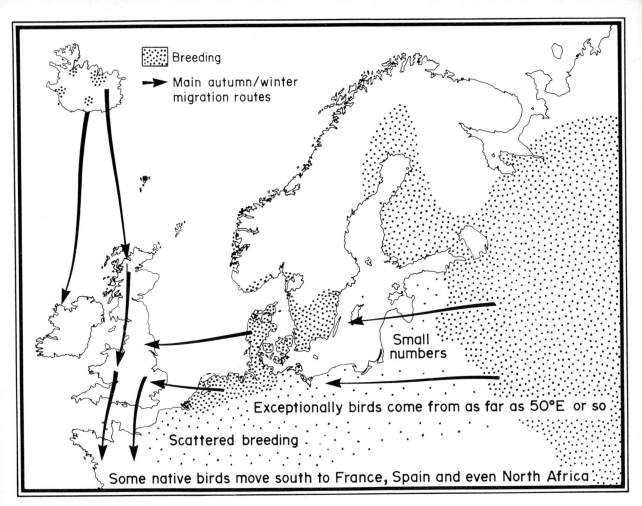

Legend:
- Breeding
- → Main autumn/winter migration routes

Small numbers

Exceptionally birds come from as far as 50°E or so

Scattered breeding

Some native birds move south to France, Spain and even North Africa

Shoveler — main autumn/winter migration routes of British-involved populations

shy and suspicious, and with man about generally keeps well out on the water where it swims with its front end held low and bill tilted down.

Some say shoveler are relatively easy to shoot but this is not particularly so for the flight is rapid and powerful with fast wing-beats; it appears faster than it actually is but is slower than the mallard's. Yet these birds are very active fliers, especially in early spring when both male and female circle their territory in courtship flight. The flight is not unlike the wigeon's and they twist and turn a lot. They rise fairly easily from the water with a characteristic drumming rattle of wings and once underway their pinions make a distinctive whistling.

POPULATION: The breeding stock is put at about 1,000 pairs. The population usually peaks in the autumn with the main influx of passage migrants, and had remained fairly constant in recent years until the big UK increase in 1981/82 to 8,370 in November. The average maximum for 1976/77 to 1980/81 was 6,370.

Shoveler (above) — duck (below) and drake; pintail (below) — duck (above) and drake

R. McPhail

R. McPhail

OPEN SEASON: Throughout the British Isles: 1 September to 31 January, but in England, Scotland and Wales extended to 20 February in or over any area below high water mark of ordinary spring tides.

IN THE POT: In 1804 Bewick wrote: 'In the opinion of many, inferior to none in the delicate flavour of its flesh, which is red, juicy and tender'. In 1893 Dixon commented 'variable according to diet' and in 1946, when palates had become that much more fussy, Vesey-Fitzgerald wrote 'scarcely worth shooting for the flesh, though quite eatable, is muddy to taste'. There is no doubt that this is the least palatable of the generally good surface-feeding duck but overall it is good when the animal content in the diet is low.

THE FUTURE: Species which favour shallow fresh waters have fared badly in this country this century, though the trend has been offset somewhat by climatic amelioration, and are unlikely to do much better as regards habitat in the next century. While quite a few new waters are being created these are mostly deep, such as in disused gravel pits, and have scant vegetation, so that it is chiefly the diving ducks such as the tufted which are attracted. Agriculture is unlikely to throw away the chance to increase profits and stop drainage. Prime sites kept as nature reserves are of course very important for they act as reservoirs from which the birds can spread, irrespective of whether or not they are managed by non-sporting organisations. However, wildfowling clubs and landowners, given generally very limited resources, are increasingly helping to provide suitable habitat for very specialised species such as the shoveler. Some even maintain waters on behalf of owners many miles from their shooting areas. This selfless-ness needs encouraging in areas where sport is easier to come by to provide a greater surplus and potential colonists.

GADWALL
(*Anas strepera*)

At first it may seem strange that this relatively unknown duck with a fairly small winter population should remain on the British quarry list but the reason is that it is very common elsewhere and its population and range are expanding. Though not boldly marked, it is a beautiful bird with delicate colours and its retiring manner and sporting behaviour make it a very welcome occasional addition to the bag.

HISTORY: Throughout recent history the bird has been scarce in Britain, even in winter. In 1801 Bewick wrote that they 'breed in the desert marshes of the north'

Pochard (*above*) — drake (*below*) and duck; gadwall (*below*) — duck (*above*) and drake

and it was not known to breed in the British Isles before about 1850 when a wing-clipped pair was turned down at Narford in the Brecks and subsequently bred. By 1875 there was a substantial population in Norfolk and by 1895 they had crossed into the Suffolk side of Breckland. Just ten years later they were breeding in the valley of the River Lark and in marshes at the head of the River Waveney. Further colonisation was probably aided by the increasing number of winter visitors being encouraged by feral flocks to remain to breed.

Although by 1906 some 1,400–1,500 birds were said to favour just one Breckland water such numbers were almost certainly maintained by intensive winter feeding for no such numbers have been seen there recently. Expansion from Breckland was slow and east Suffolk was not colonised until the 1930s when over sixty full-winged young flew away from St James's Park, London and bred at Barn Elms Reservoir in 1935. Subsequently a feral population was established in Greater London, though that in west Kent is thought to derive from later releases by wildfowlers. Later other feral populations were established through wildfowlers' release schemes; some grew following escapes from wildfowl collections.

Breeding was recorded at Loch Leven in Scotland in 1909 and first confirmed in Ireland in 1933. While most English stock is thought to be of feral origin, the Scottish and Irish birds are probably natural colonists. Nests were found regularly in the Norfolk Broads from the 1950s when the Ouse Washes and east Essex were colonised.

The gadwall has also recently spread in North America and Europe. It is now more numerous in Iceland; France was colonised in 1920, West Germany in 1930, Switzerland in 1959 and Norway in 1965.

RANGE AND DISTRIBUTION: The gadwall is widely distributed across Europe, North America and Asia but the main breeding range is well to the south of those of most European dabbling ducks and it is mostly absent from Scandinavia, Finland and the forested taiga of the USSR. West of Russia its breeding distribution is patchy in mainland Europe but in western USSR alone there are approaching 175,000 nesting pairs.

Though there has been expansion, this is still among Britain's scarcer breeding duck. The centre is East Anglia but the Essex and Kent coasts, parts of Surrey, Somerset and Yorkshire, and the Loch Leven area, have been colonised.

The gadwall's winter haunts are mainly near the southern limits of the breeding range, which itself is quite southerly. A few reach the tropics. Migrants on passage will be seen resting on our sheltered estuaries and coasts in winter but mostly they will be encountered on quiet inland waters. The winter distribution is wide but local.

HABITAT: As a dabbler the gadwall favours shallow, lowland fresh waters with thick vegetation, often with little open water, but it frequents some reservoirs and slow-moving streams as well as lakes, meres, marshes and floods. In winter a greater variety of waters is visited according to the severity of the weather and, as mentioned, estuary saltmarsh is used on migration.

126

Gadwall — summer/winter distribution in the British Isles

IDENTIFICATION: At a distance both sexes appear grey-brown but both have the distinctive white speculum; no other British duck has this white wing-patch. Seen from below, the male's generally white underparts are distinctively clear-cut against the dark head and neck but the female is less pale below. Above, the female is much like the female mallard but slightly smaller. Also look for the male's black undertail-coverts. The juvenile is like the female but streaked and spotted below and darker above.

Both sexes go into eclipse and this may start very early and be complete in early June. The return to full plumage generally commences in August and is rarely complete by mid-October. During eclipse the male loses the crescent markings on the breast and his bill assumes the colour of the duck's.
    The flight is wigeon-like and the wings more pointed than the mallard's.
    The length is 51cm (20in).

VOICE: The female's quack is softer, higher-pitched, drops off more at the end of a series and is uttered more frequently than that of the mallard. It gives the general impression of sounding more excited than the mallard. The drake has a soft whistle and a single croaking note, plus a few variations during courtship.

BREEDING: The nest is usually under 15m (50ft) from water and is thus easier to find than that of most ducks but may be found in dry vegetation such as heather. It is always well hidden in thick vegetation. The duck lines the hollow with sedges, dead leaves and down and lays 8-12 (7-16 recorded) yellow-buff or light green eggs from early May to June. Incubation is for 26-28 days by the duck alone. On hatching, the ducklings are led immediately to water, are tended by the female only and fly at about seven weeks. There is a single brood.

FEEDING: This duck is a dabbler that concentrates on vegetable matter such as roots, leaves, seeds and buds of water plants, taken by immersing the head, though rarely up-ending. Some animal food is taken, including snails and worms. It occasionally grazes on agricultural land and visits the stubbles in autumn. The gadwall feeds chiefly by day where undisturbed but is a fairly rest-less bird and will spend a considerable amount of time flying between its roost and feeding ground.

An interesting, apparently recent, development has been the establishment of a winter feeding association with the coot. The gadwall waits to feed in the very disturbed water where the coot dives and may even steal the coot's weed.

MOVEMENTS: English breeders are mainly resident but Scottish breeders move south in winter to Ireland and England. A few English birds drift over to the Continent or Mediterranean in severe weather.

A fairly small influx of winter visitors appears on our coasts and estuaries to rest but they do not stay there long for they prefer quiet, inland waters and dis-perse quickly. They arrive from Iceland, the Baltic, North Sea countries and the Continent from mid-August, reaching a peak in October and tailing off in November. The return migration is in March and April.

BEHAVIOUR: This shy bird is agile on the land and it loves to creep among rank

Gadwall — main autumn/winter migration routes of British-involved populations

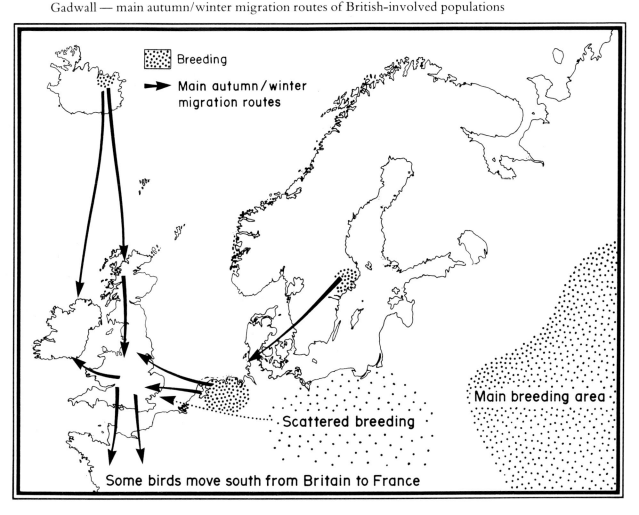

The drake gadwall — a bird of quieter waters·*(Dennis Green)*

vegetation. However, it mixes well with other duck and swims high in the water. It is often one of the first birds to respond to danger.

Although the wing-beats are more rapid and it appears faster, it is actually slower than the mallard and the whistling of the wings is lower pitched. Unlike mallard, gadwall are seldom seen together in large numbers.

POPULATION: The breeding population of the British Isles is put at 250–300 pairs. For 1981/82 the UK Wildfowl Counts put the species at over 3,000 for the first time in autumn. The peak was 3,690 in November, over half being in East Anglia. The average maximum for 1976/77 to 1980/81 was 2,070; 1980/81's peak of 3,130 was also then a record when the highest single count was 503 at Gunton Park, Norfolk.

OPEN SEASON: Throughout the British Isles: 1 September to 31 January, but in England, Scotland and Wales extended to 20 February in or over any area below high water mark of ordinary spring tides.

IN THE POT: This is one of the most delicious of duck at all times.

THE FUTURE: In the British Isles it is a little uncertain as to whether the most significant aspect of the range expansion has been man's aid or the natural factors

130

which have provided the stimulus elsewhere. Whatever the case there is considerable scope for an increase in rearing/release schemes in conjunction with an increased awareness of the need to preserve the quieter and wilder marshes which the species needs. Some landowners are probably unaware of gadwall presence.

TUFTED DUCK
(*Aythya fuligula*)

This is by far the commonest and most easily identified of the three diving ducks which remain on our quarry list. It is one of a small number of bird species which have fortuitously gained enormously from man's exploitation of the countryside.

HISTORY: First known breeding in the British Isles was in Yorkshire in 1849, followed by Nottinghamshire in 1851, Sussex in 1853, Perthshire in 1872, Kinross in 1875 and Ireland in 1877. Rapid expansion followed. The initial impetus was probably climatic amelioration and at first the species favoured large fresh waters but it soon adapted to the many small waters created by man's industry, particularly through gravel extraction.

Although by the 1930s most suitable sites in Britain had been colonised, an expansion in the gravel extraction industry and in the number of reservoirs provided scope for further steady increase. These outposts in turn supplied the birds which would later filter out to more remote and inaccessible natural waters, previously uncolonised, such as in Scotland and even Shetland. Expansion continues with some Irish counties colonised only since 1970. Most of the spread into western Europe has occurred since the late nineteenth century.

RANGE AND DISTRIBUTION: Although it has adapted to smaller waters the tufted duck still generally requires waters with an area of at least a couple of acres and breeding is unusual above 400m (1,300ft). A widespread and abundant resident in the Old World from Iceland across much of Scandinavia, northern Europe and Siberia to the Bering Strait, the species is absent from Spain and most of the Mediterranean.

In the British Isles summer distribution is widespread but sparse among the hills of the north and west. Many birds winter south of their breeding range in the temperate to warm temperate zones to the Mediterranean, the coast of North Africa and east to Iraq, Burma and the Pacific coast. British birds winter on sheltered coasts and estuaries as well as larger inland waters, the emphasis being on the reservoirs of the south and east of England.

HABITAT: Favourite breeding haunts are large inland stillwaters with islands and fringed with reeds and other dense, aquatic vegetation, but quiet rivers and city

131

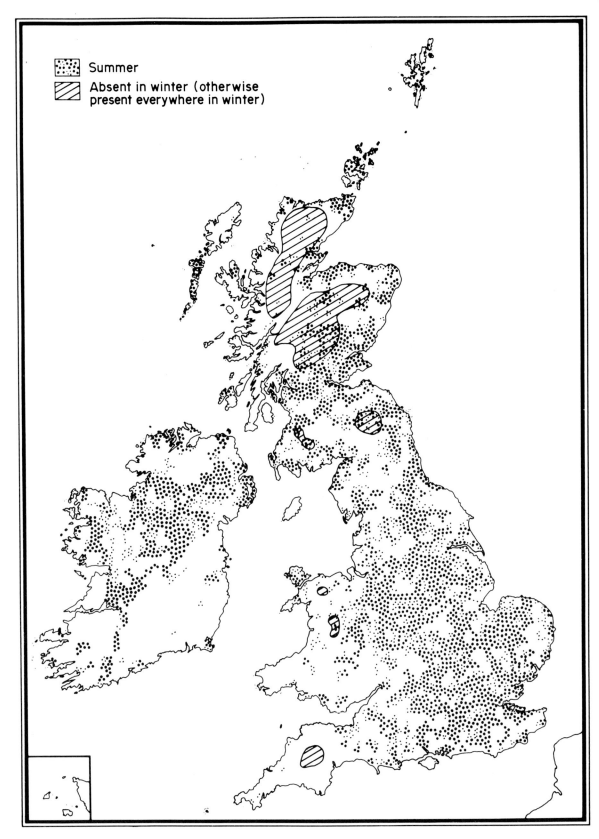

Tufted duck — summer/winter distribution in the British Isles

ponds and lakes are also used. The preferred depth is 3-5m (9ft 9in-16ft 3in).

In winter peripheral vegetation is less important and bare reservoirs are frequented as well as other larger inland waters, and to a lesser extent estuaries and calmer coastal waters. Brackish and saltwater haunts are generally chosen only during migration and in a severe freeze-up.

IDENTIFICATION: The male is readily identified with his black and white plumage and long, neat crest drooping from the hind crown. The female is rich, dark brown and her crest much shorter, though long enough to give that angular look to the head. In flight both sexes are readily identified by the white bar right across the wing. The juvenile resembles the female but is duller.

Sometimes the male is confused at long distance with the male scaup but at moderate ranges the latter's grey back may be visible. Also, sometimes there is serious confusion between the females of these two species when the white which is often found at the base of the tufted's bill is more pronounced than usual.

In eclipse the male resembles the female but is darker. This begins from the end of June but is rarely complete by mid-August, sometimes lingering until November. The full handsome plumage is rarely regained before December.

The average length is 43cm (17in), and average weight 709g (25oz).

VOICE: The tufted duck is generally a quiet species, especially in winter, but in courtship the male whistles softly. The female utters a harsh, crow-like *karr-karr* in alarm on rising and sometimes a gentler rolling note.

BREEDING: In simple but charming courtship the male tilts his head back and whistles while the female dips her bill repeatedly into the water while growling. They probably pair for life.

In selecting a site the 'tuftie' is dependent on the proximity of limestone or other non-acid formations. Favourite nest places are gravel pits with sufficient rank herbage, sluggish stretches of rivers and even town lakes where it will take food hand-outs and become almost as tame as the mallard. Most nests are on dry ground in thick vegetation within 10m (33ft) of water, but sometimes they are over water on reed platforms or old coot nests. Communal breeding is not unusual on islands such as St Serf's on Loch Leven where about 600 pairs have nested together alongside several other duck species.

Laying begins in mid–April but is mostly from mid–May, considerably later than most wildfowl, and broods are seldom seen before the end of June. The 5-12 (up to 18 recorded) pale grey-green eggs are laid on a foundation of grass and reeds lined with down. Sometimes several birds will lay even larger numbers in one nest. Incubation is for about 24 days by the female only. The ducklings swim and dive within a few hours, are tended by the female only and fly after about six weeks. There is only a single brood.

FEEDING: The diet is predominantly animal — molluscs, crustaceans, insects, frogspawn, tadpoles, frogs, small fish etc, but the leaves and seeds of aquatic plants are taken in varying proportions depending on local abundance.

One staple food in England may well have been significant in assisting the species' range expansion this century. The introduced zebra mussel was first found in the London Docks in 1824. It spread so rapidly that by 1950 it was found in forty-two vice-counties, the favoured habitat being the increasing number of reservoirs and gravel pits which tufted ducks also find to their liking.

Preferred water depths are between 3 and 14m (9ft 9in-45ft 6in), considerably deeper than those favoured by pochard. Sometimes birds feed and roost at the same site. Where undisturbed they will feed by day, chiefly during the morning and evening, but generally they are night feeders.

MOVEMENTS: The species is a resident, winter visitor and passage migrant. British and Irish breeders disperse, most in a southerly direction, but they do not usually emigrate in winter. Outside Britain most birds winter south of their breeding range, some reaching as far as North Africa and India.

Immigrants from Iceland, Scandinavia, north-west Europe and Russia start to appear on our northern and eastern shores from mid-September, and may keep on coming until the end of November, but they peak in October before many have passed through to Ireland. Large numbers carry on to France if the cold becomes severe. Much movement is at night. The return migration begins in late February and carries on until the end of May, according to location.

BEHAVIOUR: Outside the breeding season the tufted duck rarely visits land and during the day on an inland water it usually keeps well out from the shore, often preening and sleeping in the centre of a lake. It is gregarious and usually found in parties of a few dozen, though it may assemble in huge rafts in winter, mixing freely with pochards and coots. In the protection of a park or urban environment it is much less wary.

This is one of our best divers and submersions lasting over a minute are common. If pursued it always prefers to dive or swim away; sometimes several hundred birds dive simultaneously at the sound of a shot. It swims well and rapidly with the body low in the water.

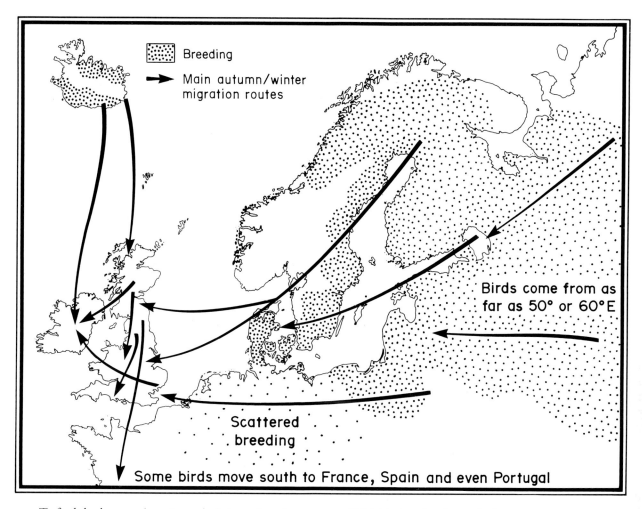

Breeding

Main autumn/winter migration routes

Birds come from as far as 50° or 60°E

Scattered breeding

Some birds move south to France, Spain and even Portugal

Tufted duck — main autumn/winter migration routes of British-involved populations

On rising from the water the feet strike the surface in the manner of the coot so that when a large flock takes wing the splashing can be heard a long way off. It gets up rather more easily than the pochard does. The flight is rapid and straight, with quick wing-beats, well sustained, easy and smooth, and the wings make a characteristic rustling sound.

POPULATION: The British Isles breeding population is put at 6,500-7,000 pairs. The 1981/82 UK Wildfowl Counts gave the highest autumn figure ever — 43,440 for November — suggesting further increase in the breeding population. The record level up to 1983 was 50,900 in January 1981, the highest single count then being at Loch Leven — 4,273. The average maximum for 1976/77 to 1980/81 was 41,250.

OPEN SEASON: Throughout the British Isles: 1 September to 31 January, but in England, Scotland and Wales extended to 20 February in or over any area below high water mark of ordinary spring tides.

Tufted duck; in flight both sexes are readily identified by the white wing bar right across the wing *(Brian Gadsby)*

IN THE POT: Some writers have described the flesh as rank and fishy when the bird has been on the coast and also suggest that it is best when feeding inland on a predominantly vegetable diet. However, the diet, as mentioned, is mainly animal but despite this most sportsmen agree that this is a popular table bird and, as Bewick said, the flesh is 'seldom otherwise than excellent'.

THE FUTURE: Prospects appear good for this species with the increase in numbers of gravel pits and reservoirs continuing and established ones settling down to develop a more flourishing flora and fauna. In addition there is more pressure on developers nowadays to landscape and generally reinstate excavations. There is more awareness of water biosystems, of which plants are more valuable and grow more quickly and of the need to establish a 'living' bed to the water rather than leave a sterile bottom which would take many years to recover unaided. A great deal of pioneering work has been done in this area by Game Conservancy biologists working at the Amey Roadstone Corporation complex at Great Lindford, near Milton Keynes, Buckinghamshire.

POCHARD
(*Aythya ferina*)

The 'poker', 'dunbird' or 'great-headed wigeon' is the least conspicuous of the three British diving quarry duck but it is equally interesting and, being faster than the mallard, presents a very testing mark.

HISTORY: Although thought to have bred in Britain for centuries it seems that the pochard was rare here until about 1840 and possibly restricted to East Anglia. Earliest breeding records are Yorkshire 1844 and Tring Reservoirs about 1850. There followed a slow expansion and increase, mainly eastwards. Scotland was colonised in 1871, with Caithness being reached in 1921, and Ireland in 1907. Since World War II the slow increase has continued in England, especially in East Anglia and the Thames Basin, but there has been marked decline in Scotland. The north Kent marshes were colonised in 1946. In some areas, such as the inner parks of London, increased breeding has helped colonisation in recent years and escapes have helped to establish feral flocks in the south and east.

The species has not been the subject of serious rearing and release schemes as it is a shy breeder with rather low fertility. Although the ducklings do quite well on artificial foods, as a diving duck the pochard has legs set well back on the body so that it is awkward on land and unless adequate swimming is provided exercise will not be sufficient to avoid undue fattening.

Since the mid-nineteenth century the pochard has also spread west and north into Scandinavia, Iceland, Ireland, Netherlands, Belgium, France, Switzerland, Austria and southern Bavaria.

RANGE AND DISTRIBUTION: The pochard breeds across the whole of Eurasia and in Europe belongs to the boreal and temperate climatic zones with the main population centres south of those of many other wildfowl species. It winters in the temperate to subtropical zones.

As a breeder the pochard is absent from Devon, Cornwall and Shetland and only sparsely distributed in western Britain and Ireland. Elsewhere it is scarce and local. Perhaps half are found in coastal counties from Kent to Lincolnshire with Greater London and Hampshire next in importance.

In autumn and winter small parties are often seen on lakes in town parks but

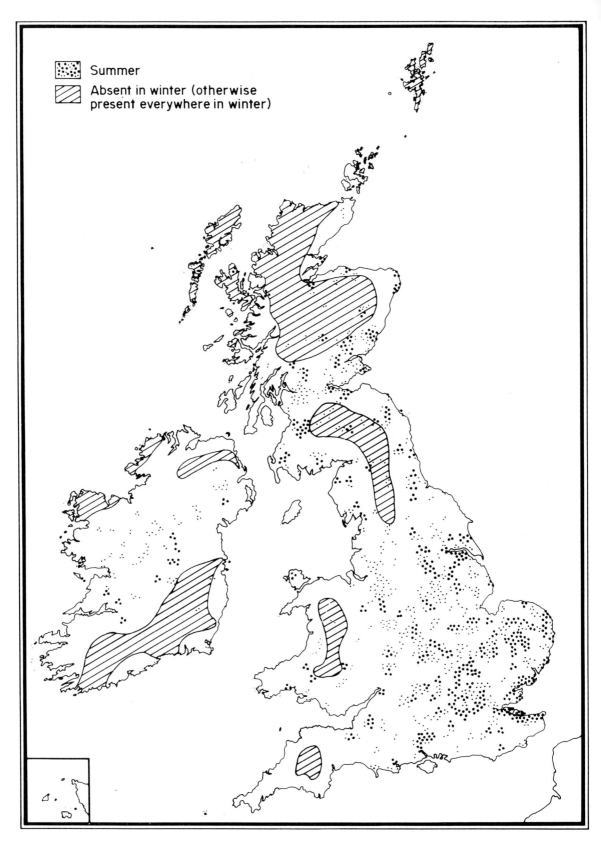

Pochard — summer/winter distribution in the British Isles

most large parties are at this time found on large inland waters such as reservoirs and lochs. Gravel pits are also used.

HABITAT: In the breeding season it requires a thick, marginal growth of emergent and waterside vegetation, preferring overgrown islands. Slow-moving rivers are sometimes frequented. In areas of high density smaller waters are also used.

Fresh water is always preferred but in winter use is made of saline or alkaline water and the pochard is found on sheltered brackish waters and estuaries. However, even in midwinter it is not a true maritime species and is most likely to be found on reservoirs and lakes, even very open waters with no cover.

IDENTIFICATION: The male's chief identifying features are his chestnut-red head and neck, and very pale grey upperparts and flanks. He is distinguished from the drake wigeon by an absence of cream on the crown and forehead and lack of white forewing. In flight both male and female are distinguished from the tufted duck by their grey wings without a white bar.

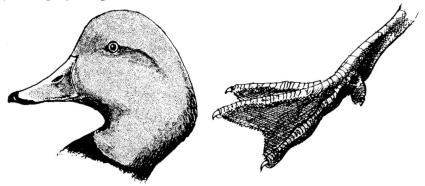

In eclipse (July to September) the male resembles the duck but has a greyer back. It is sometimes much later than September before the full plumage is resumed. The female does not go into eclipse but has what is called a 'summer plumage'. The juvenile closely resembles the female.

The length is 46cm (18in) and the average weight 822g (29oz).

VOICE: Outside courtship the species is mostly quiet. The male has a low, soft whistle and a nasal call and the female a low, but harsh, rasping croak — *kurr* or *karr*.

BREEDING: Confined to altitudes below 300m (975ft), the chief nest sites are large inland stillwaters but marshes and slow-moving streams are also used, especially where there is a wide bed of aquatic vegetation. The pochard has not taken to breeding much on the increasing number of gravel pits as has its fellow diving duck the tufted, and reservoirs too are not great favourites. The restricted breeding habitat has severely limited the species' range expansion.

139

The nest is usually on a substantial base of aquatic vegetation over water or in marshy ground such as a reed-bed but may be up to 10m (33ft) from water, well-hidden in thick growth such as sedge or gorse. It is lined with down by the duck.

In courtship the male puffs out his neck, holds up his head and whistles softly while the female growls back. After mating the drake plays no part in raising the single brood.

The 6-11 (up to 18 recorded) grey-green eggs are laid from mid-April to early May and incubated for 24-26 days by the female only. The ducklings swim and dive well within a few hours of hatching, are tended by the female alone and fly after about seven or eight weeks.

FEEDING: A predominantly vegetable diet is taken mostly in water from 1-2.5m (3-8ft) deep. The pochard dives with a leap from the surface to take roots, buds and leaves of aquatic plants, stoneworts and pondweeds being favoured. Small water animals, fish and tadpoles are also eaten but the proportion varies according to the season and location. Sometimes this diver up-ends like surface-feeding duck.

Where undisturbed the pochard feeds by day but is generally most active early and late in the night, and there are often strong dawn and dusk flights to better food waters.

MOVEMENTS: Although most British breeders are resident they move away from the nesting areas in winter and a few emigrate to western Europe and the Mediterranean.

Large flocks appear in autumn on Scottish lochs and English broads and lakes. Many of these immigrants from northern Europe and Siberia are passage migrants but others remain for the winter, arriving between September and November and dispersing to inland fresh waters throughout the British Isles. The return migration is from the end of March into April.

BEHAVIOUR: The males often form flocks as early as June. Throughout the winter they are gregarious, usually found in small, dense packs but sometimes forming huge rafts. Reputed winter preponderance of males might well be partly an illusion owing to their greater conspicuousness.

Most of the pochards' time is spent on water where they dive frequently and well. They seldom venture onto land where they waddle awkwardly and rather erect for only short distances. Pochard are fine swimmers with their legs set well back on the body but this makes them front heavy and clumsy on land. Generally they roost together on the open water where they sit low.

Booth noted that they are easiest to approach with a punt just before daybreak when they are 'disinclined to take wing, drawing all together and swimming in a compact body'. They are certainly reluctant fliers, preferring to paddle further

Greylag goose *(top left);* Canada goose *(top right);* pinkfooted geese *(bottom left)* — adult *(sitting)* and juvenile; whitefronted goose *(bottom right)* — adult *(foreground)* and juvenile

R. McPhail

R. McPhail

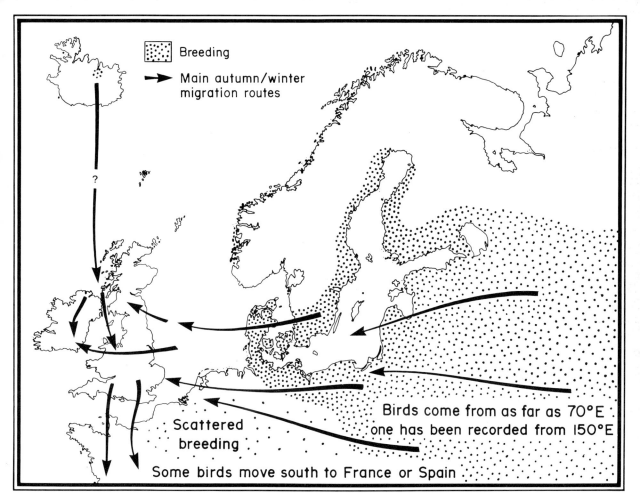

Within the map:

Breeding

→ Main autumn/winter migration routes

Scattered breeding

Birds come from as far as 70°E one has been recorded from 150°E

Some birds move south to France or Spain

Pochard — main autumn/winter migration routes of British-involved populations

out at the approach of danger. To take off they have to patter across the water in typical diving duck manner and are quite slow to get going, usually rising into the wind with rapidly beating wings. The flight is fast and direct, like that of the tufted, and on short journeys usually in tight, compact formation. On longer flights they may form long, rather irregular lines or ragged spearheads at a height to offer testing shooting. They are faster than mallard but often land very untidily headlong on the water, for the undercarriage is too far back.

POPULATION: The total British Isles breeding population is probably only 200-400 pairs. The UK Wildfowl Counts for 1981/82 gave a maximum of 31,820 in November and the average maximum for 1976/77 to 1980/81 was 35,630, but with the Irish flock the total is probably about 45,000. Several areas boast flocks of over a thousand, including the London reservoirs. The largest concentrations are found in central and southern England and the Scottish lowlands.

Moorhen *(top)*, feral pigeon *(bottom left)* and collared dove

Drake pochard feeding. The diet is chiefly vegetable and mostly taken at night to avoid disturbance *(Dennis Green)*

OPEN SEASON: Throughout the British Isles: 1 September to 31 January but in England, Scotland and Wales extended to 20 February in or over any area below high water mark of ordinary spring tides.

IN THE POT: Pochard always make a good meal and are excellent when shot over fresh water.

THE FUTURE: Despite a main breeding range more southerly than those of most waterfowl, the pochard should continue to increase its range along with some other ducks if the mean temperature continues to drop. No doubt, too, many of the currently shunned gravel pits and other waters will become more acceptable for breeding sites as aquatic vegetation increases.

144

GOLDENEYE
(*Bucephala clangula*)

Unlike the other two species of diving quarry duck, the goldeneye, not surprisingly named after its bright yellow eye, is predominantly a coastal bird in winter. As it is less gregarious than other duck it does not often enjoy the safety of flock feeding, and in the old days the professional fowler would take advantage of this to creep up on the birds in stages between the very frequent dives.

HISTORY: This is one of the species which have spread their breeding ranges southwards into Scotland following the general lowering of the mean temperature in the second half of this century.

In the nineteenth century it was common along much of the Scottish coast in winter, frequenting the firths, and it also visited inland lochs. However, it was much scarcer in England, except in severe winters. First recorded nestings in England were in Cheshire in 1931 and 1932 in rabbit burrows but since then its willingness to accept artificial sites has aided its colonisation.

RANGE AND DISTRIBUTION: The breeding range is circumpolar, from Scandinavia across northern Eurasia to Canada, Alaska and Newfoundland in the forested taiga zone but the species is absent from Greenland and Iceland. There are a few southerly outposts on alpine uplands.

In Britain it is a very rare breeder. In the area of Inverness-shire its establishment as a breeding bird is partly due to the extensive erection of nestboxes, because most of the ostensibly suitable Highland lochs surrounded by trees lack suitable nest sites.

In winter birds move from their breeding haunts in the boreal and cool temperate zones south and west in the boreal to warm temperate zones. In the British Isles winter visitors favour Scotland but there are many good English locations and the wide distribution includes Wales and Ireland.

HABITAT: It breeds where forests provide tree holes for nesting near fresh water with little aquatic vegetation. However, the vast majority of European birds spend most of the winter on estuaries, sheltered bays and coasts. Smaller parties also use suitable fresh waters but, although they are less perturbed by severe weather than most duck, sustained frost will drive them out to the coast.

IDENTIFICATION: The golden eye is not a prominent field mark but the curious triangular head will identify both sexes even at long distance. This shape is accentuated by feathers, but it has been suggested that the underlying dome's large air sinuses above the skull carry a reserve supply of air which may enable the bird to prolong its dives.

In flight the white wing-bar of both sexes is noticeable. The male is mainly black and white with harlequin pattern upperparts in flight. His head has a green

145

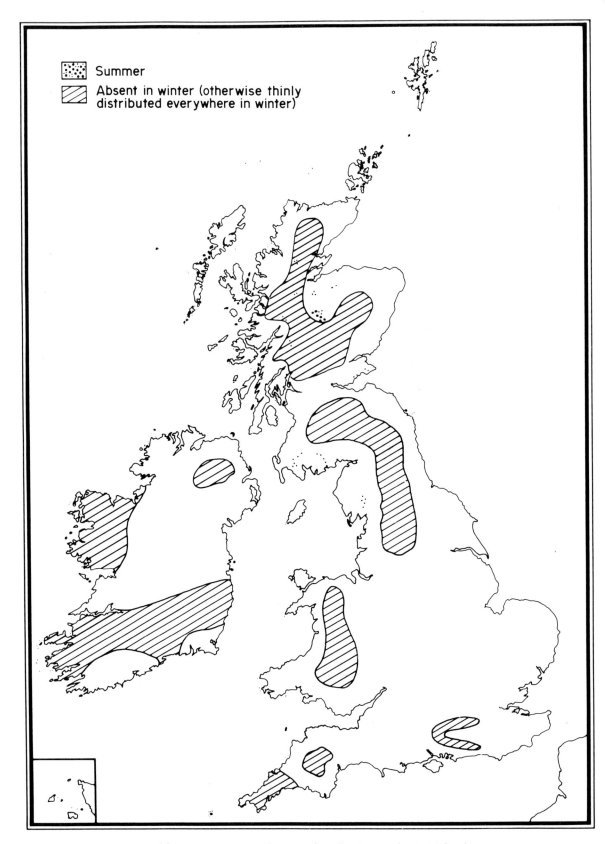

Goldeneye — summer/winter distribution in the British Isles

sheen and the white circular patch between his bill and eye is noticeable even at a distance. The female is grey with a brown head and white collar.

Both sexes go into eclipse. In complete eclipse between August and September the male resembles the female but keeps some dark green head feathers. Full plumage is not resumed until the end of October and even as late as Christmas. Juveniles resemble the duck but are duller and lack the white shoulders.

Overall the species' shape is rather squat and in flight it looks short-necked. The length is 46cm (18in) and the weight 738-908g (26-32oz).

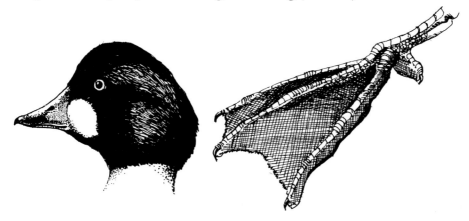

VOICE: The goldeneye is a very quiet bird but the male has a harsh, wheezing *zeee-zeee* and the female a grunting, growling *kurr*. She is also said to screech and utter a rapid *kah-kah-kah*.

BREEDING: The courtship ceremony is complicated, with the male swimming around the female while lifting his tail and head and sometimes kicking up water. He also lays back his head with the bill pointing skywards.

The natural nest site is invariably in a deep tree hollow so that without nestboxes suitable sites would be very rare in the Scottish base because the woods are chiefly coniferous, too young and too well managed generally to have hollows. Sometimes a rabbit burrow or a cavity under rocks or logs is used. Abroad goldeneye use large holes excavated by black or pileated woodpeckers, mostly at heights of 10-15m (33-50ft). The nest is always near fresh water but exceptionally may be several miles away from the loch or stream where the female will take the ducklings just one day after they hatch and tumble to the ground.

Breeding in Scotland may be rather more frequent than recorded for the species is difficult to observe, most sightings being of the downy young accompanying the female. Colonisation is also slightly delayed because the goldeneye does not breed until its second year.

The single clutch of 6-11 (up to 15 in some latitudes) blue-green eggs are laid in mid-April on a bed of wood chips, feathers and down provided by the female. Incubation is for about 30 days by the female only and fledging is after 55-65 days but the ducklings are quite independent after about 50 days.

FEEDING: This diver generally operates in water to 4m (13ft) deep where it gathers mostly animal food. On the coast it always feeds near the shore. In summer it takes insects and their larvae, tadpoles, leeches and shrimps by probing with the strong bill among stones on the beds of rivers and lakes. It also takes small fish, molluscs, crustaceans and aquatic vegetation.

The goldeneye is chiefly a day feeder, especially in summer when days are longer and there is greater security on the generally very remote breeding grounds. Sometimes in winter it may roost far from feeding grounds and in disturbed areas may flight at night to feed on fresh lakes or quiet, brackish waters.

MOVEMENTS: Mostly a passage migrant and winter visitor, the goldeneye is a rare resident. The small British population probably moves only locally.

Winter visitors and passage migrants, mostly from Scandinavia, arrive from mid-September, peak in October and tail off in November. At first they disperse inland as well as settle on estuaries and sheltered coasts but in mid-winter they are more concentrated on the less icy coasts. The return migration begins at the end of March and reaches a peak in April but some birds remain on inland waters into May.

Goldeneye — main autumn/winter migration routes of British-involved populations

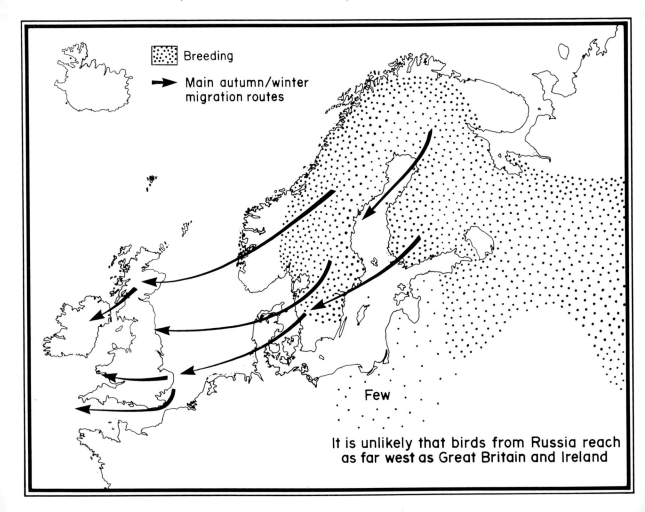

Breeding

Main autumn/winter migration routes

Few

It is unlikely that birds from Russia reach as far west as Great Britain and Ireland

A party of goldeneye. The curious triangular head will identify both sexes and the male has a white face patch. The golden eye is not visible at distance *(Robin Williams)*

BEHAVIOUR: Less gregarious than most duck, the goldeneye is usually found in small parties but flocks of 1,000 or more can be seen regularly at sites such as the Firth of Forth. It rarely mixes with other duck and if on the same water as other species will usually form an exclusive goldeneye group. The females and young appear to be more easily approached than the old males.

It swims well and lightly but when alarmed is apt to sink the body, stretch up the neck and puff out the head feathers so that they look even more swollen than usual. If danger continues to approach the bird usually dives and reappears further away. It is a tireless diver and even appears to prefer travelling under water rather than paddling across the surface. Land is rarely visited for it is clumsy there, though less so than the other divers.

Altogether this is a restless bird which spends a good deal of time on the wing. It rises more easily than the other diving ducks, directly into the air rather than pattering across the water, though it does strike the water several times with its feet when there is little or no wind. The flight is strong and fast and the rapidly beating wings produce a whistling rattle — hence *clangula* in the name.

POPULATION: The British breeding stock comprises only about fifteen pairs, but about 10,000-12,000 winter here and the European population is put at over 150,000 birds. The 1981/82 UK Wildfowl Counts gave a maximum of 10,080 in February and the average maximum for 1976/77 to 1980/81 as 9,470.

OPEN SEASON: Throughout the British Isles: 1 September to 31 January, but in England, Scotland and Wales extended to 20 February in or over any area below high water mark of ordinary spring tides. The species is protected by special penalties during the close season in England, Scotland and Wales.

IN THE POT: I do not recommend giving goldeneye to the average guest for the dark flesh is definitely an acquired taste. With a high percentage of shellfish in the goldeneye's diet some people find its meat unpalatable.

THE FUTURE: Increasing afforestation should encourage the species to colonise further areas of the British Isles but unless more woodland is left to mature further and develop more hollows then there will be continuing reliance on nestboxes. However, no doubt British-bred birds will learn to exploit other sites and with the incentive of sustained lower temperatures may slowly extend their range.

CANADA GOOSE
(*Branta canadensis*)

This long-lived bird, once merely 'a great ornament on ponds near gentlemen's seats', has spread to such an extent this century that it is now a pest in some areas. It has adapted well to life in Britain and is increasingly valued as a sporting and table bird.

HISTORY: First known in captivity in England in 1678, this North American wilderness species was introduced here as an ornamental bird to grace the lakes of wealthy landowners. By 1785 it was already breeding freely, by the 1840s flocks wandered at will in England and by the 1890s it was breeding ferally in scattered groups as far north as Westmorland.

In its native North America the Canada goose was domesticated long ago and on its spring and autumn migrations was hunted by Indians for many centuries. It was also rounded up for food by Eskimos on the bird's tundra breeding grounds during the annual flightless period.

By the 1930s there were over 2,000 on Scottish estates but during World War II winter feeding had to be discontinued and in 1953 there were only 150. In the early 1950s farmers in England began to complain about damage to cereals and puddling of fields in wet weather and wildfowlers were sometimes called in to shoot the birds, though egg destruction was also tried. However, sportsmen were also keen to introduce birds to other waters, and during the 1950s and early 1960s they often rounded up some birds during the flightless period in areas where they were not wanted, and transported them to haunts where they would add welcome variety to the bag. This redistribution led to major increases in the

1960s and 1970s and temporarily depleted colonies soon recovered as non-breeders found room to establish territories.

At first there was considerable disappointment in this goose as a sporting bird but its habits appear to change as rapidly as the population grows.

RANGE AND DISTRIBUTION: The natural breeding range is over most of Canada and the northern USA. Apart from Britain and Ireland it has been introduced to New Zealand, Norway, Sweden and Finland.

It is widespread over most of lowland England but sparsely distributed in Scotland and Wales. There is a strong population at Strangford Lough in Northern Ireland but very few in Eire. There is little seasonal variance in British distribution as our population is not internationally migratory. (*See* Movements.) The largest concentrations in 1980/81 were in September at Shavington, Staffordshire (1,600), Stratfield Saye, Hampshire (1,460) and Kedleston, Derbyshire (1,050).

HABITAT: In its native North America the Canada goose haunts marshes and lakes in wooded country but in Britain its unnatural occurrence is chiefly on park lakes. However, as its range extends it is increasingly breeding on town lakes, reservoirs with vegetated margins, flooded gravel pits, marshes and slow-moving rivers. It also occurs on smaller ponds and flooded meadows and exceptionally in sheltered harbours.

IDENTIFICATION: The best field marks are the white cheek-patch contrasting with the black head and neck, the dark grey-brown upperparts and the white undertail-coverts. The sexes are alike. There is considerable variation in size and colour. The juvenile is virtually indistinguishable from the adult in the field in its first winter but has a darker chin strap and is rather duller with pale edges to the wing-coverts.

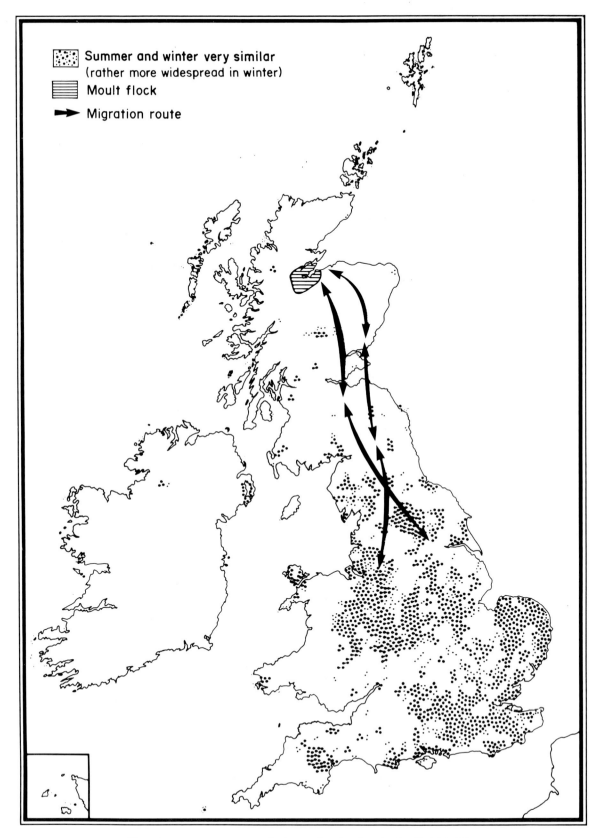

Canada goose — summer/winter distribution in the British Isles

The Canada is far larger than our two other 'black' geese, the barnacle and brent, which are black and grey rather than brown on the body. It is easily distinguished from the 'grey' geese by the black head and neck.

The general colouring of British Canada geese is similar to the *canadensis* race but in size they approach the *moffiti* (giant Canada goose) and there may well be some mixing, for documentation of introductions is poor. Smaller races are occasionally seen in Europe, especially in Ireland and western Scotland. These are mainly *hutchinsii* and *parvipes* and are usually genuine wild vagrants accompanying barnacles or Greenland whitefronts.

The long and rather narrow bill and long neck have evolved to facilitate stripping seeds off standing stalks of grasses and sedges, probing in marshland and grazing.

The average length is 91–101 cm (36–40 in). The average weight of the male is 4,880 g (10 lb 12 oz) within a range 4,170–5,410 g (9 lb 3 oz–11 lb 15 oz), and of the female 4,390 g (9 lb 11 oz) within a range 3,670–4,950 g (8 lb 1 oz–10 lb 14 oz).

VOICE: The Canada goose gives a distinctive and far-carrying *aa-honk* in flight and a swan-like hissing at intruders near the nest.

BREEDING: Pairing is a noisy time with much trumpeting and in the so-called 'triumph ceremony' the male and female run together. Courtship also involves neck stretching with the head and neck held parallel with the ground.

On larger waters the birds are colonial nesters, often close to the grazing marshes. Sites are usually close to water and well-hidden in scrub or thick vegetation, often on an island where there is greater security from predators. Sometimes colonial nesting results in territories of minimum size and some birds unable to breed through lack of space. However, the species is highly sedentary and the 'extra' birds are unlikely to colonise new waters without the aid of man.

The female lines the ground nest depression with grass, dead leaves and down and lays 5–6 (2–11 recorded) dirty-white eggs any time between early April and the end of May. Incubation is by the female alone for 28–30 days but the male stands guard nearby. The goslings leave the nest soon after hatching, are tended by both parents and fly after about nine weeks. The single brood remains with the parents throughout the winter. Adults with young begin their 30–35 day moult 14–21 days after hatching but non-breeders become flightless earlier.

FEEDING: The diet is almost completely vegetable and chiefly grass throughout the year. Some aquatic plants, clover and sedges are also taken as well as insects in summer and grain from the stubbles after harvest.

Most feeding is by day and birds often walk from the roost to the feeding grounds when within range and there are no great obstacles such as main roads in the way. Exceptionally they may flight up to about twenty miles to feed and under such circumstances offer good shooting.

MOVEMENTS: Although Canada geese are highly migratory in their native

Canada geese feeding on stubble. In many areas these birds pose a serious threat to agriculture and must be controlled *(Tony Miller)*

North America, where they are also much more gregarious, British birds are resident. Birds introduced to Sweden migrate south to winter in Denmark. Some of our birds leave their inland haunts in winter to feed in estuaries and on saltmarshes. However, a moult migration to Scotland started among the non-breeders of Yorkshire in the 1950s and the habit is extending gradually to birds breeding further and further south. These pre-breeding yearlings which would otherwise compete for food spend the moulting period from June to August on the Beauly Firth in Inverness-shire.

BEHAVIOUR: These sociable birds can form flocks of several hundreds outside the breeding season. Although their general habits are as those of the 'grey' geese, which are also diurnal feeders, they do not share the latter's regular flight times. Obviously where they do not flight at all sport can be poor but there is no doubt that the birds rapidly become wary after a few shots and an increasing amount of fieldcraft is necessary to catch up with them.

Although their flight is generally not very high in this country and they appear deceptively slow and heavy, they are fast and direct with deep, regular wing-beats and probably even faster than 'grey' geese. Thus the species can present a sporting mark and is a valuable addition to any sporting estate where shooting is sensibly restricted. On long journeys the familiar V formation is adopted.

154

POPULATION: The population growth has been remarkable since the first British Trust for Ornithology national census in 1953 when there were thought to be 2,600–3,600 birds in Britain. The Wildfowl Trust survey of 1967-9 revealed 10,000–10,500 birds, and the UK Wildfowl Counts 1981/82 recorded 19,640 in September dropping to 10,270 in March. The average maximum for 1976/77 to 1980/81 was 14,510.

OPEN SEASON: England, Scotland, Wales: 1 September to 31 January, extended to 20 February in or over any area below high water mark of ordinary spring tides. Northern Ireland: may be shot under licence from the Department of Agriculture (Conservation Branch) at Stormont if it can be shown that the birds are causing crop damage. Irish Republic: full protection.

IN THE POT: These large birds are truly delicious and on no account should they be skinned for the thin layer of surface fat imparts a magic flavour when roasted. Hanging is, as with any bird, a matter of taste and depends on the weather and the age of the bird. The tail feathers of immature geese have notched tips whereas the adults' are pointed. Also the primaries of immatures are more liable to wear and fading and are pointed whereas the adults' are more rounded until the summer moult.

THE FUTURE: Prospects are bright for this bird. The population continues to increase with the aid of sportsmen who value it as a table bird. As the number of population centres grows there is an increasing chance of natural colonisation of nearby waters. However, since the introduction of the Wildlife and Countryside Act 1981 a Department of Environment licence is needed to release the species into the wild. All the while the species is adapting to the British way and becoming a more worthy quarry. The Canada eats common foods, chiefly grass, and is not particularly fussy about its habitat. It appears to be exploiting a vacant niche in our fauna and there seems to be little reason why the population should not expand considerably.

GREYLAG GOOSE
(*Anser anser*)

This is Britain's only native breeding goose and the ancestor of most of our farmyard sentinels. Originally it was called the common wild goose or grey lag goose, the latter probably because it is the one goose that lags behind when the others return north. Another derivation of the name might be from a bird which grazed the fields or 'leys' — 'ley goose'.

Much of the information which applies to the greylag also applies to the other 'grey' geese, all of them holding a position of awe in the hearts of true wildfowlers.

HISTORY: Before the grand drainage schemes of the early nineteenth century the greylag had nested as far south as the Cambridgeshire and Lincolnshire fens and was probably even more widespread in preceding centuries, before we imported Dutch drainage expertise. In the first half of the nineteenth century the breeding range was restricted to remote parts of the Scottish Highlands and islands, though in 1876 there were still sufficient birds to inspire Booth to comment 'Great numbers rear their young in the more remote parts of Ross-shire, Sutherland and Caithness'.

Increasing tourism and general disturbance by man also took their toll. Fortunately the formation of feral flocks saved the day in the 1930s and since then, with the help of landowners, but especially local wildfowling associations, we have managed to build up a British breeding range which is probably wider than at any time in recent history. Unfortunately the international picture is more gloomy as many remote areas are 'developed' for tourism and agriculture in countries with less interest in bird conservation.

For once agriculture has dealt us a lucky hand in Britain, for as the climate ameliorated over the first half of this century an increasing acreage of barley was grown in Scotland and this has proved a great attraction for wild geese.

RANGE AND DISTRIBUTION: The greylag breeds in boreal to temperate zones, to the south of most other geese, from Iceland, through Britain and Scandinavia to eastern Europe, Russia, central Siberia and Japan.

In the British Isles truly native birds are found only in the Outer Hebrides (notably Loch Druidibeg) and adjacent parts of the Scottish mainland in Wester Ross, Sutherland and Caithness. Elsewhere breeding birds exist in feral populations, notably the Scottish Solway (largest), southern Lake District, Norfolk, County Down (Belfast area), the Midlands and Kent.

Greylag winter in temperate to warm temperate zones south of the breeding range. Our winter population is constantly changing its distribution but generally the main concentrations are on Scottish lochs and firths, and also in parts of northern England and Ireland. Greatest concentrations are in central and eastern Scotland in agricultural areas. In very wet weather birds will disperse to inland floods and shooting is then less predictable.

As with the pinkfoot, the 1981/82 winter distribution was affected by the exceptionally clean harvest. In the traditionally main area of east central Scotland numbers were the lowest for years but further south there were more than usual. However, on one farm of 146ha (360 acres) in Easter Ross the barley had not been harvested and phenomenal numbers took advantage. On 8 November 20,000 were in the area but by mid-November there were 38,000 (40 per cent of the British population). They roosted at Loch Eye but in a few weeks all were gone.

HABITAT: For breeding, fresh marshes, lakes and reed beds adjacent to grassland, farmland or swamp are ideal, but there is considerable variation including near-tundra, heathland and steppe. Scottish sites include heather moorland with

156

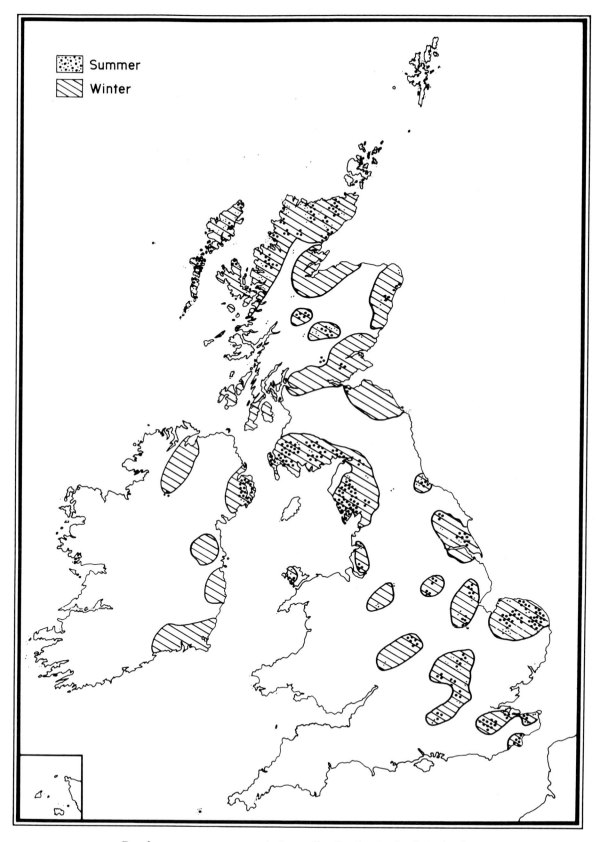

Greylag goose — summer/winter distribution in the British Isles

scattered lochs, the famous Machair (herb-rich grassland) of the Outer Hebrides and small coastal islands. Our feral birds, being less shy, are less fussy and also use reservoirs, lochs, flooded gravel pits and even protected park lakes.

In winter many large, fresh, brackish and salt waters are frequented, especially those near suitable foods such as grass.

IDENTIFICATION: Distinction between grey geese is not easy at a distance and is not helped by considerable plumage variation. In the field the greylag's general colouring appears grey-brown. At rest watch for the folded wings which do not reach beyond the end of the tail, the barred back, large orange bill with ivory nail, pink legs and feet, thick neck, and pale grey rump. In flight the best mark is the very pale grey forewing (absent in our other geese) which contrasts with the darker saddle and primaries, but the heavy head is also noticeable. The sexes are alike, being larger and paler than the other grey geese. At closer ranges you might note that the underparts are often flecked with black, though almost always less than the barring of the whitefront.

When flying very high it is almost impossible to distinguish the grey geese by sight but their calls are distinctive. On the ground, too, they are very much alike in general habits and behaviour.

At close range the juvenile might be distinguished by its less definite transverse lines on the back, less continuous pale line along the edge of the folded wing, paler bill and legs, and general lack of spots. The timing of the moult is related to weather and latitude but is generally between late May and early August.

Length is 76-89cm (30-35in). Average weight of the male is 3,799g (8lb 6oz) within a range 2,740-4,250g (6lb 1oz-9lb 6oz), and of the female 3,170g (7lb) within a range 2,070-3,960g (4lb 9oz-9lb 1oz).

Woodpigeon

R. McPhail

R. McPhail

VOICE: The exciting clamour of a distant flock has been likened to a pack of hounds in full cry and even the baa-ing of sheep. Whatever is most accurate, it carries a long way and the suspense is electric when the concealed fowler tries to trace a skein's direction as the calling lives and dies, between hills and gusts of wind. There is a wide repertoire of calls but perhaps the most familiar is the deep, sonorous, clanging *aahng-ung-ung* of two to four syllables, more throaty than other grey geese and reminiscent of domestic strains. There is also a gabbling *gaa-gaa*.

BREEDING: Each year a pair strengthens its ties in the 'triumph ceremony' when the gander produces a resonant note like that used when it has successfully driven off an intruder. Their year-round devotion may lead to the survivor also being shot on returning to investigate why its mate has fallen. Unlike most male ducks, male geese are devoted parents.

Islands are favoured nest sites because of their greater security and nests are almost always near water and well-hidden in reeds or other thick vegetation, especially heather in Scotland. The female will use the feathers and down lining the nest hollow to cover the eggs when leaving.

In Scotland the 4-6 (occasionally 3-9) white (often stained) eggs are laid between late March and May depending on the weather. In Iceland the weather is less predictable and spring later so the average clutch of 4 within a range 1-9 is generally laid from the end of April. Incubation takes the female 27-28 days while the male keeps watch at a distance. The goslings leave the nest within a few hours of hatching, are tended and aggressively defended by both parents and fly after about eight weeks. However, they remain in family parties until well into winter and not surprisingly gosling survival is good. There is only a single brood.

After hatching, the families of this loosely colonial species usually join up and may form large gatherings in which there is frequent re-allocation of young between broods. They do not breed in their first season.

FEEDING: The greylag's adaptability to foods has brought the species success but also conflict with the farmers whose crops it exploits. The strong bill has tooth-like serrations along the upper mandible and hard, horny lamellae, and was evolved for digging up the starchy roots of marsh plants before man proliferated and began extensive drainage. On native breeding grounds the summer food is mainly new shoots of reeds and other marginal plants.

Goose damage was remarkable even in 1804 when Bewick wrote 'Wild geese are very destructive to the growing corn in the fields where they happen to halt in their migratory excursions.' In 1862/63 Booth noted that in East Lothian geese were so destructive to young corn that it was necessary to employ 'herds' to keep them away. Today many farms on mainland Scotland and crofts in the Outer Hebrides suffer regular and considerable damage and welcome sportsmen to

Jay *(top)* and magpie

control the geese, especially as paying customers. Others are less scrupulous and let shooting in areas where scarcely a goose visits.

The seasonal pattern of feeding varies according to availability but in Scotland a cycle of barley stubble, potatoes and grazing is often followed. The biggest boon has been the tremendous growth in cereals acreage and, while stubbles are the main attraction, geese also sometimes take grain from standing stalks around field edges. It would be fair to say that the present high population level is dependent on arable farmland in Britain. On arrival 70 per cent of greylags feed on barley and oat stubble, and most of the remainder on grass.

When the grain has been exhausted or the stubbles ploughed in greylags turn with pinkfeet more to grass and root crops. Digging up of unharvested potatoes is only occasional and generally little harm is done. Most potatoes taken are those left on the surface after harvest and softened by frost. Indeed their removal may be beneficial in that such tubers often harbour disease. The potato supply usually lasts only until November because about three-quarters of the fields are then planted with winter wheat and only a few survive to March when spring barley is planted.

Another complaint is that geese graze winter wheat and serious damage can occur in wet conditions, but there is also some value in the fertiliser provided by goose droppings. Swedes are also taken regularly in Scotland and in severe weather the birds may turn to rape, kale and brassicae.

Grazing must be considered seriously by the farmer because the protein content of grass reaches a peak in April and May in Britain when many of the geese are still here, and this is when the early growth is particularly valuable to the farmer's stock to improve milk yields and body condition. Grass protein does not peak until July or August in Iceland. Geese probably migrate to subarctic regions to breed in order to take advantage of the longer feeding day at a time when extra reserves are needed for egg laying. In addition the increased daylight keeps the nutritive content of the food plants higher for longer than in southern Europe where droughts occur. The goslings also gain in that the wetlands of the far north are swarming with mosquitoes and other insects which provide the protein so essential in early life.

Where they are not heavily persecuted greylags mostly feed by day in terrestrial habitats, normally flighting to the feeding ground at dawn or soon after and returning to the roost at dusk, unless they are disturbed. However, they do not necessarily feed by day and the sportsman must study the local pattern to stand a chance of a shot. In tidal areas most feeding is nocturnal, between two-and-a-half hours before sunset and one-and-a-half hours after sunrise.

Notwithstanding this diurnal preference, when the moon is bright geese will flight to feed and remain on the ground all the while the moon is up, presumably because the light is sufficient to spot predators by. After such a night the birds may flight to the coast to take grit in the form of sand to aid digestion.

MOVEMENTS: British breeders are mostly resident but move locally. Elsewhere greylags are essentially migratory, wintering in and beyond the southern parts of

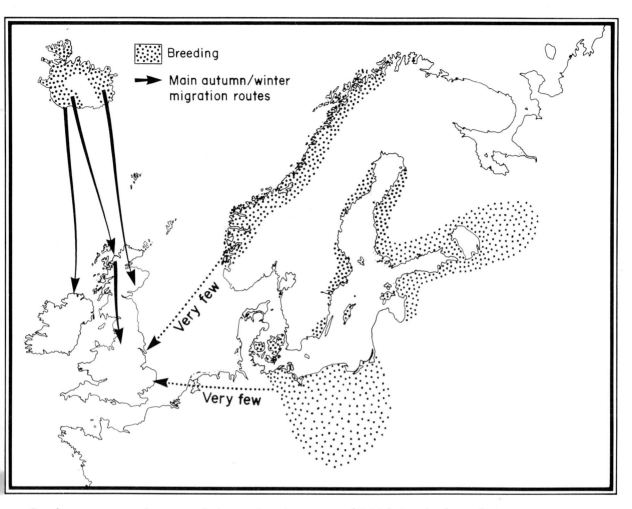

Greylag goose — main autumn/winter migration routes of British-involved populations

the breeding range. Scandinavian birds winter mostly in south-west Europe but the entire Icelandic population winters in the British Isles. They arrive mostly in late October and November in Scotland and many pass on or go straight to northern England or Ireland according to the year's harvest and weather. The return migration of Icelandic birds usually begins in mid-April.

BEHAVIOUR: There is a great deal of lore relating to the greylag, some based on fact, much on fiction. While these geese are certainly wary and difficult to approach, they do not post sentinels as the old books suggest. The truth is that in a large flock at any one time there are bound to be some birds looking up from feeding.

They also have a reputation for intelligence but for birds that are hunted so continually and frequently they can be surprisingly slow to learn and sometimes show a perplexing devotion to certain feeding grounds. Sometimes they are even less wary than other geese, feeding in small fields close to cover which could conceal predators or men. They graze near livestock and even eat roots put out for sheep.

Another myth is that the famous V formation is always led by an old gander and this is the one bird that should not be shot as it will be tough on the table. I have shot the leader of a skein and it was definitely a young bird. In these Vs the leadership is constantly changing as birds maintain even distance from their neighbours and take turns in deriving benefit from the slipstream of the bird in front.

When immigrants first arrive they are fairly unpredictable because they are so unsettled but once settled these very gregarious birds are creatures of habit.

They can spring easily from land, almost vertically for some height, but they are not so clever at rising from water and prefer to take off into the wind, though this is not essential. The flight is very direct and powerful and the regular beats of the broad wings propel the bird at a speed much greater than is apparent. Hardly surprisingly, most novice goose shooters are behind with their first shots and many others never get sufficient practice to master the art. On landing there is a characteristic flutter of wings.

Most roosts are in inaccessible places where there is a good all-round view and some proof against predators such as foxes. However, greylags are less fussy than other grey geese and may use small lakes, and floods where they will usually sleep on the margins rather than the water, as well as sandbanks and large lakes and estuaries. When greylags share a feeding area with pinkfeet the greylags usually restrict feeding to areas near the roost and feed in smaller flocks. When the two species share a roost the greylags tend to leave later and return earlier from the feeding grounds.

The study of goose flighting is one of great fascination for the wildfowler who will need to consider several major natural elements if he is to put a greylag or two in the bag. Light is probably most important but wind, weather and tide also help to determine the line of the morning flight, the height at which the birds come in and to a lesser extent the time of the flight. The wildfowler's traditional love of foul weather is well known and there is some sense in this for in fine weather geese come in regularly and in large parties but when it is stormy they arrive irregularly and mostly in small skeins so the flight lasts longer.

Wind is the most important influence on the line of approach, perhaps by as much as two miles. Geese do not like to fly across a strong wind but prefer to drift way off line before turning to drive into the wind towards their goal. They are surprisingly aware of areas which are likely to conceal guns but good shooting chances come on days of strong wind when the great birds slip in low, and during a gale they may be low enough to knock off your hat! With a light or even moderate wind they usually come in high or very high but their size makes them look deceptively low and in some notorious areas inexperienced and extremely irresponsible guns will pop away at them hoping to bring off a fluke shot, but generally succeeding only in 'pricking' (slightly wounding) a few.

When it is snowing geese fly lower, as in fog when they are even more uneasy and unpredictable. Time of arrival and direction may also be upset by the tide — an early flood may wash geese off their feet before the light is up so that they start to flight several miles wide of the roost.

Greylags over a Scottish marsh. Today most British breeding greylag originate from feral flocks *(Laurie Campbell)*

Evening flight is less popular with the goose shooter because it is inevitably shorter, the birds assembling in large flocks and moving together despite the weather. However, light is then important and it is only on evenings when there is no moon that the geese are punctual to dusk. Moonlight makes the birds irregular and they will not flight until it has gone. Also a flight will be postponed when there is snow on the ground and bright starlight too may influence geese.

Finally, in planning a flight the fowler must remember that geese will flight earlier in the morning and return later in the evening on the short days of mid-winter in order to get sufficient food energy. Times of departure and arrival will also vary according to the distance between roost and feeding ground.

POPULATION: Of the 700–800 breeding pairs in the British Isles at least 75 per cent are of introduced stock, under 200 wild pairs breeding in Scotland, mostly in the Outer Hebrides.

The recent UK Wildfowl Counts have recorded the greylag as our most numerous winter goose. The population for the United Kingdom alone rose from 26,000 in 1960 to 76,000 in 1973. There was a decline to 62,000 in 1977 but in 1980/81 a record level of 90,000 was reached, only to be surpassed by the 96,000 in the following November despite the poor breeding season indicated by 13.9 per cent young and an average brood of 2.0.

OPEN SEASON: England, Scotland, Wales: 1 September to 31 January, extended to 20 February in or over any area below high water mark of ordinary spring tides. Northern Ireland: in 1983 may be shot 1 September to 31 January and imminent legislation is expected to continue this. Irish Republic: fully protected. The greylag is protected by special penalties during the close season in the Outer Hebrides, Caithness, Sutherland and Wester Ross only.

IN THE POT: Excellent eating, a plain-roasted bird will please most palates when not hung; a very old bird could be hung for two weeks in cold weather and then made into paté.

THE FUTURE: The outlook is good for the greylag in the western parts of its range where it is holding its own in some areas and increasing in others. Interest in developing feral flocks in Britain is playing an important part but in some areas, notably Kent, this has led to new complaints of agricultural damage, and in 1983 a study of this was launched. However, most farmers will probably be more than compensated by interest in the birds and income from letting the shooting.

There are problems with over-shooting in parts of Scotland, mostly deriving from landowners and farmers letting too many shooting days in order to derive the maximum income, but also through permitting undue disturbance at roosts. Unless the sanctity of existing roosts is respected and new ones encouraged the geese will not be able to exploit further feeding grounds. It has been estimated that shooting accounts for most of the 20-25 per cent annual mortality of Icelandic stock and the 33 per cent in Continental Europe.

PINKFOOTED GOOSE
(*Anser brachyrhynchus*)

This is the smallest of the British grey geese. In most years it is virtually as numerous as the greylag and similarly treated by the farmers whose crops it takes. But when 'the pinks are in' southern fowlers head north, for one or even two special weeks every year, to 'have a go at the geese'. Sadly some leave their sense behind and succumb to the 'goose fever' which can result in desperate shooting and wounded birds. Even guns close to goose haunts are sometimes guilty of 'cowboy' behaviour.

HISTORY: In the past this bird was rounded up by Icelanders during the moult but that has now stopped. However, there is still a short open season at the end of summer in Spitsbergen.

As with the greylag, the pink's population has grown with the acreage of cereals, particularly barley, following improvement in climate and agricultural knowledge over the first half of this century. More importantly, the weather has allowed a succession of good breeding years. The result has been that pinks have fed for longer in Scotland before being forced south, though the trend has been reversed in recent years as improved techniques have resulted in cleaner harvests.

The species does not seem to have been recognised much before the 1830s and it is difficult to assess its early status because of confusion with the bean goose. Even today ornithologists have not decided whether they are separate species or simply races of the same species.

RANGE AND DISTRIBUTION: The species' range is very restricted. It breeds in the Arctic, being confined to the east coast of Greenland, Iceland and Spitsbergen. It does not breed in the British Isles.

Birds from Spitsbergen winter mostly in the Netherlands, to a lesser extent in Denmark and Germany and a few in eastern England. The entire Greenland/Iceland population winters in the British Isles: therefore we have a great international responsibility for the species. Loch Leven has often been the main arrival point and the chief centre is eastern Scotland, but the birds also visit northern England, the Wash and Ireland. The Solway is particularly important in spring.

In the early 1970s an efficiently gathered cereal harvest in Scotland meant that less food was available for the pinks in October and November and they started to go south to the Lancashire mosses where they have considerably damaged crops, especially carrots. At first about 5,000-10,000 visited Lancashire but an exceptionally clean Scottish harvest in 1975 sent 26,000 pinks to Lancashire and in later years large numbers retained the habit despite more food becoming available again further north. In the severe weather of 1981/82 there were 18,240 in Lancashire in November but this rose to 36,580 in January probably taking advantage of the slight snow cover and rotting crops following two thaws.

HABITAT: Pinks breed on higher ground in open tundra, on low mounds, rocky hillsides and outcrops, in gorges and on Arctic deltas and oases. They winter in Britain on estuaries, coasts and lakes and to a lesser extent on moors within range of suitable feeding.

IDENTIFICATION: This is the greyest of our grey geese and, unlike the greylag, at rest the folded wings reach beyond the end of the tail. At any distance the best field marks are the dark head and neck contrasting with the light body. In flight the grey forewings contrast with the dark primaries, though they are not so pronounced as in the greylag which is a heavier bird. No other grey goose has pink on the bill *and* pink legs. It has a greyer back and paler forewing than the bean and whitefront, the bill is much shorter and shallower than the bean's and it is more buoyant in flight than the bean which has orange legs and orange on the bill. Usually the only bean geese which occur in Britain are the 100-200 which visit south-west Scotland and Norfolk in winter.

Pinkfoot sexes are alike. In early winter the juveniles are rather darker and browner above, somewhat mottled below and generally duller than the adults. They are also less rounded in outline and their wing-coverts have less distinct pale edges than the adults'.

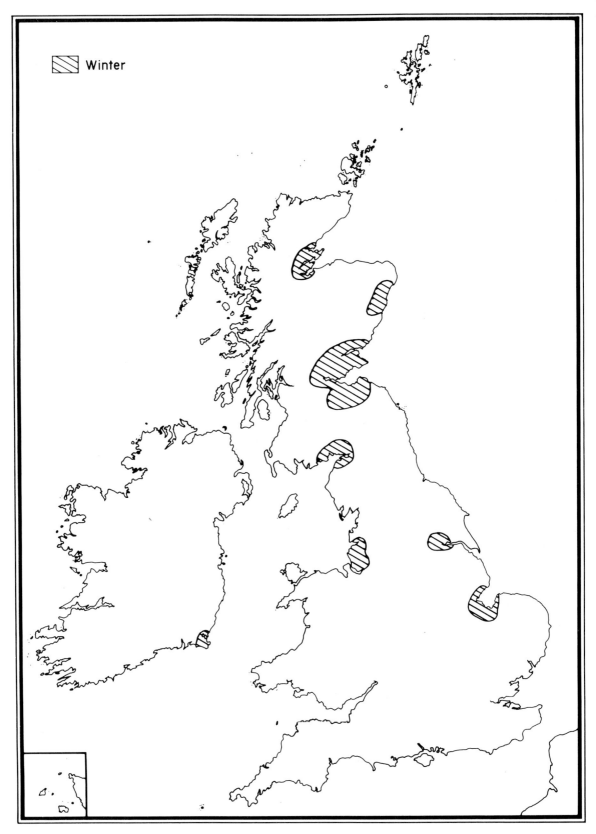

Pinkfooted goose — summer/winter distribution in the British Isles

The adult length is 61–76cm (24–30in). Average weights are: male 2,770g (6lb 2oz) within a range 1,900–3,350g (4lb 3oz–7lb 6oz), and female 2,520g (5lb 9oz) within a range 1,810–3,150g (4lb–6lb 15oz).

VOICE: A noisy bird, the pinkfoot has a shrill medley of calls — *wink-wink* or *wink-wink-wink, ung-ung* or *ung-unk* — not so deep as the greylag's, lighter and higher-pitched than the bean's and less musical than the whitefront's laugh.

BREEDING: The nest scrape on tundra, river bank, cliff ledge or rocky slope is lined with down or moss and often sheltered by low rock or a willow shrub. Sometimes in a loose colony, it is occasionally fairly isolated.

The 4–5 (occasionally up to 8) creamy-white eggs are laid within a few days of the birds' arrival between late May and June (peak hatching second half of June) and incubated for 25–28 days by the female only while the male stands guard nearby. The goslings leave the nest soon after hatching, are taken to water, tended by both parents and fly at about eight weeks. During the time when both moulting adults and young are flightless large packs are formed. Pinkfeet have single broods only.

FEEDING: Some insects are taken in summer and are especially valuable to the young which need the protein for rapid growth. They also take leaves and flowers of plants around the nest but at 21–28 days their diet resembles the adult's and includes roots of *Polygonum viviparum,* horsetail shoots, grass, willow leaves and buds, sedges, crowberries and seeds of bog plants.

In winter in the British Isles the large population exists through the courtesy of agriculture and is virtually dependent on it. There is considerable seasonal variation according to local abundance. Wild shoots and roots are also taken. On arrival cereals are the main attraction, mostly stubble grain. The pinkfoot is more fastidious than the greylag in its preference for old barley fields and will fly up to thirty miles from the roost to a suitable site, though in Scotland most feeding is within fifteen miles of the roost. Scotland's barley harvest takes place up to six weeks later than in England and wasted grain is more likely. Also more Scottish barley fields are undersown with clover and grass because the stubbles are not so readily ploughed as in the drier south. Thus in most years there is more stubble grain in Scotland and it lasts longer. Such grain is more easily collected than wild seeds and is probably more nutritious and more easily digested, with the result that birds achieve better condition and increase their chances of surviving the winter.

After the stubbles are ploughed in pinkfeet turn to ley or pasture grass and potatoes. This may be beneficial to farming in that valuable trace elements are introduced through goose droppings. Although in attacking the Lancashire carrots only the tops of the roots are eaten even this makes them unsaleable and financial loss may be great. Brassicae are also affected similarly.

Very little natural habitat is now used in winter feeding, though there are occasional large gatherings on semi-natural (grazed) or natural saltmarsh in spring. The main winter target is grass, especially where heavily fertilised. White clover is also taken on grassland. Grassland grazing is mostly insignificant for the farmer but close grazing at high density may be specially harmful in spring when weeds may be encouraged and there is competition with livestock.

Risk to standing corn is greater now with the increasing use of winter varieties, especially in floods on heavy soils, and in spring these growing cereals and grass are the exclusive diet. However, severe damage is usually only very local and there is the possibility that yields are increased through the promotion of tillering. For the birds there is the risk of poisoning from eating seed dressings and other introduced chemicals.

Generally pinkfeet feed by day unless they are heavily persecuted, flying in at dawn or soon after and returning to roost at dusk unless disturbed. They may, however, reverse this routine and feed at night when the moon is bright, flighting to the shore at dawn to take sand to aid digestion. Indeed, this is the species of goose most frequently shot under the moon.

MOVEMENTS: The earliest arrivals usually come at the end of August (second week of July exceptionally recorded) but the main influx is in the first half of October. When they first arrive they concentrate on upland or inland farms before settling down in lowland marshes about six weeks later. Some move straight to their eventual wintering areas further south. In spring most birds are in south and east-central Scotland, though more dispersed than in autumn. They leave in April and early May.

BEHAVIOUR: This is a highly gregarious species, often assembling in flocks of several thousands which break up as winter progresses, partially reuniting again in spring. A single loch roost in Scotland can hold 25,000 birds but larger sites, especially estuarine mudflats, are preferred when within reach of feeding grounds. Roosts are inevitably inaccessible places for pinkfeet are very wary. At a freshwater roost, however, they usually sleep on the margins rather than the water. The do not feed all day and in dry places may return to the roost at midday

170

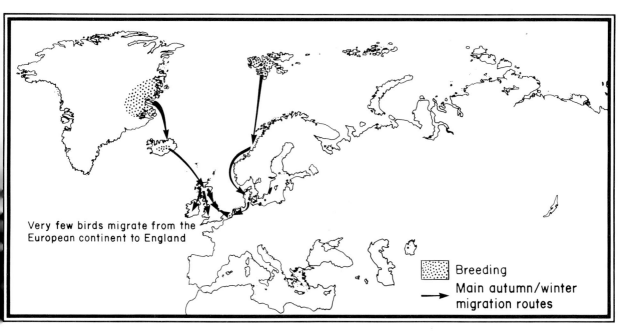

Very few birds migrate from the European continent to England

Breeding
Main autumn/winter migration routes

Pinkfooted goose — main autumn/winter migration routes of British-involved populations

to drink and bathe. Where they are feeding far from the roost they may establish a subsidiary roost in a fairly safe spot near the feeding ground and take a midday rest there.

The flight is fast and direct, and, like the greylag's, is more rapid than it appears. The 'whiffling' spiral descent from height is a marvellous sight. Their general flighting habits are similar to those of the greylag and they are generally affected by the same elements, especially light. They will not visit feeding grounds until the light is sufficient to see predators by and they will leave when the light level drops again. However, the safer the area the more likely they are to feed at night and moonlight feeding is more common when the day length is short. In some areas artificial street or industrial lighting will induce night feeding but then some wildfowling clubs ban night shooting because of the unsporting advantage.

POPULATION: The 1981/82 UK Wildfowl Counts showed a peak of 90,000 in November, a slight drop on the 1980/81 record level of 95,000 following below average breeding success (15.7 per cent young; average brood 1.9). The 1950 population of 30,000 rose to 89,000 in 1974 but a succession of poor breeding seasons brought a decline to 69,000 in 1977 before the upturn. Average annual mortality is 12 per cent.

OPEN SEASON: England, Scotland, Wales: 1 September to 31 January, extended to 20 February in or over any area below high water mark of ordinary spring tides. At the time of writing it may be shot in Northern Ireland between 1 September and 31 January but imminent legislation is expected to give protection. Irish Republic: full protection.

Pinkfooted geese on a Solway evening. The dark head and neck is a good pointer to identification *(Jack Orchel)*

IN THE POT: As excellent as the greylag, the pinkfoot needs no special treatment.

THE FUTURE: Nationally goose damage is often exaggerated and only rarely is it so serious as to bring local disaster and ruin a farmer. Unfortunately geese are reluctant to abandon traditionally good feeding grounds and the threat of excessive disturbance and over-exploitation is ever present.

The pinkfoot population is currently thriving and able to withstand shooting pressure at its present level but we must always be alert to a succession of poor breeding seasons and act responsibly for Britain is host to much of the world population of this species. At the same time there is the danger that because the pinkfoot and other grey geese have become so dependent on an artificial food supply they could not adapt quickly enough to avert catastrophic decline when the next sweeping change transforms the face of farming.

WHITEFRONTED GOOSE
(*Anser albifrons*)

This grey goose was named by Thomas Pennant in 1766 and has long been a favourite of wildfowlers. However, in recent years there has been concern over the numbers of one of the two subspecies which visit the British Isles and in September 1982 the Irish Republic banned its shooting for a trial period of three years while the situation is studied.

HISTORY: As with other geese the whitefront used to be harvested by man in the Soviet arctic but recent decline is probably related more to habitat destruction in the winter range than to pressures in the more remote breeding range. Ireland is particularly important as a wintering area for the Greenland whitefront and has unfortunately suffered extensive habitat loss in recent years as a result of drainage, afforestation and peat production. The European race is similarly threatened but the winter range is much wider so the problem is less acute.

RANGE AND DISTRIBUTION: The whitefront does not breed in Britain. The European race breeds in arctic Russia and Siberia and winters in a number of separate populations mostly in western and southern Europe and on the Mediterranean coast. It visits England and South Wales, with major concentrations at Slimbridge (Gloucestershire), Avon Floods, north Kent, Swale (mid Kent) and the Towy Valley.

The Greenland race has a very restricted range, breeding only in western Greenland and wintering almost entirely in Ireland, western Scotland and western Wales, with a few visiting England. UK concentrations include Islay and the other Western Isles, Kintyre at Campbeltown and opposite Gigha, Loch Ken, Anglesey and Tregaron. In Ireland the Wexford Slobs in the south-east are most important. Elsewhere in the country it is well scattered with each gathering under 300.

The above two races are distinct and overlap little in range. A third race breeds in arctic North America where it is the only real 'grey' goose.

HABITAT: The whitefront breeds on low, shrubby tundra near water (mostly fresh) and on offshore islands. In winter it haunts many diverse areas including fresh and saltmarshes, flooded grassland and, to a lesser extent than the other grey geese, arable farmland.

IDENTIFICATION: This is the easiest of the grey geese to recognise with the white feathers around the base of the upper mandible and the black-barred underparts (very variable) showing up well in flight and at rest, even from moderate distances. The grey-brown plumage is marked by a white line beneath the folded wing. Also look for the white undertail-coverts.

The Russian or European race (*A.a.albifrons*) is paler and slightly smaller than

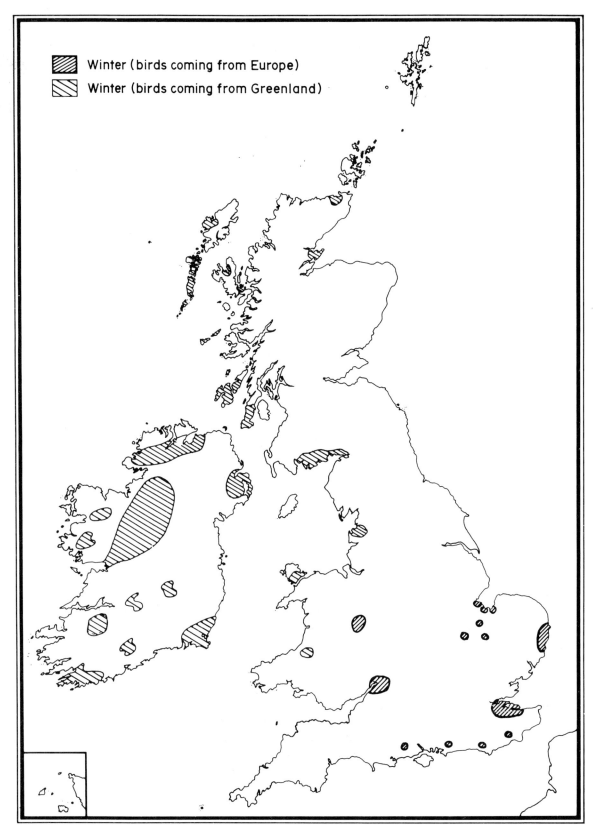

Whitefronted goose — summer/winter distribution in the British Isles

the Greenland race (*A.a.flavirostris*). The European's pink bill is shorter than the yellow-orange bill of the Greenland and there is usually more white at the base of the European's bill.

The sexes are alike. The juvenile lacks the barring underneath (some get a few flecks in spring) and the white at the base of the bill. It has an indistinct white line along the edge of the folded wing in early winter, the white on the forehead appears later in the winter and the black belly markings in the following summer.

In the field the adult appears darker than the greylag and pinkfoot, which are both larger and noticeably greyer, and the pink's dark head and neck help to separate. The whitefront has a much smaller head than either the greylag or bean goose, the latter lacking the white barring on the wing-coverts. The whitefront is also more slender than the bean. Another species sometimes found in association is the lesser whitefront, a rare vagrant which is smaller and has more white at the base of the bill.

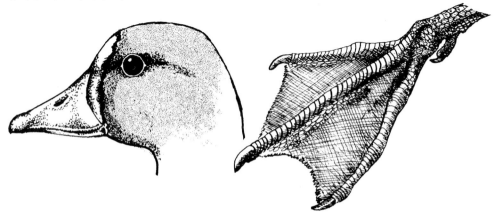

Moulting time is late June to mid-August, the non-breeders starting two to three weeks earlier. The adult's length is 66-76cm (26-30in). Average weight for the male is 2,552g (5lb 10oz) within a range 1,790-3,340g (3lb 15oz-7lb 6oz), and for the female 2,293g (5lb 1oz) within a range 1,720-3,120g (3lb 13oz-6lb 14oz).

VOICE: The gabbling *kow-yow* or *kow-lyow* is high-pitched, louder and more musical than the pinkfoot's call and has earned the species the name 'laughing goose'. The flock's chorus can sound like bells. Another call is *gar-wa-wa*.

BREEDING: The single brood is often raised further inland than that of other geese, nesting being semi-colonial, frequently in tall grass on a small hill or rise and usually near water. The ground hollow of heather, grass or lichen is lined with down. The 5-6 (sometimes 4-7) creamy-white, frequently stained eggs are laid from late May but mostly in June (peak mid-June). They are incubated by only the female for 25-27 days (sometimes 23-28) while the male mounts guard nearby. Peak hatching is in late June and early July. The goslings leave the nest soon after hatching and are tended by both parents. *Albifrons* fledges at about 46 days and *flavirostris* at about 53 days. They migrate as a family to the winter quarters.

FEEDING: The species is much less dependent on farming than the other grey geese. The diet is chiefly vegetable and in the breeding season sedges, grasses and horsetail are important, with berries taken at the end of summer.

In the British Isles the chief winter food is grass, with a preference for the heavily fertilised new seed mixtures rather than the less nutritious old pastures. However, the whitefront is also fond of grazing on saltmarsh plants. Flooded fields are favourite feeding grounds.

Grain is taken, and in the major haunt at Wexford in Ireland the birds move from the stubbles to potatoes but grass always remains important, with clover as a side dish. In spring the basic grass diet is supplemented with sprouting winter wheat and a little newly sown grain. As for all geese, grit and water are essential. Although fresh water is preferred they can survive on brackish or even salt water for considerable periods.

True to its tribe, this goose is a day feeder unless heavily persecuted, and will even roost on the feeding ground if undisturbed. It flies in to feed at daybreak or soon after and leaves at dusk unless disturbed but does not feed all day long. It also feeds under the moon, after which it is likely to flight to the shore for sand.

MOVEMENTS: Winter visitors only, whitefronts arrive between early October and January according to the severity of the weather where they come from and in areas they pass over. The Europeans (also known as 'Siberians') leave in March and April but the Greenlands do not leave much before late April and often stay into May, probably because their journey is shorter. Much larger numbers of Europeans winter in Holland and northern Germany than in southern England and South Wales.

Whitefronted goose — main autumn/winter migration routes of British-involved populations

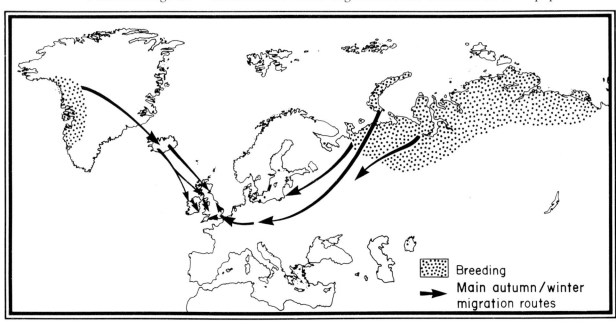

Whitefronted geese on the Solway. Apart from the white base to the bill the heavily barred underparts are a good aid to identification (*Pamela Harrison*)

BEHAVIOUR: The whitefront is less gregarious than the other grey geese and often occurs in small parties or pairs. When the birds first arrive they are naturally rather unsettled and it is not until winter sets in that their flighting is at all predictable. However, they do mix with pinkfeet and greylags.

On estuaries they move with the tide and flight to inland marshes and fields at high water. Roosts are usually inaccessible places offering considerable protection against predators, and a good field of view is particularly important. At freshwater roosts they usually sleep on the margins rather than the water.

Whitefronts are well known as masters of air manoeuvre. They prefer to rise into the wind but if pressed can take off almost vertically with a sudden spring. They are probably more adept on the wing than the other grey geese with which they share the same direct, powerful flight and deceptive speed. However, the flight is less heavy than the greylag's and more often in V formation. Like the greylag, whitefronts will swoop from a height towards the feeding grounds in a whiffling, spiral dive with the wings half-folded. They are very alert to danger and sportsmen say the birds can 'reverse engines' rapidly to take them out of gun range after coming almost to a dead stop.

POPULATION: The two races which visit Britain are enjoying very opposite fortunes. The world population of the whitefront is put at 700,000 to one million and that of the European race is probably increasing following a succession of good breeding seasons. The high February figure of 6,910 Europeans in the 1981/82 UK Wildfowl Counts suggested that more than usual had been forced across the North Sea in mid-winter, though to a lesser extent than in 1979. The main resorts were: Slimbridge, Gloucestershire 4,508 (February); Swale, Kent 1,500 (December); Hampshire, Avon river 1,500 (January); north Kent marshes 635 (February); Dryslwyn, Dyfed 720 (January). Of these a third were

177

juveniles and the average brood size 2.5. The average maximum for 1976/77 to 1980/81 was 4,300.

The Greenland whitefront, however, has been having a bad time following below-average breeding success. In 1981 (14.3 per cent young in winter flocks) the two main UK centres (Islay and the Mull of Kintyre) showed substantial declines to 3,300 and 650 respectively in November compared with 4,300 and 1,160 in 1980. Elsewhere, however, UK numbers were normal with maxima of 330 at Loch Ken, Dumfries and Galloway, 480 at Stranraer and 250 in Caithness. In addition to the 6,000 or 7,000 in Scotland about 8,000 winter in Ireland (about 6,000 in the Wexford Slobs area) but there appears to have been decline there too in recent decades.

OPEN SEASON: There is no distinction in British law between the two races. England and Wales: 1 September to 31 January, extended to 20 February in or over any area below high water mark of ordinary spring tides. Scotland (where usually only the declining Greenland race is found): full protection. Northern Ireland: 1 September to 31 January but the Wildlife (Northern Ireland) Order is expected to rescind this in 1983. Irish Republic: full protection introduced for a trial period of three years from 1 September 1982.

IN THE POT: Equally as good as the other quarry geese, birds shot inland are marginally better than those from saltmarsh.

THE FUTURE: This is still the most common grey goose in winter in the western British Isles and probably still the most widely shot goose in the USSR and north-west Europe. With the population trend of the European race upwards shooting should continue in England and Wales, though some wildfowlers and wildfowling clubs have their own local bans, especially in those few areas where there is occasional overlap with the Greenland race.

The position regarding the Greenland race has been vague and the Irish government has sensibly erred on the side of safety with their three-year moratorium, which is not popular in many quarters. The population has not been properly censused and this gives an opportunity for much-needed study.

The population of *flavirostris* is less than those of all but two of the world's distinct subspecies and as virtually all Greenland whitefronts winter in the British Isles we must demonstrate our international responsibility in ensuring their survival. There have been poor breeding seasons but the position is made much worse by Ireland's continuing land 'improvement' schemes and eradication of marshland. In addition, the whitefront's reproduction rate is said to be very low, but it is not known if this is normal for this long-lived bird. The bird's breeding success is, unfortunately, largely out of our control — we can only hope for favourable weather, but we can try to solve the winter habitat problem.

In November 1982 the first-ever complete census of the Greenland whitefront was carried out through the Greenland Whitefronted Goose Study Group and in 1983 a spring survey was carried out.

COOT
(*Fulica atra*)

In the shooting world there certainly are fashions which dictate the extent to which species are pursued, but in some cases, such as that of the coot, they are not hard to explain. With its black plumage the coot does not generally appeal as a pot bird, especially in today's pernickety society, and this probably has a lot to do with its fall from favour. As a sporting bird it is certainly underrated. The population is healthy but there is very little reason to shoot it as a pest. Diminishing interest is probably more to do with the sportsman's desire to promote a good conservationist image, for generally the layman sees this bird only in semi-tame settings, such as town lakes, and it is hard to explain its sporting value in wilder settings.

HISTORY: On the one hand the coot has probably suffered extensively following land drainage over the last few centuries, but on the other it has taken great advantage of the many new waters such as flooded gravel pits and reservoirs. It was certainly very common indeed throughout Britain during the nineteenth century when battues were organised at regular intervals during the autumn and winter. Often a whole village or community joined one of these exciting occasions, frequently on a public holiday such as Boxing Day.

Some of these coot shoots were annual events, for example the famous one on Hickling Broad, and the eastern counties offered some of the best venues for this activity. Boats full of guns would drive the birds across the water to another line

of guns. When the birds took off they would wheel about and provide surprisingly testing shooting. At Slapton Ley in Devon in January 1891 1,700 coots fell to twenty guns who claimed the English record. I shudder to think of the damage such an exercise would do to sporting PR today.

RANGE AND DISTRIBUTION: A very widespread bird, the coot breeds throughout temperate Europe, Asia and North Africa, to Japan, China, India and Australia (separate race).

In the British Isles it breeds in every mainland county but it is very scarce in north and west Scotland, and absent from many of the islands in the Hebrides and Shetlands. Elsewhere it is generally absent only above 230m (750ft). However, altitude alone does not appear to be the controlling factor for it is common at Malham Tarn in West Yorkshire at 380m (1,240ft) and has been found nesting in Scotland at above 500m (1,640ft). The reason is thought to be ecological for most Highland waters are deep and lack submerged and aquatic vegetation.

HABITAT: For breeding the choice of habitat is rather narrow, coots being dependent on aquatic vegetation for security. They prefer large, open waters such as lakes, flooded gravel pits and reservoirs but also use large ponds, land-locked arms of the sea, reed-fringed drainage dykes of coastal marshland, navigational canals, and, less occasionally, are found on slow, quiet stretches of rivers and streams. Generally they require a water area of not less than an acre. In winter they often resort to estuaries, especially in severe weather.

IDENTIFICATION: This is our only all-black freshwater bird and with its contrasting white bill and frontal shield showing well at considerable distances there is little chance of confusing it with anything else. The sexes are alike and the juvenile is dark grey-brown with a whitish throat and front of neck.

The length is 38cm (15in) and the weight about 794g (28oz). The thighs are placed well behind and the distinctive, huge feet are semipalmated.

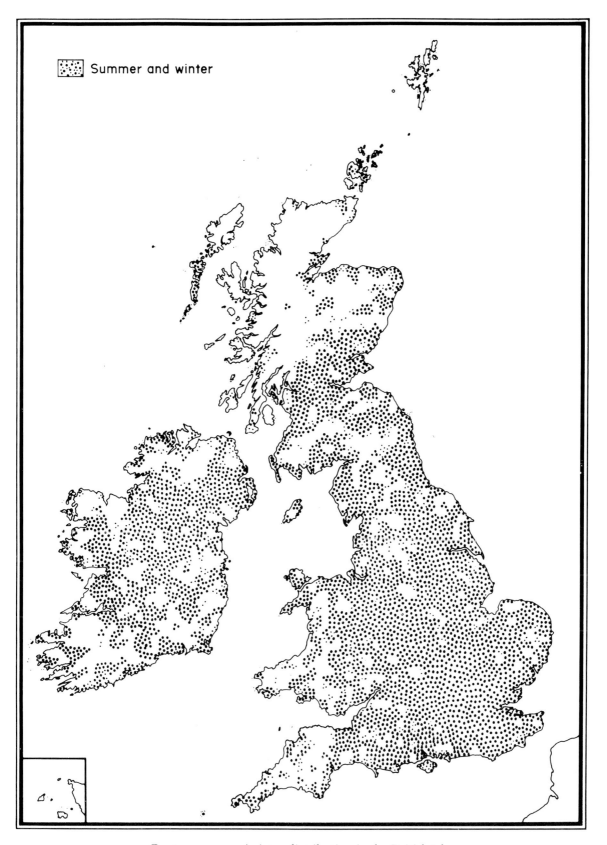

Coot — summer/winter distribution in the British Isles

VOICE: The coot gives a loud, high-pitched cry, an explosive *teuk,* and a clear, far-sounding *kö.*

BREEDING: In courtship the neck is stretched out until almost touching the water and mutual preening strengthens the pair bond. In a sophisticated invitation display one of the birds ruffles its head feathers, and, with neck arched, points its bill towards its feet and almost freezes. Sometimes both birds act thus side by side and occasionally the entire head may disappear under water for several seconds.

Because the substantial nest is often so obvious, a water barrier is essential against predators but the mound of debris, twigs and aquatic vegetation is built up from the bottom rather than floating like that of the great-crested grebe. It is often among dead reeds and sometimes on a fallen tree or just an odd branch in the water, usually among emergent vegetation. Nesting is sometimes loosely colonial and sometimes in towns artificial winter feeding often induces attempted nesting at unusual sites such as among flower beds and on grassy banks. Both sexes build.

The 6-9 (occasionally 4-15) elongated oval eggs are stone-coloured or buff spotted black-brown and laid from mid-March to May. The 21-24 day incubation is shared by both parents and starts with the first or second egg. The chicks leave the nest 3-4 days after hatching, are tended by both parents and become independent after about eight weeks. There are usually two broods and sometimes three. Before they are independent the young return to the nest or to a specially constructed brooding platform.

FEEDING: The diet is predominantly vegetarian and food is taken from the bottom or by up-ending. Most dives are to a depth of 2m (6ft 6in) and the bird surfaces before eating. Feeding is easiest in relatively shallow, eutrophic waters. As well as aquatic weeds, shoots of reeds, roots of water plants, corn, seeds, newts, tadpoles, small fish, dragonfly nymphs and occasional eggs and chicks of other birds are taken. In winter coots graze on grassland near water and in severe weather may take hips and haws.

MOVEMENTS: The coot is a resident and a winter visitor. Northern birds move south within the British Isles and many others move to lower altitudes. Some European birds winter as far south as northern tropical Africa. Our large influx comes from as far east as Russia, with peak arrival in October. They mainly winter in east and south England and return in March and April. Continued frost will drive them to harbours and tidal rivers.

BEHAVIOUR: The coot threatens with lowered head and raised wings. It is very aggressive with a highly developed territorial sense which leads to long chases in the breeding season. However, in the winter it is gregarious and may form very large flocks, especially on reservoirs where the breeding population is small because of the concrete embankments and lack of cover.

It walks fairly well, though inelegantly, and swims very buoyantly with the

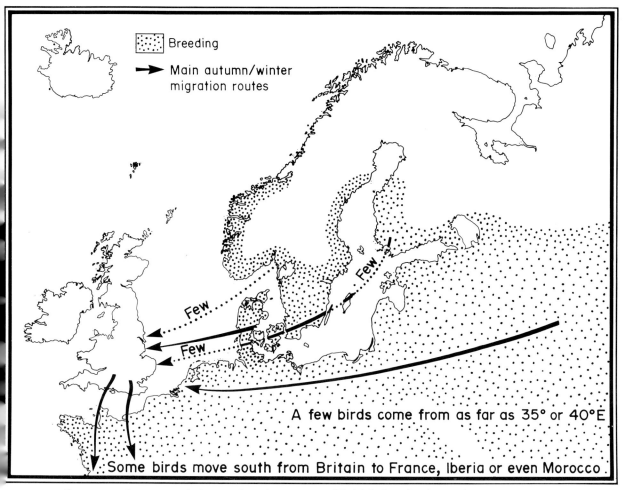

Coot — main autumn/winter migration routes of British-involved populations

same head-bobbing movement as that of the moorhen. The great feet make the dive look rather clumsy but it resurfaces like a cork. The coot can submerge completely until only its bill shows above the surface like a snorkel.

On taking off the legs hang down as if broken. It is said that the coot kicks up water spray in the face of enemies and that if a bird of prey swoops on a flock they will paddle to security so furiously as to raise a cloud of spray. It takes off only after lengthy pattering across the surface. The low flight over the water looks heavy and laboured but when the coot is shot at it will fly high and well with the feet stretched out behind, offering good sport in travelling at considerable speed.

Coots sometimes roost in trees and are always very wary and suspicious; occasionally at night they fly about their haunts in circles calling loudly at regular intervals.

POPULATION: There are about 100,000 breeding pairs in Britain.

OPEN SEASON: England, Scotland, Wales: 1 September to 31 January. Northern Ireland and the Irish Republic: full protection.

183

Coot with young. In earlier times the species was the focus of great annual community shoots *(Roy Shaw)*

IN THE POT: In the eighteenth century many people liked the strong, marshy taste of this bird. Even at the end of the nineteenth century the flesh was still considered by no means unpalatable, if obtained from fresh water, and the bird was commonly bought in the market-place. Today it has fallen from favour. The best birds are those which have been eating grass or grain and the worst are from muddy estuaries.

THE FUTURE: The bird is very adaptable and should continue to thrive as long as suitable new waters appear faster than the natural marshes disappear. It would help if more reservoirs had less emphasis on leisure activities such as water-skiing and yachting and more 'reserved' corners with natural margins rather than sterile, concrete embankments.

Some people still value the coot's sport and enjoy eating its flesh. It is very important to retain it on the quarry list to add variety to the bag, provide shooting for the maximum number of people and spread the load among as many species as possible.

MOORHEN
(*Gallinula chloropus*)

This very common but extremely wary bird is certainly not to be despised as a sporting mark and it is often the first species of water bird to be shot by the young gun. It has a fascinating natural history which has helped nurture many a sporting naturalist.

HISTORY: The species is particularly susceptible to severe winters and therefore its population has probably fluctuated considerably with the climate over the last few centuries. In the eighteenth and nineteenth centuries it appears to have been as widespread as it is today but very scarce in some areas and abundant in others. However, recovery is rapid from major decline and there is no evidence of long-term change in status. Adaptability appears to have more than compensated for loss of large areas of the various water habitats the species uses.

As to be expected with a species sensitive to temperature fluctuation, there was a marked increase in Scotland over the first half of this century with climatic amelioration, but cooling off since 1950 may have brought slight decline.

RANGE AND DISTRIBUTION: This 'common gallinule' or 'waterhen' is virtually cosmopolitan and absent only from Australia in its vast range across boreal, temperate and subtropical zones. It is not found in the deserts of Arabia and Africa.

In the British Isles this is the commonest riparian lowland bird, found virtually everywhere except in some of the hillier districts of the north and west. The main areas lacking are the Scottish Highlands, peaks of central Wales, higher Exmoor and Dartmoor, Mayo, Galway and the highlands of Kerry.

HABITAT: The name moorhen has nothing to do with moors but is a corruption of 'merehen' — bird of the lakes. It is far less fussy than the coot in its choice of water. Almost any fresh water will do, from the largest lakes and reservoirs to marshes which do not even contain free water all the time. Farmyard ponds, rivers, reed beds, flooded meadows, canals, town lakes, flooded gravel pits and garden ponds all suffice. It often travels considerable distances away from water and it is not unusual to see one killed on the road.

IDENTIFICATION: The dark-plumaged moorhen could hardly be confused with any bird except the coot and then only rarely for it has a bright red forehead and red and yellow bill. There is a conspicuous white flash as it frequently flirts its tail. The sexes are alike and the juveniles dusky brown but with the same white undertail-coverts and flank line as the adults. Moorhen chicks are distinguished from coot chicks by the lack of red on the sides of the head.

The length is 33cm (13in) and the average weight 397-454g (14-16oz).

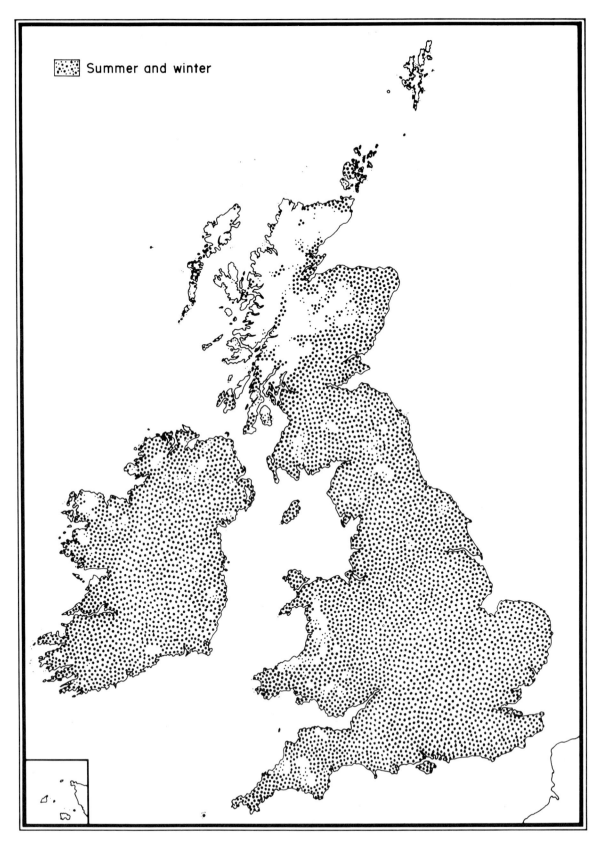

Moorhen — summer/winter distribution in the British Isles

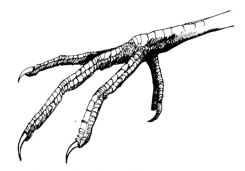

VOICE: The most common call note is a loud but rather liquid *kurruk* which often startles the passer-by. Other calls are *kittic,* a harsh *kaak* or *kr-r-rok,* the piercing *kik-ik-ik* and a *ker-r-r-r-k.* The bird is most frequently heard at dusk and commonly calls at night.

BREEDING: Most nests are in thick vegetation such as reed beds near water but the species is full of surprises and the bulky platform of dead or even green vegetation may be on a fallen tree or branch, among hanging bushes, in a field tussock, on marsh or bog, on a bare island in the middle of a town lake and even up to about 8m (26ft) high in thick shrubs or an old magpie or woodpigeon nest. Floating nests on deep water sometimes have a ramp so that the parents can enter without damaging the sides. As with the coot the nests are often conspicuous and rely on inaccessibility to avoid predators. However, the breeding season is very long and many nests fade from view as the vegetation blooms.

Territory is defended vigorously and the males can fight so fiercely in the water that they end up with broken toes or dislocated thighs. They are also aggressive to other birds and there is a record of one trying to drown a homing pigeon by holding it under water. In a special courtship posture the male leans forwards, points the wing-tips upwards and the head downwards and spreads the tail to display the white beneath.

Most nests are below 600m (1,950ft) and fast-flowing rivers or streams are avoided. As well as the actual egg nest, display platforms and brood nests are constructed. Display platforms are built from late February, mostly from twigs and dead vegetation, are also used for coition and there may be as many as five within a single territory. There may also be several brood nests, depending on the number of young. Some have ramps and are built soon after the chicks hatch. Construction is similar to that of the egg nest — a platform of dead or green aquatic vegetation with a shallow depression formed from finer stems, grasses and leaves. The species is surprisingly alert to the dangers of flooding and may build up a nest if the water rises during incubation.

The 5-11 buff, speckled red-brown eggs are laid from mid-March with a peak in the last week of April and the first three weeks of May. Two broods are common, and there are often three with laying into early August. Being so exposed early in the season, the clutches are subject to a high rate of predation which leads

187

Moorhen and young. Sometimes the chicks are fed by the young from an earlier brood
(*Eric Hosking*)

to many repeat layings. Quite often two or more females lay in a single nest
('dump nesting') to produce a clutch of up to 20. The eggs are often covered
when the nest is unattended.

Both parents share the 19-22 day incubation as well as the feeding of the
young. The downy chicks leave the nest within 2-3 days, can swim and dive immediately and may even be fed by the young of an earlier brood.

FEEDING: The moorhen eats mainly vegetable matter but has a variable diet and
can even be a pest. Natural foods taken include wild fruits and seeds, aquatic
plants, snails, worms, slugs, insects and their larvae, leaves, and eggs and chicks
of other birds. Hips and haws are taken from bushes mostly in hard weather. Not
only will the moorhen take dead rodents and their bones but also will occasionally kill and eat ducklings and pheasant chicks.

This bird will also damage crops, and is especially troublesome in areas where
high densities (up to sixty adults per 100 acres of farmland recorded) graze close
to water. Damage to standing crops is more severe than that done by ducks because moorhens tend to uproot plants. They also eat grain and other food put
down for ducks and pheasants and damage watercress beds.

MOVEMENTS: The species is mostly resident throughout the range but some
northern birds move south and west in winter. British birds too are mostly resident. They are joined by winter visitors from Denmark, Germany, Holland and
Sweden, chiefly to our east coast. Even in very severe weather they rarely visit
salt water but prefer to roam the countryside in search of food.

188

BEHAVIOUR: Although small, loose flocks are seen in winter concentrating around good food sources, the moorhen is not generally gregarious and is mostly rather aggressive towards its own kind. In fact it even defends territories in winter, though these are usually much smaller than breeding areas. In most places moorhens are secretive and skulking but in some environments such as town parks, where they are not persecuted, they may feed quite openly. Mostly they run for cover, with the tail flared up at man's approach.

If it is in danger and there is no cover close by the moorhen will patter for long distances across water and if necessary will take flight with the legs hanging down. However, like that of many swimming birds, the flight is rather weak and slow.

This delightful bird swims with a jerky motion and constant flicking of the tail. It has the amazing ability to submerge when alarmed, and to stay down with only the bill protruding like a periscope, probably by treading water and forcing air out of the plumage and air sacs.

Like the coot, it sometimes takes to the air at night and flies about for an hour or more calling shrilly at regular intervals. I have often found moorhens roosting in tall bushes, especially in ivy and evergreens during bitter weather.

Moorhen — main autumn/winter migration routes of British-involved populations

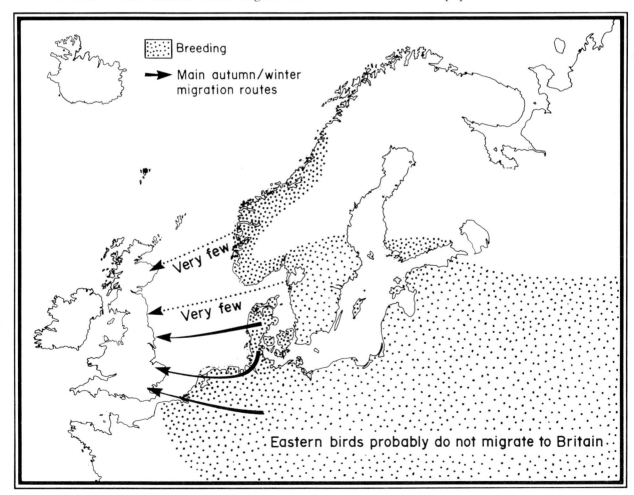

Breeding

Main autumn/winter migration routes

Very few

Very few

Eastern birds probably do not migrate to Britain

POPULATION: There are probably at least 300,000 breeding pairs and possibly far more. One authority has suggested one million pairs.

OPEN SEASON: England, Scotland, Wales: 1 September to 31 January. Northern Ireland and Irish Republic: full protection.

IN THE POT: The flesh can be very good, especially in September or October after the birds have fed on stubbles. However, there are a number of problems associated with eating the moorhen and coot, as explained by Booth in 1876:

> Cooks who are aware of the trouble of plucking them are sure to declare they require to be flayed and then steeped in water, or possibly even perpetrate some such enormity as burying them in a cloth for several hours. Let them, however, simply be treated as wild duck or teal. I always, when shooting, order the men to pluck those that are intended for home use as soon as they are collected. While warm the feathers and down may be stripped from them with but little exertion, though, should they once get cold and set, it will require nearly an hour's scrubbing with resin to remove the tenacious black down from the breast and back.

They can be skinned but this spoils presentation and dries the meat when roasting.

THE FUTURE: Unless the mean temperature drops considerably and remains low this adaptable bird should continue to thrive and is never likely to be threatened by over-shooting in this country of conservative palates.

WOODPIGEON
(Columba palumbus)

This is neither the most widespread nor the commonest species of bird in the British Isles yet it is the worst avian pest and said to cause millions of pounds worth of damage annually. Yet no one would like to see the species exterminated for it is truly sporting, provides many sportsmen of modest means with their only bird shooting and adds a very welcome variety to the notoriously plain British diet. While this is one wild bird that does regularly appear in our supermarkets, many thousands are exported annually, especially to France where they are more appreciated. Indeed, for centuries Pyrenean passes have been netted to catch these 'ring doves', 'cushats' or 'queests' as they slip low over the cols.

The word pigeon is of Norman origin and derived from the Latin *pipio* — a young, cheeping bird. However, it was not until this century that the name woodpigeon was widely adopted and even today many countrymen still call it the ring dove after the ring of white neck feathers.

190

HISTORY: Although now chiefly associated with farmland, the woodpigeon was originally a bird of deciduous forest. It still needs woodland for breeding and roosting but because it is a strong flyer it has been able to take advantage of the opening up of our countryside. However, mere removal of woodland in favour of farmland was not sufficient to bring about the species' population explosion. It needed the Agricultural Revolution to achieve this.

First records of the woodpigeon as a pest are from the eighteenth century, and by 1850, when growing turnips for winter fodder and undersowing corn with clover had become normal, the species was steadily increasing in range and numbers. Infiltration of towns did not begin until about 1830 in much of Europe. Today we are all familiar with the uncharacteristically tame birds which mingle with park feral pigeons.

More important than increasing acreage of farmland was increasing reliability of artificial food supplies, especially in winter. Staple foods such as acorns and beech-mast might come in a bumper crop one year and fail completely in the next. Stand-by foods such as ivy berries and weed seeds and leaves would not be abundant or nutritious enough to support a large population. However, because it was already able to digest natural green-stuffs, the woodpigeon could exploit the new agricultural crops such as kale, turnips, clover and other brassicae which stand green through winter. This meant that increasingly there was always something somewhere in the larder and, with the species' great mobility, more and more birds could survive the winter.

Other important factors have been an extension northwards of the cereal-growing area during the climatic amelioration of the first half of this century, the availability of spilt grain on stubbles for several weeks after harvest (specially valuable for late breeders), and the ability to exploit the new vast acreage of monocultures such as oil-seed rape in the 1970s and 1980s particularly. Now the species is more common on farmland than in its ancestral woodland habitat.

Not so long ago the Ministry of Agriculture provided a cartridge subsidy for pigeon shooting and farmers were not only happy for strangers to shoot their pigeons but would also supply the cartridges. The subsidy was withdrawn when it was realised that removal of some birds merely increases chances of survival of the remainder. Now, although crop protection is still invaluable on a concerted local scale, there is an increasing tendency for farmers to sell woodpigeon shooting by the day as more people discover the bird's sporting and culinary value.

RANGE AND DISTRIBUTION: The species is widespread throughout most of Europe, eastwards through Russia to beyond the Urals, south-east to the Middle East, south to North Africa and north to central Scandinavia.

In Britain it is also widespread, occurring everywhere except in the remotest agricultural areas. It is scarce on the higher hills of Scotland, in the Outer Hebrides and Shetland. In Ireland it is more sparsely distributed because suitable habitat is more patchy. Northern Ireland particularly, with its wetter climate, has concentrated on dairy farming rather than cereals and does not have the great numbers of woodpigeons which exist in England.

Woodpigeon — summer/winter distribution in the British Isles

HABITAT: Although in those few areas where extensive deciduous woods remain some woodpigeons spend much of their lives among the trees, most now spend their lives on farmland, resorting to trees only for nesting and roosting.

IDENTIFICATION: At long distances it appears predominantly grey but may still be identified by its distinctive flight. At moderate range the best field mark is the white wing-bar but at closer range also watch for the white patch on each side of the neck and black tip to the long tail. The sexes are alike but the female is fractionally smaller and duller and the tail tinged brown.

The squabs are covered with down at first. When fledged the juvenile resembles the adult but is duller, tinged brown and lacks the iridescent hues. The white neck ring starts to appear at about two months and is usually complete within a fortnight. The irides change colour with age: in the young they are nearly black and in the adult brilliant yellow. The young bird's breast is particularly plump and the thighs relatively thin. Its legs are pinky-orange without scales and the

 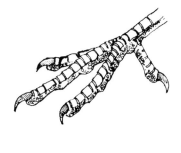

claws pinkish whereas the adult has purple-red legs and toes and dark brown claws. The juvenile also has paler skin and the beak looks disproportionately large. Although the plumage is complete after the first moult it will continue to develop intensity of colour.

The average length is 41cm (16in). The average weight of the male is 559g (1lb 3½oz) within a range 490-625g (1lb 1½oz-1lb 6oz), and of the female 540g (1lb 3oz) within a range 480-600g (1lb 1oz-1lb 5oz).

Most shooters are familiar with the woodpigeon's remarkable eyesight which has evolved to avoid capture by peregrines and other raptors, and picks up the glint of a gun or spectacles and slightest movement of the hand at long range. All-round vision is important so it has a total visual field of 340° out of a possible 360°. However, its binocular vision is only 24° — hence birds seen moving their heads from side to side to establish distance.

It is most important that the shooter does not kill the stock dove, rock dove, racing and domestic pigeons which are all now protected and may be shot only under licence. They are all smaller than the woodpigeon and lack the white wing and neck patches. Racing pigeons will not be afraid of the gun and keep on coming. Their flight is mostly high, but lower in strong wind and slower in long races, particularly in July and August. The racing season is from late March to the end of October but most birds are in large, tight, fast packs and even single birds will then be flying very straight, whereas during much of that period the woodpigeon will be preoccupied with breeding and will not generally flock.

Doves may be distinguished from juvenile woodpigeons most easily by their direct flight and pulsating wing-beats.

VOICE: The soft, far-carrying *coooo-coo, coo-coo, coo* is one of the most familiar and symbolic sounds of summer woodland. After general winter silence the woodpigeon regains its note in early spring and calls freely and continuously until September and less frequently in October. There are considerable variations to the cooing, some being more reminiscent of sighing and heard only at close range. The bird is most vocal just after sunrise, just before going to roost and, to a lesser extent, during the common early afternoon rest. Sometimes, with great stealth, it is possible to stalk a cooing bird but it is vital to move towards it only when it is calling and not when it pauses to listen, for its acute hearing will detect the faintest crack of a twig or rustle of leaves with ease.

BREEDING: The woodpigeon's courtship, with its mutual bill caressing and feeding, bowing, and diving flight with wing-clapping, is one of spring's delights.

Most nests are in trees — spinneys, tall hedges and even isolated trees as well as woods and large forests, both deciduous and coniferous. However, in areas where few trees exist these birds have learned to use tall heather and will even exceptionally nest on the ground. In urban areas they use trees and shrubs in parks and gardens and even those along pavements as well as building ledges. They probably pair for life and nest in the same area each year where not disturbed.

The conspicuous nest is a mere platform of twigs built by the female from materials supplied by the male and is more likely to be low on islands or in other undisturbed areas such as the centres of forests. Conifer plantations surrounded by farmland often have a particularly high density and their steady increase has helped the woodpigeon's range extension in northern Britain particularly.

The 2 (sometimes 1 or 3) oval, white eggs are mostly laid on successive days and have been found in every month of the year. Peak laying is rather late so that the young can take advantage of the grain harvest. On farmland breeding is chiefly from July to September but it is earlier in towns where there is a steady bread supply. The 17 day incubation by both sexes is from the first egg and the young are fed by the highly nutritious, cheesy 'pigeon's milk' regurgitated from the crops of both parents. Excreta is never removed from the nest but has a positive value in caking together to form a firm platform with the twigs to support the heavy squabs securely. They are fed for 29-35 days before fledging and there are usually two, and often three, broods.

FEEDING: While there are staple foods in the woodpigeon's predominantly vegetable diet during each season, the species is extremely adaptable and with such a choice on offer will frequently change location so that local reconnaissance on

The woodpigeon's ability to feed its young on 'pigeon's milk' — a regurgitated cheesy substance — means less dependence on specific foods and thus facilitates a very long breeding season *(David Gowans)*

every shooting day is essential. The woodpigeon eats the equivalent of its own weight every four days. When food is plentiful it usually feeds three times a day — soon after dawn, near midday and late afternoon, except in high summer when there may be a fourth main feed late in the evening. In mid-winter it is less predictable and may also continue feeding for a little while after dark in order to gain sufficient energy to survive the long, bitter nights.

To buy pigeon shooting far away in a strange area will almost always lead to disappointment, for a knowledge of local cropping is essential. Conditions vary from north to south but as a rough guide from January to March main items of interest are clover, lucerne, sainfoin, weed seeds, leaves of winter corn, ivy berries, holly berries and frosted potatoes. During very cold weather pigeons will

195

increasingly attack green crops such as rape, kale, cabbage and sprouts. However, such leaves do not contain sufficient nutriment in relation to water content to maintain condition during the shortest winter days and birds forced to feed thus will inevitably lose weight. Although they might take only the top of a plant they will destroy its market value.

From April to June attention switches to newly sown grain (unearthed and sprouting as well as on the surface), beans, maize, peas, charlock, wild mustard, sprouting kale, clover, rape, mustard and turnips. Generally they feed only on pastures where clovers are present.

From July to September they favour ripe and ripening grain where 'laid' by bad weather, clover, young kale, grass seeds, mustard, ripe peas, soft fruits, and woodland and hedgerow leaves. In summer they generally start feeding later after dawn with the extra daylight.

During autumn and early winter attention first focuses on the spilt grain of the stubbles but clover becomes more important as these are ploughed in. Worms, slugs and ripe maize add variety. In December they often resort to fields where sugar beet has been harvested but many fragments remain.

Living mainly on vegetable matter the pigeon needs a rather elaborate digestive tract and the elastic walls of the lower gullet expand into a 'crop' where food can be stored for later digestion. This accounts for the quiet periods on a shooting day. The amount of food the crop holds is often quite amazing. Not only can it take several ounces of grain (in my youth I had the patience to count 744 barley grains!) or clover leaves, but also I have counted in single crops 50 small acorns, 14 huge acorns and 27 oak apples, and I once found a 7/16in diameter ball-bearing.

The highly nutritious 'milk' which this remarkable crop produces means that the young do not need to hatch out to coincide with the peak of any critically important natural food and thus facilitates an exceptionally long breeding season. The cheesy mass is rich in protein, similar in composition to mammals' milk, and given to the young about twice a day. The nestling, too, can store it in the crop. Without this adaptation the parents would be less able to care for the young within the sanctuary of the nest.

With such a diet the woodpigeon needs to drink frequently — hence the strategic importance of water on a shoot. Several times I have made good bags by siting my hide near a cattle trough in a 'sea' of grain. The pigeon is unusual in that it imbibes continuously without looking up.

When you discover where the pigeons are feeding, but wonder where to site your hide on or around a large field, it is worth remembering that if it is windy the birds will almost always seek a fold or dip in the ground. Not only does that shelter the birds but also the crops, and in such spots growth is often more advanced. Drier situations are also preferred, for the feet quickly 'ball up' with mud. Another good plan is to set up near the gathering or 'sitty' tree where birds generally assemble before feeding. This is assuming that there is no clear flight-line (approach path) beneath which you can conveniently site your hide. If you are protecting crops or shooting for the pot then there is no reason not to shoot perched birds too.

MOVEMENTS: The species is a resident, winter visitor and passage migrant. Most birds are sedentary but some Scandinavian birds winter as far south as the Mediterranean.

In Britain there are some *northerly* flights in September and October before a southerly orientation is adopted later in the autumn. These apparently involve young birds from densely populated areas looking for space to settle and chances are often better in the more sparsely populated north.

In common with many seed-eating species which are at the mercy of varying harvests the woodpigeon displays irruptive type behaviour. Each autumn it lays down reserves of migratory fat and adopts the flights patterns of true migrants but this latent migratory urge is realised only sporadically when the main food supplies of the area fail. In Britain a bad cereal harvest plus a failure of the beechmast may send a few birds to north-west Europe, especially France.

However, the influx of Continental winter visitors is regular and varies only in quantity. They arrive from October, the peak being at the end of November on the east coast, and are more numerous when the whole of Europe is in the grip of a very cold winter. The spring passage is less discernible but begins in mid-February, peaks at the end of March and tails off in early June.

With sustained frost the woodpigeon becomes progessively bolder and will even raid small gardens. In the memorable winter of 1962/63 with one shot I killed three pigeons on a single sprout plant in my urban garden.

BEHAVIOUR: With keen eyesight, acute hearing and an apparent ability to learn quickly the woodpigeon is increasingly difficult to outwit. There is a general feeling that decoys are not nearly so effective as they were just ten or twenty years ago and their increasing variety does little to alleviate the problem. Pigeon 'shyness' probably has more to do with an increasingly greater choice and quantity of food and therefore is mostly a temporary and local problem. Young birds are, naturally, much easier to decoy.

Because they are gregarious in winter pigeons lend themselves well to roost shooting and good sport is to be had in the fir plantations and oakwoods. The ideal month is February when the game season is over, and keepers are not preoccupied with disturbance of pheasants, and before immigrant pigeons go home and home birds disperse to breed. Birds roosting in ivy-covered hedgerow trees are best taken at dawn with a gun walking down either side providing that all safety rules are observed.

For a big roost shoot it is best to wait for a dull day with a strong wind and a hint of storm in the air for then the birds will return an hour or so earlier than on calm days and will usually come repeatedly despite the gunfire and disturbance. Whether by coincidence or design, big flocks send 'scouts' in advance and it is best not to shoot these. Generally the main party will come over at a great height. Let them deceive themselves into thinking that all is well and make their final run before opening fire so that not only do you stand a chance of two shots but also to let your adjacent guns share the action. It is not essential to get right in the roost — beneath the line of approach at the edge will do, and may give better vision.

Remember, although birds leaving a covert will avoid flying against a strong wind, those returning will invariably approach into the wind to gain greater flight control. In my experience, because pigeons are more unsettled and active on windy days they offer more steady shooting and present more sporting marks. In fog they will not move far, if at all, from the roost. Roost shooting should stop while pigeons are still coming in to ensure that the site continues to be used and to allow pheasants to go up to roost.

Decoys should be placed downwind of the guns because no matter from which direction the birds enter the field they will turn upwind to settle and you need as much notice of their approach as possible. Still conditions give more flexibility. However, feeding birds do not all face the wind and therefore it is not necessary to pattern your decoys in this manner. Some sportsmen say that all decoys should be head-down as a head-up alert posture may warn off approaching birds.

POPULATION: The British Isles breeding stock is put at 3-5 million pairs but the population at the end of July probably doubles by the end of September and then gradually falls through winter. The number of winter visitors can only be guessed at. Average annual mortality is estimated at 36 per cent, average life expectancy is 2.3 years and the maximum age recorded in the wild is 21 years.

OPEN SEASON: The woodpigeon may be shot at any time by authorised persons throughout the British Isles.

IN THE POT: This bird makes a good meal for which there is a ready market. Old birds make a delicious base for paté and even when roast need no sophisticated treatment. They are very easy to pluck but if you have many birds to process it is worth remembering that most of the meat is on the breast and it is far quicker to peel back the skin and cut out the 'steak' either side of the breastbone.

Two of my favourite dishes are pigeon and mushroom pie washed down with a bottle of claret, and curried pigeon with chilled hock to refresh the palate. Hanging is unnecessary.

THE FUTURE: In recent years there has been considerable conjecture over reputed pigeon decline but there is no real trend other than that in many areas they are generally harder to decoy. There is considerable scope for further research. Indeed, prospects are good with continuing extension northwards throughout the range this century. As with geese, the big danger is that a species which depends on agriculture to sustain such an artificially large population may not be able to respond quickly enough to further change to avoid significant decline. However, I cannot see this happening because the species is so adaptable. On the contrary, the population will almost certainly continue to increase. Disease does occur at high density, and bodies gathered from beneath roosts should be burnt.

Control methods have included poking-out of occupied nests, large-scale co-ordinated winter shoots and the use of stupefying baits, but poking is labour

The woodpigeon is unusual among birds in that it imbibes continuously without looking up *(E. A. Janes)*

intensive, stupefying bait not practical on a large scale and shooting in autumn and winter merely removes individuals which would, in any case, die during the period of greatest food shortage in February and March. However, growth of interest in pigeon shooting in recent years has reached a scale which may well have a depressive effect on the population in some areas. Nonetheless, although millions are shot in Britain each year, it has been suggested that the bag is still only half that which would satisfy the farming community.

Shooting control is real if more birds are shot than would die anyway but depleted breeding areas are soon topped up. There is value in killing birds *before* they damage crops, though this is usually only of local benefit for most birds escape to feed on a neighbour's land. With the amount of shooting not changing significantly from year to year it is an arbitrary cull not in proportion to crop damage. Truthfully, although most pigeon shooting is secured under the guise of crop protection, sport is the prime motivator and no *sportsman* really wants to deplete the pigeon stock significantly.

Although young birds are more easily shot than adults until mid-winter they learn rapidly and from February are just as wily as adults. But, as their mortality rate is higher, winter shooting can significantly alter the age structure of the population without affecting the following summer's number. Therefore if a serious attempt to reduce the population were to be made in the future it should concentrate on shooting during late winter when the pigeon's larder is nearly bare and its population already naturally thinned. However, most shooters are glad of the plentiful supply of woodpigeons and are the first to express concern over local numbers. Many impose their own restrictions such as not shooting during the breeding season so that orphans are not left to starve in the nest, but that is largely

199

a futile exercise as both parents are unlikely to be killed. Because the present system of dominance by game shooting means that great acreages of coverts offer sanctuary to pigeons during the pheasant breeding and shooting seasons, when keepers will not permit disturbance, the pigeon cull will never be really effective.

The export trade in frozen and fresh pigeons is thriving and even home sales seem to be increasing with more and more supermarket outlets as well as interested butchers. They may stimulate increased bags but I doubt if this will ever be significant.

The number of pigeon shooters is on the increase because the sport is cheap and generally near home (particularly important during general economic recession) and the pigeon shooting accessories market has been selling hard. Strangely enough, for sportsmen this increased interest is not all bad, for if a number of guns are out at the same time in one area the birds are kept on the move, and as a result bags are often larger. In the past quiet week-days were favoured but now weekends are frequently more productive.

FERAL PIGEON
(*Columba livia*)

Although this species is not one which the sporting shooter would usually deliberately go after, some mention of it is necessary because it can be a significant agricultural pest and there may be confusion with the protected rock and stock doves. The rock dove is the ancestor of the feral pigeon.

HISTORY: In medieval times semi-domesticated dovecote pigeons were an important source of food and the birds were free to find their own food in the countryside. Contact and interbreeding with wild rock doves was easy and many birds soon established completely wild populations. With the growth of pigeon racing in the nineteenth and twentieth centuries many individual birds have been lost and joined up with feral pigeons to influence the genetic composition further.

Today pure rock doves survive best in the areas where dovecotes were always scarce and where arable land is so restricted that very few pigeons are attracted and there is little competition for food.

RANGE AND DISTRIBUTION: The feral pigeon is widespread throughout the world. In Britain it is most common in eastern districts and areas concentrating on arable farming. It is also common in towns and cities. Truly wild rock doves are now found only along the coasts of north and west Scotland down to Kintyre and on the northern, western and southern coasts of Ireland. Elsewhere even coastal birds are well mixed with feral stock.

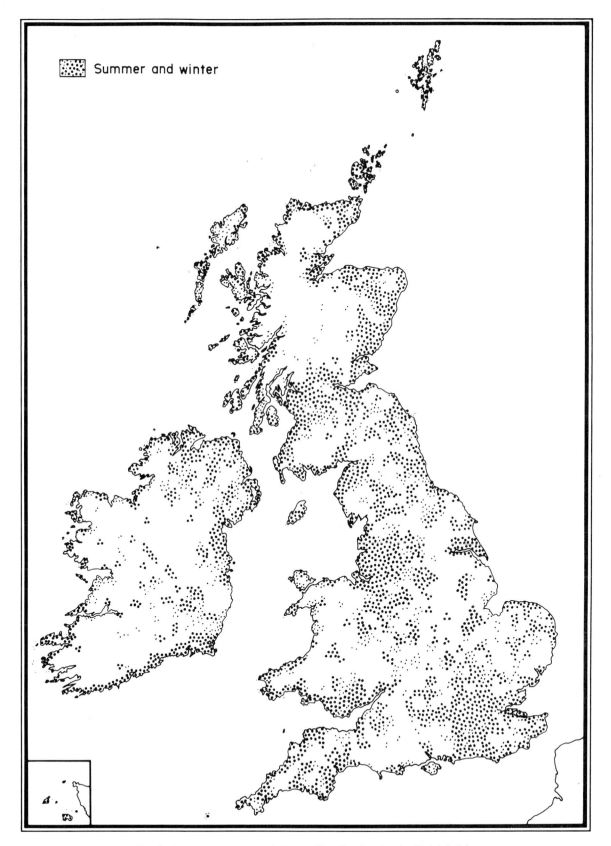

Feral pigeon — summer/winter distribution in the British Isles

HABITAT: It is thoroughly at home in the urban environment where it nests and roosts on large buildings. In many areas flocks swarm out of the towns into the surrounding countryside to take advantage of arable hand-outs in the appropriate seasons. Because of their general tameness it is not often realised that these are completely wild birds.

IDENTIFICATION: The variety of plumages is immense and very confusing. If in doubt then do not shoot for you could kill a valuable racing pigeon, pure rock dove, stock dove or one of your neighbour's treasured tame pigeons. Knowledge of the area and careful observation of bird behaviour will generally tell you which are the truly feral birds.

At 33cm (13in) the feral pigeon is 7.5cm (3in) smaller and considerably less heavy than the woodpigeon, though it is the same length as the rock and stock doves. Although the variety of plumages is confusing there are several common types. The most familiar are the 'blue', which resembles the rock dove apart from the stouter bill and enlarged cere common to all domesticated and semi-domesticated strains, and the 'blue chequer' which has the wing-coverts spotted with black. Other common colours are cinnamon-brown, mostly black, all white and any combination of black and white. In flight, you can often see the rock dove ancestry in the double black wing-bars or white rump, which will distinguish from the stock dove. However, many feral pigeons are similar to the stock dove and in these cases the feral's greater gregariousness, tameness and more leisurely flight are useful pointers. The sexes are alike.

VOICE: The familiar cooing from town roosts — a repeated *oor-roo-coo* or the quiet *ooo* — is not significant in the shooting field where the bird is quiet in flight.

BREEDING: Feral pigeons interbreed freely with the rock dove. On those coastal cliffs of England, Wales, the Isle of Man and Scotland where they have totally replaced rock doves, they have assumed the nesting and feeding habits of their predecessors. Inland colonies occupy old, disused or ruined buildings, especially on farms, and town populations nest on the ledges and in the recesses of large buildings.

Because they live in such close association with man, taking his year-round food hand-outs and enjoying the warmth and protection of his buildings, feral pigeons enjoy a long breeding season. Both sexes build the shallow nest of grass and twigs. The 2 white eggs can be laid in any month but mainly March to Sep-

The feral pigeon population is restricted by its dependence on buildings *(Brian Martin)*

tember. Winter breeding is much more common among town birds, and melanistic birds are more likely to be continuous breeders. Both parents share the 17–19 day incubation and feeding the young which fly after 35–37 days. There are usually two to four broods and five are not uncommon.

FEEDING: Town birds take almost anything including bread, chocolate, apples and bacon rind but join their country cousins to take grain, weed seeds and a few insects and snails. They can be a considerable nuisance in joining with wood-pigeons to take freshly sown grain, laid corn and other crops.

MOVEMENTS: The species is sedentary. Local movements follow the food supply.

BEHAVIOUR: On the ground they behave quite differently from the wood-pigeon, strutting about and indulging in breast-puffing courtship at almost any time of year. The flight is mostly slow with much circling and dipping on arched wings. Feeding is more continuous throughout the day than that of the wood-pigeon or stock dove. Roosts are generally at the nesting sites or nearby.

POPULATION: The total feral pigeon plus rock dove population has been guessed at 100,000 pairs.

OPEN SEASON: England, Scotland, Wales: may be shot by authorised persons at all times. Northern Ireland: may be taken when it is necessary for the owner or occupier of any land, or a person or persons authorised in writing signed by him to act on his behalf, to kill or take these birds on the land of the owner or occupier in order to protect the crops or property. Irish Republic: may be shot at any time.

203

Feral pigeons use delapidated buildings for roosting and nesting *(Brian Martin)*

IN THE POT: Most feral pigeons are as good as if not better than woodpigeons to eat and it is a shame that so many are wasted because the generally unfamiliar plumage is offputting and not conducive to easy sale. Even home consumption is avoided by many shooters, probably because there is often a nagging suspicion that a protected bird has been shot.

THE FUTURE: There is likely to be little change. The population will not increase significantly unless the bird adapts to a greater variety of breeding sites. On the contrary there may be some decrease as general tidying-up of old farm buildings continues and pest control in towns becomes more efficient. With the extension of arable farming west and north prospects look bleak for continuance of pure rock doves for increasingly there will be feral pigeons on their doorstep.

COLLARED DOVE
(*Streptopelia decaocto*)

Against all the odds imposed by man's proliferation this bird has found a vacant niche (possibly linked to the dovecote decline) in nature to exploit and its world population has exploded since about 1930. Its range continues to increase. Although it was not even recorded in Britain until 1952 it has since been so successful that it is now on the quarry list. Rather fittingly, that first sighting was in Lincolnshire, at Manton — a name synonymous with guns.

HISTORY: During this century the species has spread north-westwards right through Europe from a range once restricted to Turkey, Albania, Bulgaria and Yugoslavia and it is still increasing. Hungary was reached in 1932, Czechoslovakia in 1936, Austria in 1938, Germany in 1943, the Netherlands in 1947, Denmark in 1948, Sweden and Switzerland in 1949, France in 1950, Belgium and Norway in

1952 — nearly 1,000 miles in twenty years.

The first recorded British nesting was at Cromer in Norfolk in 1955 and during the first decade here it spread at the incredible rate of 100 per cent per annum. Town suburbs and villages were first to be colonised, particularly in low-lying areas of coastal counties, and as the optimum habitat was taken colonisation slowed down but still continued into rural areas and town centres. The Common Birds Census recorded a five-fold increase on farmland 1969-73. Early in the 1970s it was even breeding in the Faeroe Islands and Iceland.

The bird had spread to south-east Europe from northern India by the sixteenth century but expansion then ceased. Why this pause to 1930 occurred is unknown though it has been suggested that a genetic mutation occurred which has less restricted needs. Increased arable farming in the wake of climatic amelioration no doubt helped. Strangely, pre-1950s deliberate attempts to introduce the species to Britain failed.

RANGE AND DISTRIBUTION: Apart from the countries above there has been a small spread into Turkmenistan and Japan. Outside Europe the collared dove is found in southern Asia and North Africa and there have been many introductions around the world. In the British Isles it has bred in every county and is widespread except in hilly districts, especially in the north and west.

HABITAT: With the species' unusual history, its original habitat is obscure but the link with man is long-standing and throughout the range towns, villages, parks, palm groves, gardens, farmyards, roadsides and cultivated areas as well as woods, oases and open arid regions are frequented.

In Britain initial concentration was on coastal lowlands but consolidation has brought infilling even to many uplands where farmsteads act as nuclei. Favoured sites are parks and large gardens where ornamental evergreen trees such as pines and cypresses provide suitable sites for extended breeding and permanently sheltered roosts.

IDENTIFICATION: This dainty, generally pink and buff bird is likely to be confused only with the turtle dove in this country. Its distinctive marks in flight are the tail's white terminal band and the virtually white underwing-coverts, and at rest the neat, white-edged, black half-collar on the hind neck and the plain upperparts.

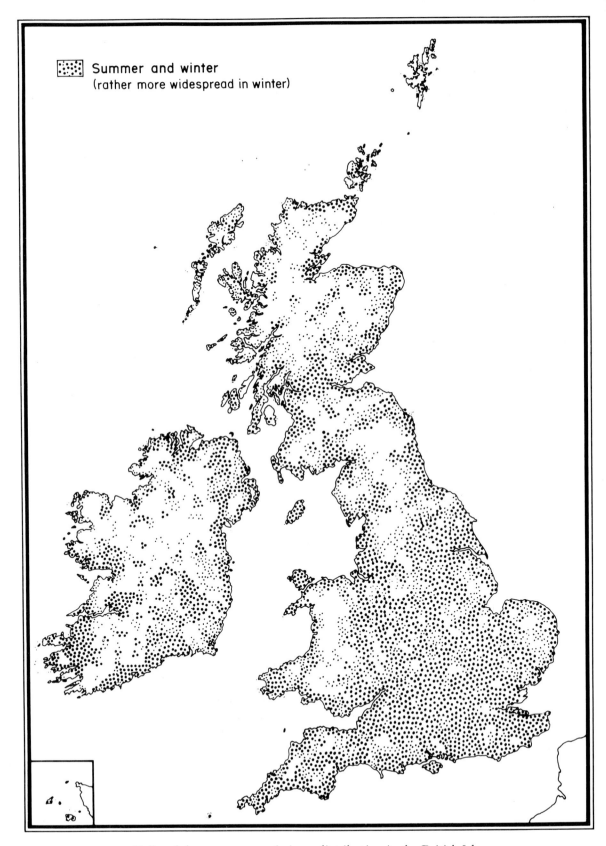

Collared dove — summer/winter distribution in the British Isles

The smaller, creamy-buff barbary dove is similar but lacks the dark-grey in the tail and black wing-tips. It is often kept in captivity and some escapees breed ferally.

Collared dove sexes are alike. Average length is 32cm (12½in).

VOICE: Almost everyone must be familiar with the persistent *kuk-koo-kook* which can annoy when next to the bedroom window. The male has a repeated alighting call.

BREEDING: The flat, flimsy nest of twigs and stems is built by both sexes, generally rather higher than that of the woodpigeon and more commonly in evergreens which offer year-round protection. Sometimes a building ledge is used.

Clutches of 2 white eggs are found in every month but most are laid from March to September. The incubation of about 14 days and feeding the young are shared by both parents. Chicks fledge at about 18 days and finally leave the nest a few days later. At least two broods are normal and five are commonly attempted. Indeed, at the height of the breeding season successive broods sometimes follow so closely that the parents have to feed fledged young in between incubating the next clutch. Such intense breeding has helped sustain the dynamic range expansion.

FEEDING: Predominantly a vegetable feeder, the species' close association with human settlement has brought conflict with man. Weed seeds and some wild fruits such as elderberries are taken and collared doves are often seen picking about the kitchen garden, but the main attraction is grain. They increasingly feed on stubbles along with woodpigeons but damage to laid corn is probably negligible. Most complaints arise from their habit of gathering around stocks of harvested grain at mills, maltings, docks, farmyards, hen-runs and pheasant rearing pens where there is often spillage. More seriously, they frequently get inside large stores and then foul grain and fodder crops with their droppings, in which case control may be easiest with an airgun inside the buildings.

MOVEMENTS: Throughout the range the species is sedentary but long-range dispersive movements occur. Immigration is probably continuing into the British Isles and surplus birds press north-westwards into uncolonised or less populated areas.

BEHAVIOUR: Despite its fondness for man's habitations and rather frail flight the collared dove certainly does not give itself up and can provide moderate sport with its rapid springing and unpredictable manoeuvres. These birds gather in large numbers at suitable feeding grounds and substantial bags may be had. Cattle water troughs are good points at which to lay ambush and early morning appears to be the period of greatest activity.

POPULATION: The Common Birds Census indices indicate a continuing increase

The collared dove was first recorded in Britain as recently as 1952, yet it is already a considerable pest *(Eric Hosking)*

in recent years and there are probably at least 50,000 pairs (possibly even double that).

OPEN SEASON: England, Scotland, Wales: may be killed or taken by authorised persons at all times. Northern Ireland: protected but may be killed or taken using poisonous or stupefying bait under licence from the Conservation Branch of the Department of the Environment, Stormont Castle. Irish Republic: fully protected but may be killed under licence or by specific exemption from the Forest and Wildlife Service.

IN THE POT: Delicious. Far better than the woodpigeon.

THE FUTURE: Concern has been expressed that should this bird ever reach the prairies of North America and replace the extinct passenger pigeon in the world's greatest grain store it could spell disaster for mankind. It was assumed that such dynamic expansion could easily bridge the Atlantic from Ireland. However, the species has already been *introduced* to America and is naturalised in some areas but expansion is much slower than in Europe. As in Britain, it seems that it will only really proliferate when nature gives it the signal.

As a sporting bird the collared dove should become increasingly popular as pressure on a reduced quarry list increases and successive generations of home-bred birds adopt more evasive behaviour. The population should continue to rise as further food sources and nest sites are exploited. If climatic amelioration was significant in assisting the range expansion over the first half of this century then it will be interesting to see what effect any continuance of the steady drop in the mean temperature since the 1950s will have.

MAGPIE
(*Pica pica*)

Long regarded as the black-hearted villain of birdland, the wary magpie has not only survived the heyday of professional gamekeeping but also has become progressively bolder and more common. It has even taken to visiting garden bird tables.

HISTORY: Already very common, the magpie was one of the species to gain significantly from the great increase in hedgerows provided by the enclosure of open fields, especially during the late eighteenth and early nineteenth centuries. However, the magpie's proliferation was soon arrested by the advent of intensive keeping later in the nineteenth century. Even today the breeding distribution is a legacy of past keepering.

Because of its predation on game chicks and eggs the magpie was widely trapped and shot in Victorian times and even eliminated from some game-rearing areas. There was marked decrease in much of England and Scotland and as early as 1876 Booth remarked that it was 'becoming scarcer every year'.

As with the other crows, the magpie's all-time low was at the beginning of this century during the 'golden era' of formal driven shooting. The impact of keepering first became apparent when the activity lapsed during World War I. With the guns out of the woods and turned on the Germans magpie numbers made substantial increases and were helped by an Act of 1911 which prohibited the use of poisoned bait.

However, in many of the shooting strongholds of east and south-east England the magpie stock remained suppressed until the 1930s. Expansion in numbers and range during the 1930s and 1940s was accelerated by another lapse of keepering during World War II. The process has continued ever since and has been particularly noticeable during the last five years. Some decline since the 1950s in parts of eastern England is probably related to grubbing out of hedgerows and general loss of habitat to prairie farming rather than a resumption of intensive keepering. However, hedge removal has slowed markedly very recently. Further recent magpie increases are probably related to exploitation of a wider variety of habitats, particularly urban and suburban.

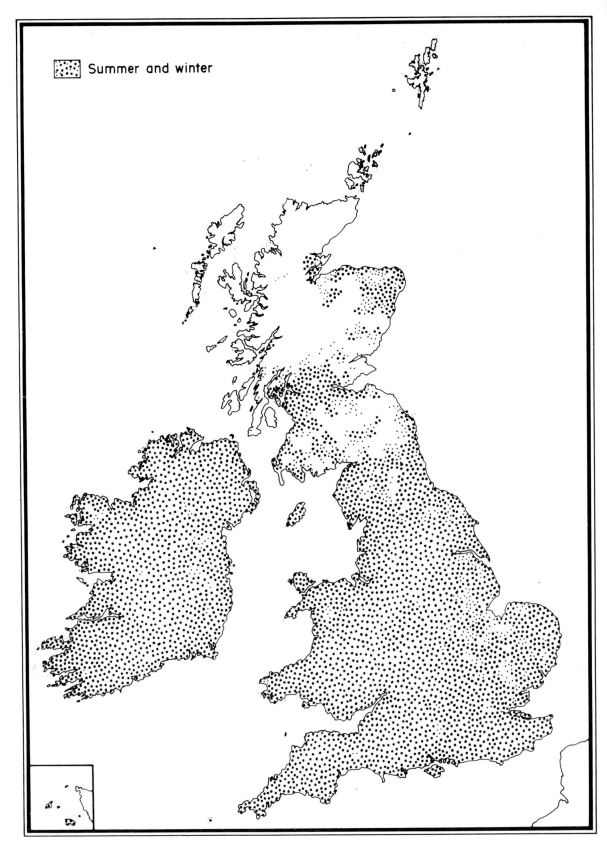

Magpie — summer/winter distribution in the British Isles

The first Irish record is from County Wexford in 1676. There too expansion was temporarily arrested through intense persecution but now they breed there in every county.

RANGE AND DISTRIBUTION: The magpie has a vast breeding range throughout Scandinavia, Europe, much of Siberia and central Asia to southern China, Pakistan and the Bering Sea. It also occurs in much of western North America from southern Alaska south to Kansas and California. There is an isolated population on the Arabian peninsula.

In England, Wales and Ireland it breeds in every county but is absent from the Border hills and parts of eastern England. It is more local in Scotland and absent from the Highlands and islands. Greatest densities occur away from centres of game rearing, chiefly in well-wooded suburbs.

HABITAT: This is chiefly a bird of woodland edge, the long tail facilitating balanced movement through low, often unstable, branches. It frequents all types of habitat with tree or bush cover but there is a preference for poorly managed farmland, especially grassland with thick hedgerows including a few trees and copses. Some open country is also used, especially where there is livestock, and this century there has been expansion into town gardens and parks, orchards, some city centres, coastal scrub and even onto sea-cliffs, where their nests have been found.

IDENTIFICATION: If you cannot identify this bird then you should not be shooting for the pied plumage, long, wedge-shaped tail and harsh chattering make it extremely conspicuous and there is no other British species with which it could be confused. The sexes are alike. The length is 46cm (18in), with the tail 20-25cm (8-10in).

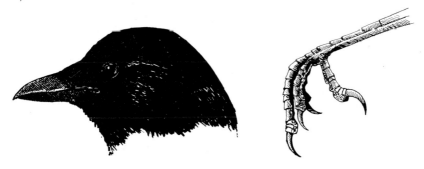

VOICE: The species' constant chattering in woodland often gives it away. Both parents are noisy during nest building and the male is particularly vocal during incubation. Apart from the familiar, far-carrying *chak-chak-chak* and a nasal, questioning *renk* there is a babbling *chook-chook* in spring and a warbler-like, crooning, gurgle heard only at close range.

BREEDING: Nest building often begins in February and in 1983 one pair started in an exceptionally mild January in my garden, very high up in a cedar of Lebanon. Most common sites are tall hedges and the edges of woods and copses where there is a good view. Thickets and single thorn bushes are also used. The birds are very conspicuous in nest building before the leaves are out. Frequently it appears that the virtually completed nest has been deserted and it might be two months before the eggs are laid. The big structure of sticks strongly lined with mud, grass and roots is constructed by the female from materials brought by the male. Usually over the cup there is a thorny dome with a side entrance so that it resembles an unfinished squirrel's drey. Being so conspicuous the nest relies on inaccessibility.

The 5-8 (up to 10 recorded) light blue-green eggs, closely speckled with grey-brown, are mostly laid from early April to May but I have found them in March. Incubation takes 17-18 days by the female only. Both parents feed the nestlings which leave after 22-24 days but the noisy family usually remains together for some time after that. The magpie has only a single brood.

FEEDING: This is a very unpopular bird with the gamekeeper as it takes game chicks and eggs but predation on pheasant and partridge nests is fairly high only because they are relatively exposed and vulnerable. The nest of the woodpigeon is even more open and that is probably the magpie's most common victim. Range extension into gardens this century is bad news for songbirds for the magpie takes many of their eggs and young too.

The bulk of the food is invertebrates, especially defoliating insects and larvae, so the species does do a great deal of good and in some countries it is protected! Other foods include beetles, flies, mosquitoes, small mammals, carrion, cereals, fruits, berries, frogs, snails, worms, cereals, nuts and potatoes. It has taken particular advantage of the huge number of animal and bird carcases provided by increasing road traffic.

Another habit which makes it unpopular is that of perching on the backs of livestock but it is only looking for insects disturbed by the animals' feet and the ticks and parasites in their hair. Bird tables are increasingly visited and this has led to opening egg cartons left on the doorstep and eating the contents.

MOVEMENTS: The species is sedentary but in America it wanders far east in winter. It is resident in Britain with very few local seasonal movements.

BEHAVIOUR: With slow, direct flight the magpie appears to be an easy target but you have to get near it in the first place. The wing-beats are rapid and it changes direction with ease. Parties usually travel in single file across open space — a sort of 'I'll see if the coast is clear'. On the ground, where most feeding takes place, it walks about deliberately, with occasional brisk hops sideways when excited, the tail a little raised.

Outside the breeding season it is commonly found in small parties and a hundred or more may gather at roosts in mid-winter. There is ceremony at-

The magpie is a great predator of small birds *(Dennis Green)*

tached to large gatherings, in which they chatter, jump about on branches and chase each other, but this is not fully understood. The suggestion that this enables unmated birds to pair seems unlikely, because such gatherings have a preponderance of paired birds. Flighting magpies into such roosts is a good method of control. Large evergreens deep in mixed woods are popular roosts.

If you have only a small number to shoot, a large owl decoy is extremely useful, for not only will magpies mob it but will also give you warning of their approach with excited chattering.

The wary magpie is resourceful and adaptable. Like other crows it even scavenges bright or shiny objects which it hoards along with food.

POPULATION: There are probably over 300,000 pairs.

OPEN SEASON: The magpie may be killed at any time by authorised persons throughout the British Isles.

IN THE POT: This bird is not generally eaten at all nowadays. The earlier name of maggot-pie probably originated through the bird's habit of picking ticks from sheep's wool. Today's 'pie' element in the name may derive from the original word for a mix of colours. However, it was once believed that eating a pie made from ground-up magpie would cure epilepsy, the assumption being that consuming a chatterer would neutralise the 'chattering' disease.

THE FUTURE: As professional keepering continues to decline and marginal habitats are further developed by agriculture the magpie's range should continue to expand and the population increase, especially in suburban areas where there is little shooting. This will be counteracted somewhat by continuing eradication of areas of backward or poor farming which the species favours.

JAY
(*Garrulus glandarius*)

Few birds have obtained such unenviable notoriety as the jay. Abhorred by the husbandman, farmer and gamekeeper, the jay, in the reign of George II, was considered such a desperate character that an Act of Parliament was passed empowering certain authorities to pay a reward of threepence per head for every slaughtered bird.

Thus wrote Swaysland in *Familiar Wild Birds,* 1883. His contemporary, Edwin Arnold, in *Bird Life in England,* 1887, wrote

I am certain that all the crow kind within our four seas do less harm to agriculture in the aggregate than a single shower when the hay is down, or corn is ripe; and much less harm to game than a thunderstorm (or an inch of snow on the high grounds), when grouse and patridge chicks have grown too big and bulky to shelter under their mothers' wings. Jays do but little harm to the game of our woodlands, it is on the small birds that they chiefly wage war.

How enlightened these men were, for today research shows that the jay is certainly not as black as painted and is even welcomed as a sentry on some shoots. Game chicks are taken only infrequently and predation on ground nests is less than by other crows.

HISTORY: Primarily a woodland bird, the jay has hardly been affected by changes in farming but it must have suffered overall decline as most of our forests disappeared down the centuries. However, it was still very common in 1800.

As with the magpie, the jay reached an all-time low at the end of the nineteenth century when keepering was most intense and anything which threatened the keeper's livelihood had to go. In addition, in the age of the collector taxidermists sought the jay for its bright plumage, and boys took it for a pet. During this century there has been steady increase in range and numbers brought about by decline in keepering and taxidermy, lapses in keepering during the two world wars and an increase in afforestation since the Forestry Commission was established in 1919.

Now it visits gardens and suburbs more openly and even Central London was colonised in 1930. Ireland, too, has shared the expansion, especially since the 1930s, and there has been occupation of new ground in the west as well as recolonisation of old haunts. Although the jay has a special relationship with oakwood it has made use of the new great acreage of conifers.

RANGE AND DISTRIBUTION: The species is widespread in boreal to warm temperate zones across Eurasia to Japan, China and the Himalayas, north to the treeline, south to the Mediterranean, Middle East and the tip of North Africa. Plumage variations occur in some areas.

In the Britsh Isles it is widespread and absent only from the treeless areas of the Pennines, Scotland's Highlands and islands, the Fens and parts of the north and west of Ireland. It is rather scarcer in Ireland generally but the geographically distinct subspecies is increasing with continued afforestation. Its sedentary nature probably explains absence from the Isle of Man.

HABITAT: This is the most arboreal member of the crow family. It prefers open woodland with tall undergrowth in summer and in winter favours oakwoods for their important food, the acorn. Jays help to propagate oakwood by burying acorns, some of which are not subsequently eaten. This is especially valuable in extending oakwood uphill. They also occur in beech, chestnut, mixed and coniferous woods and have a special liking for coppiced areas near mature trees. Generally they prefer thick cover.

Most suburbs with trees have been colonised, as have many city parks, large gardens and orchards.

IDENTIFICATION: A colourful bird, hardly likely to be confused with anything else in the British Isles. The best field mark is the square white rump contrasting

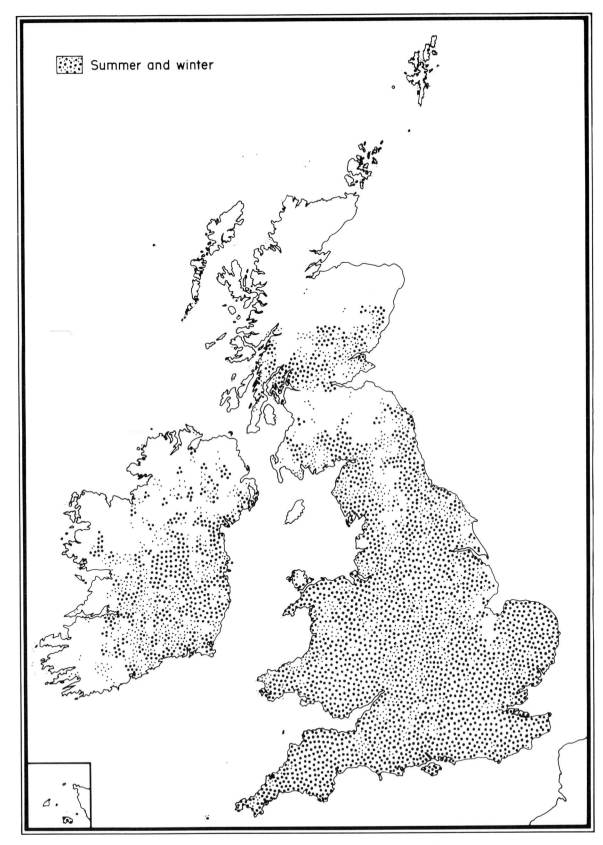

Jay — summer/winter distribution in the British Isles

with the black tail, usually the first thing you notice as the bird makes off. In good light the blue and white on the short, rounded wings (ideal for manoeuvrability in woodland) shows well. The sexes are alike.

The Irish race (*G.g.hibernicus*) is slightly darker than the British (*G.g.rufitergum*), though this is not noticeable in the field. The British race has more chestnut than its Continental cousins, probably because it is rather isolated on an island and is at the extreme endpoint of range variation. The greyer, paler Continental bird (*G.g.glandarius*) occurs in south-east England in winter but can only be identified in the hand.

The average length is 34cm (13½in).

VOICE: The screech of jay parties is one of the most familiar of woodland sounds and echoes for long distances through the trees, no doubt to effect good communication in the dense woodland habitat where other species such as the nightingale and tawny owl also produce particularly penetrative notes. The jay is a great imitator, including the lamb, cat, horse, cock, buzzard and squirrel in its vocal repertoire. Bewick noted that 'When kept in a domestic state they may be rendered very familiar and will imitate a variety of words and sounds.' Later, in Victorian times, many were kept for this novelty.

The Latin name *Garrulus* means talkative. Most remarkable was the realisation that jays have several different 'words' for danger and are known to give specific calls for certain predators. Frequently these resemble the cries of the predators themselves and it has even been suggested that a popping noise alludes to a gun.

There is also a soft, crooning warble, as produced by other crows, but this is audible only at close range.

BREEDING: In early spring jays gather to chase one another on slowly flapping wings. Courtship consists mostly of posturing and spreading the wings and tail.

The jay keeps a low profile when nesting and often resorts to the thickest part of a wood so that the nest is the most difficult to find of all the crows. It is at any height between 2 and 20m (6ft 6in-65ft) in undergrowth, a tall bush or the crown of a big tree. Bewick described it adequately as an 'artless nest composed of sticks, fibres and tender twigs' but in fact they vary tremendously in skill of building. Both sexes build. An exceptional site is in long heather.

The 5-7 (3-10 recorded) greenish eggs with olive-brown freckles are laid from late April into May and less frequently in June. In his *History of British Birds* 1851–57 Reverend F. O. Morris noted how they vary in size and 'degree of polish' but perhaps their most surprising point is their generally small size in proportion to the bird. Incubation from the first egg is mostly by the female and lasts about 16 days. The chicks are fed by both parents and fly at 19-20 days. Incubating birds sit very tightly and generally only fly off when the tree is climbed.

Although the jay is usually single-brooded, some observers have recorded two broods in the warmer south, and it is there that they tend to stay in family parties until later in the spring before they separate to form new pairs.

FEEDING: Although they do not take too many game chicks and eggs jays do raid many songbird nests, especially those of blackbird and song thrush, though this may well be simply because those species are particularly common in the jay's habitat. There is very high predation on woodpigeon eggs and young, though again this is probably because the species is common in the habitat and certainly partly because the woodpigeon's nest is so exposed. Coles suggested that three of each five woodpigeon clutches are taken by jays, magpies and other predators.

Other animal food taken includes reptiles, amphibians, fish, snails, slugs, worms, cockchafers, gall insects, spiders and beetle larvae. To the bird's 'credit' (as if one can, without guilt, evaluate a species' worth simply from an economic standpoint) it does destroy pests such as mice (skinning them neatly before eating), click beetles (wireworms in larval stage), winter moths and defoliating caterpillars.

Yet this is a true omnivore and a wide variety of vegetable food is taken including fruits, seeds, acorns, beech and hazel nuts, pine seeds and grain. Although it does love peas and cherries in particular it is the wild harvest that it relies on — flowers of cruciferae and nuts and fruits in the widest sense. Of these the acorn appears to be the most significant and most interesting. The Latin name *glandarius* means 'eating acorns and beechmast'.

It might be said, though this is not proven, that the jay has a symbiotic relationship with the oak. Some researchers have found that it feeds its young mainly on lepidopterous larvae from oak foliage. Not only does the adult feed on acorns but also it stores them away in holes in trees, under leaves and about an inch below turf to recover them later not only when winter's larder is truly bare but right through to spring. It can carry up to six acorns at a time — one in the bill and the rest in the oesophagus. It will even search for them under snow. Fresh-looking, buried acorns are recovered as late as June, at a time when most have rotted or been eaten, or have otherwise produced seedlings. Surprisingly the jay can recognise these young plants and even distinguish them from the seedlings of other species and the offshoots of roots. Murton records that 'on finding a newly-germinated seedling the jay digs down and removes the cotyledons which are still as fresh as the acorns in autumn. The young oak tree is not damaged in the process.'

MOVEMENTS: The jay is resident throughout its range. Northern forest birds irrupt southwards in seasons when food is scarce. This brings visitors to Britain (chiefly south-east England), arriving in October from the Baltic, North Sea countries and the Continent. At home there is little seasonal movement but during hard times wandering pairs and small flocks drift into areas where they do not usually breed.

BEHAVIOUR: The secretive jay is wary and restless, and difficult to observe when settled. Despite its arboreal habits it appears somewhat clumsy with heavy hops along branches and on the ground, frequently jerking its tail and making more progress sideways than forward. One reason why it is often seen flying up from

A nest full of jays. The species is less black than once painted *(Eric Hosking)*

the ground is that it is very fond of 'anting', when the bird allows worker ants to run over its plumage aggressively squirting out formic acid. It deliberately arouses them and leans back on its tail with wings spread out in front; it appears to derive sensual pleasure from this, though the true reason probably is that the ants' acid kills the mites in the plumage.

Jay flight looks flimsy and laboured in the open, with quick, jerky wing-flaps. None the less it is skilful in covert flight. Jays have regular flightlines along hedgerows and are difficult to shoot when you are alone. Probably more are shot during covert drives for pheasants than at any other other time. Flocks may be of twenty to forty birds.

This is an inquisitive bird and has even been found jammed between branches. The shooter can turn this curiosity to advantage in decoying jays with artificial owls and rabbit squealers which attract several birds to one position.

To meet an enemy the jay turns sideways, ruffling and spreading feathers to look bigger.

POPULATION: There are estimated to be at least 110,000 pairs and the number is probably increasing.

OPEN SEASON: The jay may be killed or taken at any time by authorised persons throughout the British Isles.

IN THE POT: Generally never eaten in Britain, the jay is eaten abroad in poorer countries such as Greece.

THE FUTURE: The crow family is intelligent and highly adaptable and the jay is no exception. Robbed of much of its original woodland habitat it is rapidly taking to man's environs and the vast monocultures of conifers generally planted in areas where there had been no trees in recent times. This will continue to aid the jay's range extension. In addition it looks as though continued public outcry against coniferous woodland from an aesthetic viewpoint is about to bear fruit and it is likely that more broad-leaved trees will be planted from now on. Such woods, especially of oak, will allow greater jay densities.

Shooting is no longer likely to have any significant effect on the future population. Increasingly the jay will be valued as a sporting bird rather than a pest and the blue feathers will be worn with pride in the roughshooter's hat. He will probably continue to spare a few for fishing flies.

ROOK
(*Corvus frugilegus*)

The bustle of the rookery in March is as integral a part of the British countryside as April showers, strawberries and cream and the Boxing Day meet, and something which both the shooter and farmer would never wish to be without. The rook's 'economic' value has been debated since the Middle Ages and today, though its depredations are occasionally serious on a local scale, and control is then necessary, there appears to be no reason to persecute it unreservedly as a pest.

HISTORY: In 1424 James I of Scotland introduced an Act for the destruction of the rook and at one time villagers set nets to trap the birds coming down to the corn. In 1766, in *A Society of Gentlemen*, it was observed that rooks can do considerable damage to sprouting corn (their predominantly vegetable diet not only involves taking grain but also the inadvertent uprooting of seed in probing for insects) but

> they never molest the wheat which is sown about Michaelmas [29 September], because so much of the late harvest then lies scattered about the fields, that they find it much easier to pick up that, than to search for corn underground in new-sown lands.

Overall the British population has been subject to considerable fluctuation related to weather patterns and agricultural change. In Scotland in particular, during the first half of this century at least, there has been long-term increase and expansion as a rise in the mean temperature allowed the cereal belt to move northwards with the aid of new technology.

The British Trust for Ornithology's first national survey during World War II revealed nearly three million rooks in Britain — up by 20 per cent on the 1930s. Further growth may have been due to increased tillage improving the earthworm supply. Local decline in the late 1950s and 1960s was probably due to extensive use of the now discontinued persistent organochlorine seed dressings and loss of farmland to development.

In 1975 another national census was undertaken in the UK for there had been a drop in rook numbers of 43 per cent on 1945. Studies showed that a decline in ley grassland not only immediately precedes a decline but also that population reduction stops as soon as the area of grassland stabilises. Population fluctuation does not so far appear to have been particularly related to cereals acreage, but increased stubble burning and early ploughing in of stubbles mean less grain available and have not helped.

Intensification of agriculture and increased disturbance have brought a trend to

smaller rookeries in Britain, though this does not necessarily mean a reduction in the population, rather that the birds are more dispersed. In recent years the ravages of Dutch elm disease have accelerated this process through the loss of many traditional rookeries.

RANGE AND DISTRIBUTION: The rook is widespread across the boreal and temperate zones of Eurasia from Britain to China, south to northern France and the Persian Gulf and with outposts in northern Spain and parts of Scandinavia. Successfully introduced to New Zealand between 1862 and 1873 it has spread only very slowly and still has a very limited range there. Rooks winter in and just to the south of their breeding range.

In the British Isles rooks breed in all counties and are absent only from treeless areas such as the Scottish Highlands and islands, and from London. They are scarce in the uplands of central Wales, along the Scottish border and in south-west Scotland. The Outer Hebrides were colonised in 1895 and Shetland in 1952.

HABITAT: With the starling and jackdaw this is a typical bird of the steppes of central Europe and Russia and probably spread to Britain from that region. It prefers moist grassland with an abundance of woods and copses for colonial nesting, though heavily wooded areas are generally avoided. In Britain at least this preference often leads to close association with human settlements and sometimes the outer suburbs of towns. Density is far lower on heath, moorland and marsh but all types of tree-clad agricultural country are used.

IDENTIFICATION: The rook is unlikely to be confused with the much larger raven, which is protected, or the smaller jackdaw but it is often mistaken for the carrion crow. At close range the rook is distinguished by the bare, grey-white patch on the face and base of the bill, and the purple gloss to the black plumage. On the ground you may notice the thick thigh feathers which give the well-known 'baggy breeches' effect. It walks a lot with a definite waddle. In flight it is distinguished from the crow by its finer bill, more angular forehead, lighter build and deeply slotted wing-tips. The carrion crow does occur in small groups but rarely in the large gatherings which typify rooks.

Beware of confusing young rooks with crows for they lack the bare face patch

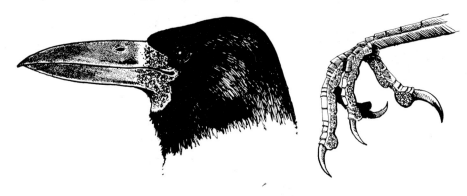

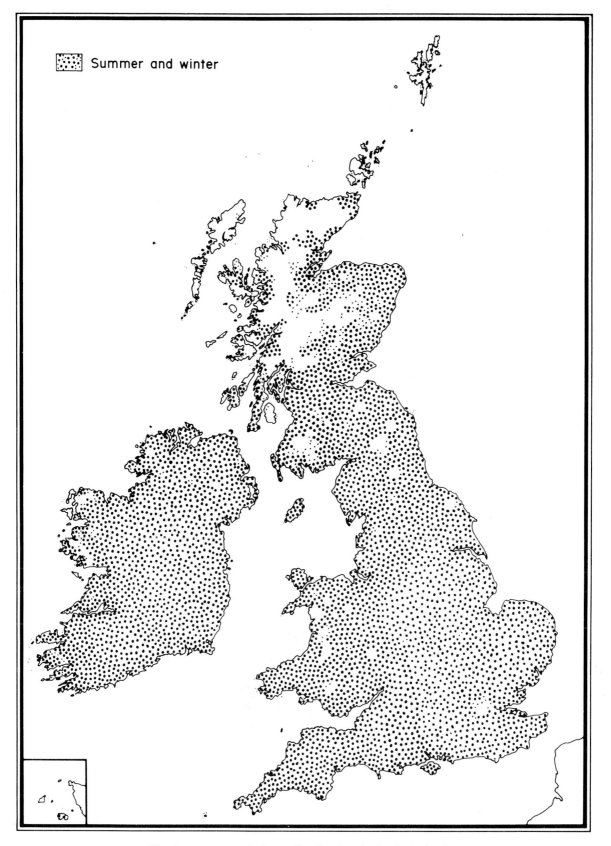

Rook — summer/winter distribution in the British Isles

and are less glossy than adult rooks but they do have the loose flank feathers. The sexes are alike. The average length is 45cm (18in).

VOICE: Everyone knows the hoarse *caw* of the rook but there is a variety of harsh notes including *caah* as well as a starling-like sub-song.

BREEDING: The dense colonies of nests known as rookeries are obvious features of our landscape and rely on inaccessibility through great height to avoid predation. Because of their security rooks are able to start nesting very early, well before the leaves are out, and use the same sites and repaired nests year after year. The largest British rookery is at Hatton Castle in Aberdeenshire where 6,985 nests were counted in 1945 and 6,697 in 1957. Single nests do occur. In Ireland few rookeries contain over fifty nests. With the destruction of so many elms through Dutch elm disease in recent years more tree species are now being used.

Birds start re-visiting rookeries in late autumn and each pair often uses the same nest annually. When making repairs they are very quarrelsome and frequently steal one another's sticks. Despite their colonial feeding they have a strong sense of territory and vigorously defend a small area around each nest.

The male feeds the female in courtship and during incubation, bowing and cawing to her high in the swaying trees. Both gather material but only the female builds the untidy nest of sticks lined with leaves, dry grass, wool and roots.

The 3-5 (occasionally up to 9) eggs, pale green to grey or pale blue heavily flecked with brown and green, are laid in late March or April and incubated for about 18 days by the female only. The nestlings (single brood) are fed by both parents and fly after about 30 days.

FEEDING: On balance it is now thought that the rook is beneficial to agriculture, though there can be serious local damage and there have been some interesting developments in recent years. It can also be a considerable thief of gamebird eggs but again this is a local problem calling for sparing control.

Like the woodpigeon, this is one of a small number of species which have adapted well to the few niches created by crop monocultures and it has specialised in their exploitation. Its gregariousness is the result of adaptation to feeding in large tracts of country where food distribution may be patchy and an individual searching alone might not encounter worthwhile feeding grounds quickly enough. Outside the breeding season very large flocks indeed may respond to individuals which have found good feeding sources. This explains the endless circling of rooks and their great traffic morning and evening.

The long bill and bare face patch have evolved to exploit soil invertebrates upon which rooks largely depend and they must breed in spring to coincide with an early peak in this food supply. But the peak population after fledging soon comes up against the worst season for food shortage — mid-summer, when juvenile mortality is at maximum. With the dried-up soil hard to probe and chief foods such as leatherjackets (cranefly larvae) and earthworms largely unobtainable rooks concentrate on surface feeding, chasing imagines with the emergence

Rooks carrying off pieces of turnip left out for sheep at Newton Stewart, Scotland, in winter *(Jack Orchel)*

of flies from pupae. But the biomass is not sufficient to sustain all the birds and it is the less resilient and less adaptable young which die first.

However, we now have an increasing acreage of winter barley and wheat so that grain is often available about three weeks earlier than it used to be, at a very critical time for young rooks. They have learned to break down the stalks to get at the ears so that many more young birds are surviving and the agricultural threat has increased. Adult rooks concentrate on grain — stubbles or sowings — when they have only themselves to feed but they resort to freshly cultivated land or pasture for protein-rich worms and other animal food when feeding young. Worms are particularly important in winter.

Damage to barley has been a particular problem in Scotland in recent years and the rook's liking for maize is sometimes troublesome in the south-west. Excavation for seed is not usually sufficient to affect crops seriously. Digging down to potato tubers is rare.

Other foods taken include harmful wireworms, insects and larvae, snails, weed seeds, fruit, occasional carrion, shellfish, root vegetables, berries, slugs and spiders. Food pellets are regurgitated.

Shooting of young rooks at rookeries is said to be pointless as so many of them will die anyway and removal of *some* merely increases the chances of survival for the remainder. A study has been made comparing areas where 'branchers' were not shot with those where they were heavily shot. It was found that hard shooting made no difference at all to the level of crop damage after July but on the other hand it did not reduce the rookery size in subsequent years.

MOVEMENTS: The species is both resident and migrant. British birds are largely sedentary but there is some late summer dispersal. Breeding birds from colder parts of the range migrate south as far as the Mediterranean. Immigrants from Holland, Germany and east to Russia arrive on our east coast in autumn. Booth said he often met large flocks when fishing on the North Sea.

BEHAVIOUR: Because the rook is vulnerable as a feeder on open grassland, its gregarious feeding has probably evolved also to give mutual warning of pre-

225

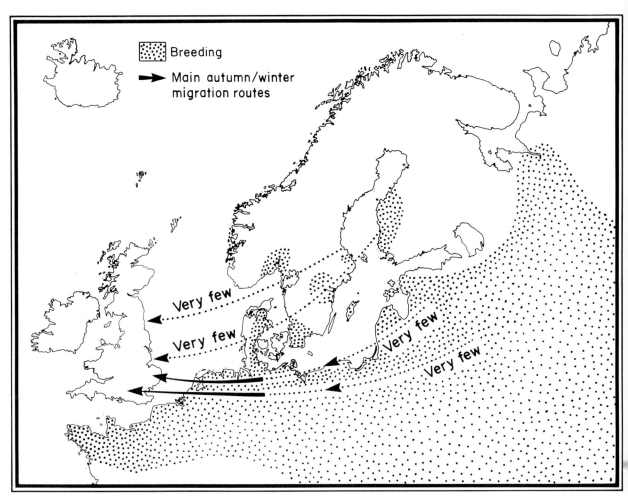

Rook — main autumn/winter migration routes of British-involved populations

dators. Small flocks have a 'peck order' for feeding which also ensures survival of some during lean times. In fact, the rook's communal life is so well developed that it has given rise to fanciful tales of rook 'parliaments' with circles of birds sitting in judgement on 'criminal' rooks. Such wrong conclusions probably originate partly from observation of rooks' aggressive defence of territory.

Rooks are not fast birds but when shot at in the open (frequently over a pigeon hide on stubbles) they are often missed behind because they tend to fly over at maximum range. Their eyesight is excellent and they will veer off at the slightest movement, appearing to have an uncannily accurate assessment of shotgun range. In autumn they tumble, twist and dive headlong through the air but this spectacular display may have no link with courtship.

Apart from the traditional shooting of 'branchers' with a ·22 rifle in May before the foliage is too dense, attempted control methods involve scaring devices at the rookeries during the breeding season, trapping and dusk flighting.

POPULATION: The British Isles hold about 1½ million pairs.

OPEN SEASON: Rooks may be killed or taken at any time by authorised persons throughout the British Isles.

IN THE POT: Adult rooks are not generally eaten in Britain but a pie made from the breasts of 'branchers' is still a traditional favourite in some rural areas.

THE FUTURE: Being so dependent on agricultural practices the rook population will probably continue to fluctuate, but is a very obvious and useful indicator of the state of health of our countryside. How much it exploits cereals will depend on the timing of sowings and the abundance of natural foods in an industry which is increasingly chemical-orientated.

CROW
(*Corvus corone*)

Today the carrion crow (*C.c.corone*) and hooded crow (*C.c. cornix*) are regarded as races (subspecies) of the same species because they freely and successfully interbreed where their ranges meet. Most gamekeepers will never allow these birds to breed on their shoots and they are unpopular with shepherds too.

Each subspecies has many local names including 'grey' or 'Royston crow' for the hooded (evidently it was once common on the downs near Royston in Hertfordshire), and 'flesh crow', 'corbie crow' and 'land daw' for the carrion. Apart from the skylark the crow is the most widespread bird in the British Isles.

HISTORY: The two races are thought to have evolved during the last ice age when European crows separated into isolated populations in the ice-free Balkan and Iberian peninsulas. Separation was long enough for distinct plumages to develop but not sufficient for variation in voice and behaviour. When the ice retreated and the two groups met again they had not been apart long enough to evolve biological incompatibility and were able to interbreed.

Crows have been common in Britain at least since the Middle Ages. Shakespeare wrote of a 'crow-keeper' and in olden times a boy would have been employed to protect the newly sown wheat before 'scarecrows' became common. However, in those days the word crow often referred to rooks and jackdaws as well.

As with other members of its family, the crow was at first unable to take full advantage of the extension and development of agriculture and animal husbandry since the eighteenth century because of the rise of gamekeepering. However, with the decline in professional keepering this century and the aid of the two world wars, during which most 'pests' flourished unchecked, the crow has found time and space to adapt well to the modern farm environment.

The hybrid zone between the two subspecies is not stable and was pushed northwards in Europe during the climatic amelioration of 1900–50.

RANGE AND DISTRIBUTION: Very widespread across Eurasia, the crow breeds in subarctic to warm temperate zones from well above the treeline in the north and southwards to the Nile Valley and Persian Gulf. The carrion crow is dominant in western Europe and the hooded in east and north Europe and most of the Mediterranean.

The carrion is widespread over England and Wales and in Scotland up to the Caledonian Canal but has a mere toe-hold in Ireland, in the extreme north. The hooded is widespread in north and west Scotland to Shetland, the Outer Hebrides, St Kilda, the Isle of Man and Ireland. It is not so local in north-west Scotland and on the islands as the jackdaw and rook.

Where the ranges overlap every combination of their plumages plus 'thoroughbreds' of both subspecies occur. In Scotland the hybrid zone has fluctuated with differing proportions of carrion types, the climate, altitude and habitat preference all having an influence. Throughout the range the width of the hybrid zone never seems to exceed 50-60 miles and is often less. Thus, even allowing for the species' sedentary behaviour, a reduced viability of the hybrids is implied.

HABITAT: The hooded is much more abundant in upland districts but both subspecies occur in all types of country from farmland and woodland to moorland,

Carrion crow

Hooded crow

heathland and coast, and even city parks and squares and tree-lined suburban avenues.

IDENTIFICATION: The hooded crow, with its pale grey underparts and wing linings and grey back contrasting well with the rest of its plumage, which is

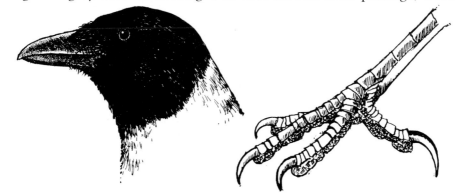

black, is unlikely to be confused with any other British bird and most of the hybrids are fairly recognisable too. The carrion crow, however, is often confused with the rook. Apart from the differences already listed under the entry for rook it is said that old rooks occasionally retain the black feathers above the beak so identification is not always so easy. Booth remarked 'It is as well to know that the colour of the mouth of a rook is a dull slate while that of a crow is pale flesh. The nestlings of both species show this difference as well as the adults.' Another way to separate young rooks from carrion crows is to examine the flight feathers. The rook's second primary from the outside is longer than the sixth while in the crow the second is shorter than the sixth.

Despite its much larger size, the raven is sometimes confused with the carrion crow but its distinctive, deep *pruk-pruk* call will identify.

The crow's average length is 46cm (18in), there being no appreciable difference between the two subspecies. The sexes are alike.

VOICE: The hooded and carrion crows have identical calls — a harsh *kraaah*, mostly uttered three times in succession, a *keerk* and a honking *konk* like a motor horn.

BREEDING: Pairs are said to stay together for life. In courtship the male bows with wings spread and tail fanned and in some areas, including Scotland, they have been seen to jump repeatedly several yards into the air.

Unlike the rook, the crow is a solitary nester, usually high in the fork of a tree but also on cliff ledges and, where there are no trees, in bushes, deep heather, on buildings and even electricity pylons. Both sexes build the large nest of sticks, earth and moss lined with sheep's wool, dead leaves, dried grass and hair. It is easily found.

The single clutch of 3-5 (occasionally 2-7) light blue-green eggs, spotted grey-brown, is laid in late March or April but sometimes in May and even June. The 18-20 day incubation is by the female only and starts before the clutch is complete. The nestlings are fed by both parents and fly after 30-35 days but may remain with the parents until spring approaches.

Carrion crow — summer/winter distribution in the British Isles

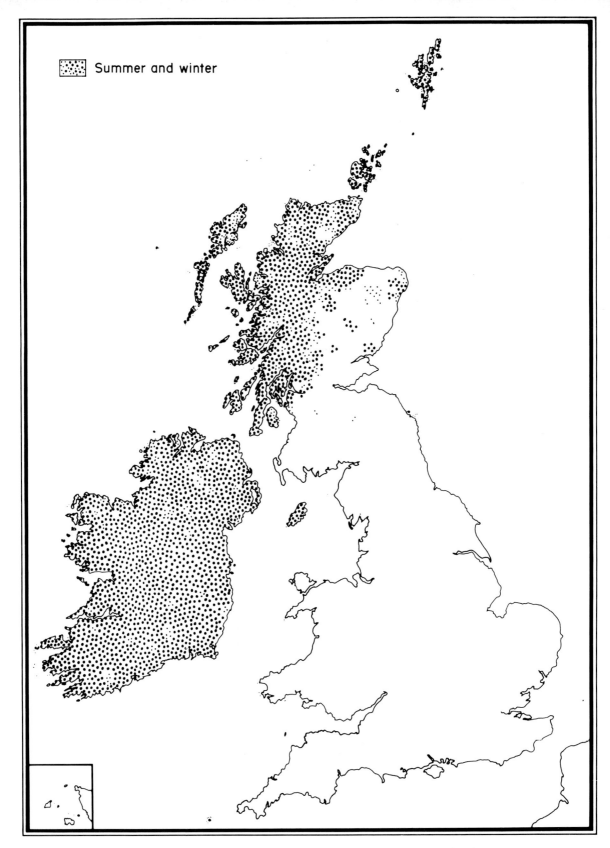

Hooded crow — summer/winter distribution in the British Isles

Carrion crow with frog for lunch — a bird with a catholic diet *(Robin Williams)*

FEEDING: The crow is regarded as the keeper's enemy as it often takes gamebird chicks and young as well as those of other species so it still often features prominently on his gibbets. It will also exceptionally take a bird as big as a partridge or fieldfare. The 'hoodie' especially is associated with the taking of grouse eggs and chicks. It is not popular with keepers of ornamental waterfowl either and will enter nesting baskets given the chance. Wild duck eggs are taken too.

Another blacklist which features the crow is that of the sheep farmer. In sheep country crows are mostly simply feeding on carrion but, of course, they always look suspicious. They do attack sickly and injured ewes and lambs but it is thought that most attacks are by non-breeding birds attracted by after-births and feed put out for sheep. Murton put the loss of lambs at well under 0.5 per cent of those at risk. The number of healthy lambs attacked is small as is the number of ewes attacked while giving birth. Many of those in difficulty, such as stuck in a snowdrift, would die anyway.

Other foods include small birds, reptiles, amphibians, grain, insects and their larvae, worms, wild fruit, seeds, orchard fruits, snails, nuts, occasional small mammals, fish, acorns and root crops. Crows are very fond of visiting the seashore where they will smash open mussels and crabs by dropping them from a great height and then prising them open with their powerful bills while holding the morsels with their feet.

MOVEMENTS: Crows are both resident and migrant. British birds are resident and generally move only locally but numbers are swollen by immigrants of both subspecies from adjacent parts of the Continent and Scandinavia. They mostly

233

arrive in eastern and central England in October and November and return in March and April. Immigration of hooded crows features more than that of carrions in British literature probably because they are much more obvious and distribution dictates that foreign hooded crows are much more likely to arrive in British *carrion* territory.

BEHAVIOUR: Although mostly found in pairs and frequently alone, family parties are common from summer to early spring. Occasionally they gather in flocks to roost in trees but are rarely as gregarious as the rook.

In exploiting carrion, crows have become good walkers and occasionally hop. Their direct flight is very deliberate with slow wing-beats but, like the rook, they will swiftly change direction at the slightest hint of a suspicious movement and are very difficult to stalk. Although the nest is easy to find it is another matter to shoot both birds there. If missed they become extremely wary. However, they seem to be poor at counting and if two men enter a hide the crows will return on seeing just one man leave the area.

Crows respond well to a reasonable imitation of their call. They seem to appear from nowhere and may gather in small flocks to mob owl decoys, swooping down almost to the point of touching, or settling in nearby trees to protest.

POPULATION: There are probably over one million pairs. There was an increase in most areas 1953–63 and the Common Birds Census indices indicate an increase in the breeding population in recent years.

OPEN SEASON: Crows may be killed or taken by authorised persons at any time throughout the British Isles.

The hooded crow differs from the carrion crow only in plumage. Voice and behaviour remain the same (*Eric Hosking*)

IN THE POT: This bird is not generally eaten at all nowadays in this country.

THE FUTURE: The crow is adapting well to human pressure and exploiting urban and suburban environments. This should lead to further expansion. It will fare much better when the despicable and illegal use of indiscriminate poisons on many hill farms and on some irresponsible game shoots is brought under control. Sadly, attempted crow poisoning often leads to scarce birds of prey and other creatures being killed illegally. Shooters discovering poisoning incidents should inform the police.

Increasing afforestation will provide more nest sites in remote upland areas where carrion is often more abundant. Cooling of the climate since 1950 should not affect the British population unduly as the species is well used to much more northerly latitudes but it may affect the range of the hybrid zone.

JACKDAW
(*Corvus monedula*)

This, the smallest of our crows, is a favourite with most countrymen. Its cheerful *tchack* call and aerial antics on the way to roost always brighten my way home at dusk. It can be an egg thief that the keeper must deal with and it does tuck in to some of our crops but most problems are very local and on a small scale.

HISTORY: Already common before the Agricultural Revolution, the jackdaw appears to have become more numerous and widespread in Europe with the increase in cultivation. This century particularly has been good for the species. During the first fifty years there was some increase northwards in Finland and Scandinavia which was probably due to spread of cultivation into forested regions rather than climatic amelioration. Increase in Scotland is probably linked to extension of cereal production. First Shetland breeding was recorded in 1943 and the six pairs which colonised Eigg in the Inner Hebrides in 1933 had risen to 100 by 1966. Ireland too has seen great increase this century and it is now much commoner there than in many equivalent habitats in Britain.

However, a severe decline came in the late 1960s and 1970s and this, as with the rook, appears to have been brought on largely by a reduction in the acreage of ley grassland for it stopped when the area of grass stabilised.

RANGE AND DISTRIBUTION: A typical species of the steppe fauna of Russia and central Europe, whence it probably originated, the jackdaw breeds right across Europe from southern Scandinavia, Britain and the Iberian Peninsula east to northern USSR and the Chinese and Mongolian borders and south to Afghanistan, Iraq, Turkey and the Mediterranean. Isolated populations occur in Algeria and northern Morocco. Many birds winter just south of their breeding range.

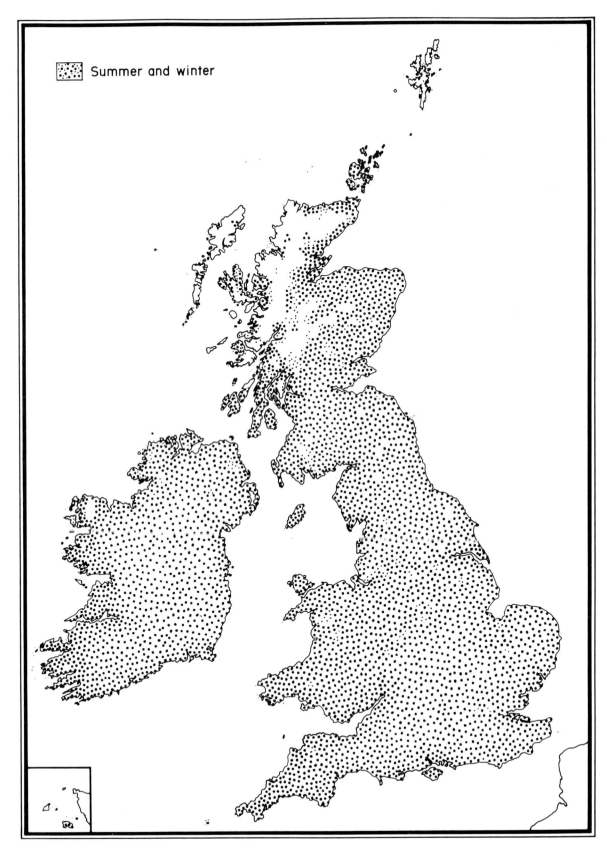

Jackdaw — summer/winter distribution in the British Isles

In the British Isles it breeds in all counties but in north-west Scotland, the Hebrides, Orkney and Shetland it is as local as the rook, avoiding higher hills.

HABITAT: The jackdaw has a preference for farmland, especially with grass, but frequents many types of country — woodland, parkland, sea cliffs, rocky moors, quarries, large gardens and even town centres, but rarely ventures above the treeline in mountainous areas.

IDENTIFICATION: In this country the only possible confusion can be with the other crows with which it often associates but at close range its grey nape and smaller size will distinguish. In flight it calls frequently and flaps less with faster wing-beats than its black cousins. The general appearance is compact and thick-necked. The legs and feet are fairly long and powerful and the stubby bill short but pointed. The sexes are alike. Average length is 33cm (13in).

VOICE: Apart from the very familiar *tchack,* which is often repeated twice or more, there is a metallic *kow* or *kyow* and the bubbling sub-song typical of crows.

BREEDING: The male's courtship involves bowing with outspread wings and tail and sometimes displaying the ash-grey nape feathers by raising the crown feathers while tucking the bill into the breast.

This acrobatic bird, formerly known as 'Jack-daw' or just plain 'daw,' can squeeze into all sorts of cramped nest sites — crevices in rocks, tree hollows, chimney pots, holes in ruined buildings, churches and castles and even rabbit burrows on cliff brows. More open structures are sometimes built in ivy or dense conifers. It breeds in single pairs, small groups and even in substantial colonies in neighbouring trees or on cliffs. The same sites are used year after year. An exceptional home is in the base of a rook's nest.

Both sexes assemble the untidy pile of sticks, and large cavities are filled until a firm platform has been constructed before the lining of wool, hair and soft vegetation is added. Small holes may simply be lined with soft materials but some large chimneys are completely choked with great accumulations of kindling.

The 4-6 (occasionally 2-9) light blue eggs with brown-black blotches and spots are laid mostly in late April and early May. The 17-18 day incubation of the single brood is from the first egg and by the female only. The nestlings are fed by both parents and fly after 28-32 days.

FEEDING: Although it has been found that jackdaws spend about half their feeding time throughout the year on grassland, unlike starlings and rooks, with which they often associate, they are mainly surface feeders. There is a heavy emphasis on animal foods, some of the most important being moth larvae, butterflies, flies and spiders. In May defoliating caterpillars are eaten and later their pupae on oaks and elms. The breeding season is considerably later than the rook's to coincide with a different peak food abundance.

Other foods include potatoes, worms, eggs, chicks, grain, carrion, weed seeds, wild and cultivated fruits and small animals. Birds will also perch on sheep's backs to pick the ticks from the wool. Useless, inedible objects are also taken and stored away.

Eggs are taken occasionally from laying pens, and in some areas, such as the South Downs, they eat a few partridge eggs but overall there is little harm to English game. However, the shells of many grouse eggs have been found in some jackdaw nests.

MOVEMENTS: Many of the more northerly foreign birds move south and west in

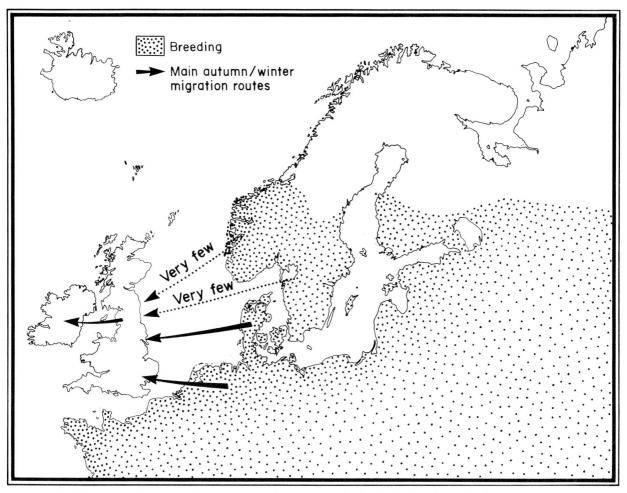

Jackdaw — main autumn/winter migration routes of British-involved populations

winter. British and Irish birds are sedentary with only local wandering but emigration to the Continent has exceptionally been recorded. Winter immigrants arrive from Scandinavia and the near Continent on the east and south-east coasts in October and November and some pass further south to France. They return between late February and April.

BEHAVIOUR: This crow is gregarious in all seasons, often associating with rooks, and is a bigger thief than the magpie. Much of its traditional unpopularity is quite unjustified and stems from the ignorant olden times when it was observed perched on horses and sheep plucking out tufts of hair or wool to line its nest. Such behaviour was often misconstrued as an attack on livestock.

Large roosts are often found at old nest sites where they set up a tremendous clamour. Their flight to roost in the late dusk is often very low and, being much less wary and suspicious (probably because they have not been persecuted to the same degree in the past), they are generally much easier to shoot than crows or flighting rooks.

Jackdaws in winter, in Wigtownshire *(Jack Orchel)*

POPULATION: There are estimated to be over 500,000 pairs and the number is probably rising.

OPEN SEASON: Jackdaws may be killed or taken at any time by authorised persons throughout the British Isles.

IN THE POT: This is not a bird that is generally eaten at all nowadays in the British Isles.

THE FUTURE: Another species whose success seems interwoven with the pattern of agriculture, the jackdaw will continue to be subject to considerable population fluctuation. However, agriculture alone can only be part of the picture for attempted introductions to New Zealand, where much of the habitat is ostensibly ideal, have been unsuccessful. Climate seems to be important too and the jackdaw appears to be doing well in the general cooling since the 1950s. It will probably continue to exploit urban and suburban environments further but, unless it adapts, will always be hampered by a restricted choice of suitable nest sites. Increasing afforestation, especially with deciduous trees, will help.

APPENDIX I

Organisations with special bird shooting interests

British Association for Shooting and Conservation (BASC) (formerly WAGBI), Marford Mill, Rossett, Wrexham, Clwyd, LL12 0HL (tel 0244 570881). Britain's largest shooting organisation. Represents interests of all bird and animal shooters. Responsibilities include scientific research into aspects of shooting, results of which contribute to greater understanding of quarry species and their needs, and hence to sound management of populations and habitats. In particular, long-term studies concentrate on quantifying and monitoring the annual kill of all quarry species, through bag and wing surveys. Immediate issues relating to both shooting and conservation are investigated as needed. All bird shooters should be members.

Game Conservancy, Burgate Manor, Fordingbridge, Hants, SP6 1EF (tel 0425 53281). An independently financed charitable organisation which researches practical shooting problems, conducts detailed research to benefit game and wildlife in a continually changing countryside, investigates modern farming pressures which restrict game abundance, assists farmers, landowners and shooters to get the best from their shooting assets, and ensures that the government and its ministries are constantly made aware of the importance of game and the necessary conservation and management that also benefit other wildlife. It has a network of trained field advisers specially concerned with habitat improvement and publishes research papers and guidance in an Annual Review and a series of advisory booklets. All game shooters should be members.

British Field Sports Society, 59 Kennington Road, London, SE1 7PZ (tel 01 928 4742). Co-ordinates and defends all British field sports interests, including bird shooting, through strong representation at parliamentary level and a very active, enthusiastic and widespread team of regional and local representatives. Membership is highly desirable for all bird shooters.

Ulster Game and Wildfowl Society, 49 Ashdale Crescent, Bangor, Co Down. A very important local link for all bird shooters in Northern Ireland. Close liaison with BASC.

Standing Conference on Country Sports, Mr R. G. A. Lofthouse, Convener, c/o College of Estate Management, Whiteknights, Reading, Berks, RGG 2AW (tel 0734 861101). Representatives of all field sports interests, including bird shooters, meet several times a year, often with leading conservationists, to discuss and act on trends and urgent issues affecting field sports. Their first major report — *Countryside Sports – Their Economic Significance* — was published in 1983.

UK Federation of FACE, The Federation of Hunting Associations of the EEC, Secretary: Mr J. Swift, c/o BASC, Marford Mill, Rossett, Wrexham, Clwyd, LL12 0HL (tel 0244 570881). FACE was founded in 1977 following tabling of the EEC Directive on Bird Conservation in December 1976 to ensure adequate representation of national hunting associations of member states of the European Community concerned with hunting, shooting and the conservation of game. The UK committee meets several times a year. Among recent concerns has been voluntary tests on shooting proficiency.

International Council for Game and Wildlife Conservation (CIC), Conseil International de la Chasse et de la Conservation du Gibier, 15 rue de Téhéran, 75008 Paris, France. A non-governmental organisation founded in 1930 by 121 game authorities from 23 countries. Members and supporters include official representatives of nations, public-law organisations, national and international agencies and private citizens interested in bird hunting, small game and big game and wildlife conservation in general.

Other organisations concerned wholly or partly with birds and their management

Agriculture, Fisheries and Food, Ministry of, Whitehall Place, London SW1A 2HH (tel 01 217 3000). Consult telephone directory for local offices.

Army Birdwatching Society, c/o Lt Col N. Clayden, MoD Defence Lands, 4 Tolworth Towers, Surbiton, Surrey.

British Museum (Natural History), Sub Department of Ornithology, Tring, Herts HP23 6AP.

British Ornithologists' Union, c/o Zoological Society of London, Regent's Park, London NW1. Our senior ornithological society. Issues the excellent journal *Ibis*.

British Trust for Ornithology, Beech Grove, Station Road, Tring, Herts HP23 5NR (tel 044 282 3461). Formed in 1933. A small professional staff coordinate observations by birdwatchers throughout the British Isles and collate and analyse the information to keep a finger on the pulse of our bird-life, monitoring abundance, productivity and movements. A most important and helpful organisation.

Eire Forest and Wildlife Service, Leeson Lane, Dublin 2, Ireland.

Environment, Department of the, 2 Marsham Street, London SW1P 3EB (tel 01 212 3434).

Environment, Department of the for Northern Ireland, Stormont, Belfast BT4 3SS (tel Belfast 768716).

Fauna and Flora Preservation Society, c/o Zoological Society of London, Regent's Park, London NW1.

Forestry Commission, 231 Corstorphine Road, Edinburgh, Scotland EH12 7AT (tel 031 334 0303).

Guild of Taxidermists, Secretary: Chris Stoate, c/o Hants County Museum Service, Childcomb House, Childcomb Lane, Bar End, Winchester, Hants.

International Council for Bird Preservation, 219c Huntingdon Road, Cambridge. (British Section, c/o British Museum (Natural History), Cromwell Road, London SW7 5BD).

International Waterfowl Research Bureau, Research Dept, Wildfowl Trust, Slimbridge, Glos.

Irish Department of Fisheries and Forestry (Forest and Wildlife Service), 22 Upper Merrion Street, Dublin 2, Ireland (tel 01 789211).

Irish SCPA, 1 Grand Canal Quay, Dublin 2, Ireland.

Irish Wild Bird Conservancy, Southview, Church Road, Greystones, Co Wicklow, Ireland (tel 01 875759). With over 3,000 members, the largest Irish conservation organisation. It manages reserves and engages in important surveys which provide the facts on which conservation is based.

Irish Wildlife Federation, c/o 8 Westland Row, Dublin 2, Ireland.

Nature Conservancy Council, GB Headquarters, 19/20 Belgrave Square, London SW1X 8PY. See telephone directory for regional offices.

Pheasant Trust, Great Witchingham, Norwich, Norfolk.

Royal Air Force Birdwatching Society, c/o Sq Ldr D. Hollin, RAF Wyton, Cambs.

Royal Naval Birdwatching Society, c/o 23 St David's Road, Southsea, Hants.

Royal Society for Nature Conservation, The Green, Nettleham, Lincs LN2 2NR. The parent body of the county naturalists' trusts.

Royal Society for the Prevention of Cruelty to Animals, The Causeway, Horsham, Sussex RH12 1HE. Their interest includes birds.

Royal Society for the Protection of Birds, The Lodge, Sandy, Beds SG19 2DL (tel 0767 80551). Founded in 1899. Received Royal Charter in 1904. Now Europe's largest voluntary wildlife conservation body with a membership of about 350,000. Their object is to conserve wild birds and their habitats, and encourage public interest in them. Its work covers all aspects of conservation, though not extending to bird welfare, and is most tangibly shown by the 88 reserves which it owns or manages.

Scottish Office, New St Andrew's House, St James Centre, Edinburgh EH1 3TD (tel 031 556 8400) and Dover House, Whitehall, London SW1A 2AU (tel 01 233 3000).

Scottish Ornithologists' Club, 21 Regent Terrace, Edinburgh EH7 5BN.

Seabird Group, c/o British Ornithologists' Union (see above).

Welsh Office, Gwydyr House, Whitehall, London SW1A 2ER (tel 01 233 6066 and 8202) and Cathays Park, Cardiff CF1 3NQ (tel 0222 825111).

Wildfowl Trust, Slimbridge, Glos GL2 7BT (tel Cambridge, Glos 333). Established by one-time wildfowler Sir Peter Scott in 1946, it is concerned with the conservation of wildfowl and their wetland habitat, research into wildfowl conservation, education leading to greater public appreciation of wildfowl in particular and nature in general, and recreation to enable people to enjoy living wildfowl.

World Pheasant Association, Harraton Square, Church Lane, Exning, Newmarket, Suffolk CB8 7HF. Aims to develop, promote and support conservation of all species of the order Galliformes.

World Wildlife Fund, Panda House, 11–13 Ockford Road, Godalming, Surrey (tel Godalming 20551).

Young Ornithologists' Club, c/o RSPB as above.

APPENDIX II

The Law

Gamebirds
* Legislation is contained within the Game Laws.
* Species within this book affected are: pheasant, grey partridge, redlegged partridge, red grouse, black grouse, ptarmigan.
* The capercaillie is not included as it was extinct in the British Isles when the 1831 Game Act was framed so that a Game Licence is not needed to shoot it.
* A Game Licence (obtainable from any Post Office) is necessary to shoot the above species plus the woodcock and common snipe which are included in the Wildlife and Countryside Act 1981.
* Gamebirds fall under the Wildlife and Countryside Act 1981 in the section detailing prohibited methods of killing or taking birds.
* To sell game species a Game Dealer's Licence must be obtained from the Post Office unless you are selling to a licensed game dealer in which case an ordinary game shooting licence will cover you. A shoot may not sell gamebirds to its members without a Game Dealer's Licence. Game may be sold only up to ten days after the end of the season.
* No game may be shot on Sundays or Christmas Day.

All other species
* Legislation is contained within the Wildlife and Countryside Act 1981 which repealed and re-enacted with amendments the Protection of Birds Acts 1954 to 1967 and the Conservation of Wild Creatures and Wild Plants Act 1975. Copies are obtainable through HMSO, 49 High Holborn, London WCIV 6HB or their other branches or through booksellers. The most important points for bird shooters are listed below.
* All birds, their eggs and nests are protected, with exceptions as detailed by legislation. Thus any species omitted is automatically protected. This includes all vagrants.
* *Species which may be killed or taken* In addition to those listed in this book the following may be killed or taken by authorised persons at all times — great black-backed gull, lesser black-backed gull, herring gull, house sparrow, starling. An authorised person is the landowner, occupier or person authorised by either to shoot on specific land.
* *Species which may be sold dead at all times* Woodpigeon and feral pigeon. No licence needed.
* *Species which may be sold dead from 1 September to 28 February* Capercaillie, coot, tufted duck, mallard, pintail, golden plover, pochard, shoveler, common snipe, teal, wigeon, woodcock. No licence needed to sell duck.
* *Wild geese* Sale strictly prohibited at all times.

★ *Special licenses* Some species which previously could be shot as pests throughout the year in certain parts of the country are now only shootable under a licensing system detailed by Section 16 of the 1981 Act 'for the purpose of preventing serious damage to livestock, foodstuffs for livestock, crops, vegetables, fruit, growing timber or fisheries'. These include goosander, red-breasted merganser, stock dove, rock dove, cormorant, oystercatcher, shag, barnacle goose, brent goose and (during the close season) greylag goose and pinkfooted goose.

Licences are issued by divisional offices of the Ministry of Agriculture, Fisheries and Food and Department of Agriculture and Fish for Scotland in accordance with guidelines which these two authorities have drawn up in consultation with the Nature Conservancy Council. Licences are issued to owners or occupiers who may authorise a limited number (usually three, or four if the licence holder is not included) of people to shoot on their behalf. Advice will be taken by Regional Pest Officers who will process each application and conditions will include provision of evidence of serious damage or reason to believe that there is likely to be serious damage. A 'bag limit' will probably be placed on each licence for which there will be a time limit and records must be kept. Generally scaring methods must be employed before shooting takes place.

At the time of writing some licences appear to have been abused and landowners or occupiers have sold such shooting. This is clearly breaking the spirit of the law. In addition this has led to birds being shot away from the area of crop damage with the use of decoys. This is illegal.

In fact a licence may be issued to kill or take any wild bird to prevent serious damage to livestock, foodstuffs for livestock, crops, vegetables, fruit, growing timber or fisheries; for scientific or educational purposes, ringing or marking; falconry or aviculture; taxidermy and photography; and to disturb any Schedule I bird for photography. In practice such licenses are strictly controlled. For example, the bullfinch sometimes needs control in fruit-growing areas.

★ *Suspension of shooting during severe weather* The Secretary of State for the Environment has the power to suspend shooting of wild birds included in Part II of Schedule I or Part I of Schedule 2 during any period outside the close season. This may apply to the whole or any specified part of the country for a period not exceeding fourteen days. Species affected include all ducks and geese which may be killed or taken outside the close season, golden plover, woodcock, common snipe, coot and moorhen. A Working Party set up under the NCC considered that the capercaillie should not be covered by future suspension orders as its inclusion in current bird protection legislation as opposed to the Game Acts is anomalous.

Criteria for triggering severe weather procedures are based on the state of ground data collated daily by thirteen coastal meteorological stations. On these criteria, the NCC will consult interested organisations, including the BASC, before advising the Secretary of State to sign an Order. When seven days of severe weather have been recorded at seven or more of the meteorological stations (or ten days including one or two days of thaw) the BASC will inform by first-class post the Secretaries of Clubs, Joint Councils and syndicates affiliated to the BASC that if the severe weather continues for a further six days, and looks likely to continue, a statutory Order is likely to come into effect. At that point voluntary restraint will be called for. Information will also be given of where notice of such a statutory Order will appear. The Order will be signed on the thirteenth day of severe weather but there will be a two-day publicity period before the Order comes into force at 9 am on the fifteenth day. Publicity will involve national and local media.

If a thaw sets in a ban may be lifted before the fourteenth day but it may also be renewed to run for a further and consecutive fourteen days. During such a crisis the BASC runs a twenty-four hour telephone answering service but advice may also be obtained from the DoE and NCC.

Procedures are subject to review after each suspension. Previous 'bans' have caused considerable disagreement among shooters, especially over the possibility of regional bans, but many have overlooked the fact that we have a national and international responsibility for bird populations and it is the total picture that is important. In addition, regional bans would be very difficult to determine (altitude must also be considered insofar as it affects climate) and police. A true sportsman does not need telling that birds have lost condition and are easier to approach: he will have stopped shooting *before* a ban is imposed.

★ *Prohibited methods of killing or taking wild birds*   (1) Any bow or crossbow; (2) Any explosive other than ammunition for a firearm; (3) Any automatic or semi-automatic weapon; (4) Any shotgun of which the barrel has an internal diameter at the muzzle of more than 1¾in; (5) Any device for illuminating a target or any sighting device for night shooting; (6) Any form of artificial lighting or any mirror or other dazzling device; (7) Any gas or smoke; (8) Articles of such a nature and so placed as to be calculated to cause bodily injury to any wild bird coming into bodily contact therewith, that is to say any springe, trap, gin, snare, hook and line, any electrical device for killing, stunning or frightening, or any poisonous, poisoned or stupefying substance; (9) Use of nets, baited boards, bird-lime or substance of a like nature; (10) Use of any sound recording or any live bird or other animal whatsoever which is tethered, or which is secured by means of braces or other similar appliances, or which is blind, maimed or injured, as a decoy; (11) Use of any mechanically propelled vehicle (including motor boats) in immediate pursuit. See Wildlife and Countryside Act for exceptions to some of the above points.

It should be noted that a motorised boat may be used to get to a general shooting area providing no by-laws are infringed. Under Section 16 an Open General Licence authorises the full use of semi-automatic weapons for killing birds on the pest schedule, including woodpigeons. A semi-automatic weapon is defined as one with more than two rounds in the magazine. It is legal to use a semi-automatic which has been plugged so that the magazine holds two rounds with a further round in the chamber without reloading. This is taken to include gas-operated and recoil inertia weapons but does not appear to include guns with a manual pump-action which appear to have unrestricted use.

The use of any gun or rifle firing a single bullet is not illegal for bird shooting but is generally discouraged as an unacceptable practice. One traditional exception is the use of a .22 rifle on 'brancher' rooks but the shot should always be aimed high into the air.

★ *Christmas Day*   Shooting is forbidden in England, Scotland and Wales.
★ *Sunday shooting*   No species may be shot in Scotland on Sundays. In England and Wales there is no Sunday shooting in specified areas. At the time of writing (1983) this means no Sunday wildfowling in the following counties and county boroughs: Anglesey, Brecknock, Caernarvon, Cardigan, Carmarthen, Cornwall, Denbigh, Devon, Doncaster, Glamorgan, Great Yarmouth, Isle of Ely, Leeds, Merioneth, Norfolk, Pembroke, Somerset, Yorkshire (North and West Ridings). Such restrictions are subject to change and should be checked locally with the police or council.
★ *Trap shooting*   It is illegal to take any part in any activity involving the release of birds as immediate targets for shooting.
★ If in doubt on any point consult the Department of the Environment in England or Scottish or Welsh Offices or your national shooting organisations.

NORTHERN IRELAND

In addition to the information given under species accounts in this book the following are among the more important points:

Gamebirds
★ Jack snipe may be shot 1 October to 31 January.
★ Partridge and grouse — illegal to sell or purchase for consumption (subject to review).
★ Pheasant (female) — illegal to sell or purchase for consumption unless exemption has been obtained from the Department of the Environment to kill them. Trading must be through an authorised dealer.
★ A Game Licence is required to shoot pheasant, partridge, red grouse, snipe and woodcock.

All other species
★ The Province is not subject to the Wildlife and Countryside Act 1981. There was a major Act in 1931 which revoked all previous bird protection Acts and provided a strong basis on which the 1950 and 1968 Acts have built. At the time of writing (1983) a proposed Wildlife (Northern Ireland) Order was about to be published and debated in the Northern Ireland Assembly. Proposals included the following main variations from existing legislation: full protection extended to all swans, geese (except greylag), common scoter, red-breasted merganser, longtailed duck, grey plover and stock dove.

* *Species which may be shot* In addition to those listed above and under the species accounts — grey plover, scaup, whimbrel, redshank, curlew, rock dove, stock dove (all 1 September to 31 January open season). Those species which may be shot at any time by authorised persons are: shag, cormorant, great black-backed gull, lesser black-backed gull, herring gull, black-headed gull, woodpigeon, feral pigeon, crow, rook, jackdaw, magpie, jay, starling, house sparrow. Coot and moorhen are fully protected and it is proposed that they should remain so.
* *Sale of dead birds* Apart from some gamebirds only the woodpigeon may be sold.
* *Night shooting* All shooting is forbidden from one hour after sunset to one hour before sunrise.
* *Sunday* No shooting.
* For details concerning special licences, temporary Orders or any other queries contact the Department of the Environment at Stormont.

IRISH REPUBLIC
* The main legislation is contained in the Wildlife Act 1976.
* *Species* which may be shot in Eire but not in England, Scotland and Wales are scaup and jack snipe (both 1 September to 31 January).
* *'Pest'* species which may be shot at any time are crow, great black-backed gull, herring gull, house sparrow, jackdaw, jay, lesser black-backed gull, magpie, pigeons (not carrier, racing or homing pigeons or doves), rook or starling.
* *Night shooting* It is not permitted to hunt any protected wild bird except a wild duck or goose between one hour after sunset and one hour before sunrise.
* *Motors* Protected birds shall not be hunted by means of mechanically propelled vehicles while being so propelled.
* *Rifles* Protected wild birds shall not be hunted with rifles.
* *State land* Hunting on the foreshore on inland waters owned by the State is prohibited except under licence from the minister responsible
* *Visitors* must be accompanied by a guide and his dogs. Firearms certificates (which cover shotguns) and hunting licenses are generally issued to those with arranged shooting.
* *Severe weather* There is statutory power to suspend game shooting in certain circumstances such as severe weather.
* *Hunting licenses* These are issued to hunt game species but are not required for 'pests'. Application to Forest and Wildlife Service. No fee.
* *Guns* Repeater and automatic shotguns must be adapted so that they carry no more than three cartridges.
* *Sale of dead birds* Although gadwall and goldeneye may be hunted they may not be sold or disposed of by way of wildlife dealing or trade.
* A guide to the Wildlife Act has been published by the Forest and Wildlife Service and may be purchased from the Government Publications Sales Office, GPO Arcade, Henry Street, Dublin 1.

NB These legal notes are offered as a guide only and are subject to constant review and change. The author and publishers accept no responsibility for their accuracy, though every care has been taken to ensure their correctness. If ever in any doubt about a point seek advice from the appropriate authorities *before firing a shot*.

APPENDIX III
Silhouettes

It is every sportsman's duty to shoot at only those legitimate quarry species which he can positively identify. Thus it is incumbent upon him to familiarise himself with every point which will not only distinguish between the quarry species but also between the frequently similar protected species. Accurate identification will also enable the sportsman to avail himself of every opportunity which comes his way.

Because of the birds' habits, much shooting, especially wildfowling, must be undertaken during periods of poor light (particularly dawn and dusk, and sometimes even by moonlight) and then knowledge of plumage coloration is almost useless. Under such conditions recognition of calls is useful but the main means of identification is through recognition of the silhouette in conjunction with the species' 'jizz' — the indefinable overall impression in the field. To help with this Rodger McPhail has specially drawn wing silhouettes of all the species in this book. Each plate is to scale so that relative sizes may be learnt along with distinctive shapes. In addition some of the 'pest' species have been drawn in a standing position as they are sometimes shot in those stances.

Shoveler

Mallard

Gadwall

Tufted duck

Pochard

Pintail

Teal

Goldeneye

Wigeon

Jackdaw

Carrion crow

Rook

Jay

Collared dove

Moorhen

Coot

Magpie

Woodpigeon

Feral pigeon

Blackcock

Pheasant ♂

Hen pheasant

Greyhen

Woodcock

Ptarmigan

Capercaillie ♂

Commo
snipe

Red grouse

Hen capercaillie

Golden plover

Redlegged partridge

Grey partridge

Pinkfooted goose

Greylag goose

Canada goose

Whitefronted goose

ACKNOWLEDGEMENTS

A book of this nature necessarily draws on a large number of other works, reports and articles in an attempt to be as comprehensive as possible. However, space precludes a full bibliography but I would like to record my admiration for the following books which have been particularly helpful: Sharrock, J. T. R. (Compiled for the BTO and IWC), *Atlas of Breeding Birds in Britain and Ireland* (Poyser, 1977); Murton, R. K. *Man and Birds* (Collins, 1971); Vesey-Fitzgerald, Brian *British Game* (Collins, 1946); Coles, Charles *The Complete Book of Game Conservation* (Barrie and Jenkins, 1971); Owen, Myrfyn *Wild Geese of the World* (Batsford, 1980); Dixon, Charles *The Game Birds and Wild Fowl of the British Islands* (Pawson and Brailsford, 1900, 2nd ed, 1st ed 1893); Long, John L. *Introduced Birds of the World* (David & Charles, 1981); Booth, E. T. *Catalogue of the Cases of Birds in the Dyke Road Museum Brighton* (King Thorne and Stace, 1901, 3rd ed); Bewick, Thomas (text by Rev Cotes) *A History of British Birds* (Newcastle, 1821; 1st ed 1797 and 1804); Salmon, D. G. (Ed) *Wildfowl and Wader Counts 1981–82, The Results of the National Wildfowl Counts and Birds of Estuaries Enquiry* (The Wildfowl Trust, 1982).

In addition I would like to thank the staff of the BASC, Game Conservancy and *Shooting Times and Country magazine;* Capt Jimmy Hamilton, Mr J. Furphy of the DoE Northern Ireland, Richard Nairn of the IWC, Mr J. Fuller of the BTO, and Michael Newton for help in various ways. Thank you also to Philip Murphy for his beak and feet illustrations, and to Chris Mead of the British Trust for Ornithology for his help with the maps. Also to the staff of David & Charles, especially Sue Hall, as well as the many correspondents who have been kind enough to share their valued observations with me in recent years, particularly through my 'Country scene' column which appears in *Shooting Times* under the pen-name 'Rusticus'.

My very special thanks go to Rodger McPhail for supplying the magnificent paintings and drawings reproduced here. Sadly, the first eight of the specially commissioned watercolours were stolen. Many lesser artists would then have abandoned the project but Rodger displayed great kindness and resolve in tackling those subjects all over again. Should the 'originals' ever surface we would be pleased to hear for they have become unique collectors' items.

Lastly I thank my wife Carol and sons Spencer and Ross for tolerating my temporary lack of application to family life.

INDEX